Killing the
Buddha on the
Appalachian
Trail

Killing the Buddha on the Appalachian Trail

WALKING ON
THROUGH
SELF-DOUBT
AND AGING

John Turner

THE UNIVERSITY OF
GEORGIA PRESS
ATHENS

© 2024 by the University of Georgia Press
Athens, Georgia 30602
www.ugapress.org
All rights reserved
Designed by Kaelin Chappell Broaddus
Set in 9.5/13.5 Quadraat Regular
by Kaelin Chappell Broaddus
Printed and bound by Sheridan Books
The paper in this book meets the guidelines for
permanence and durability of the Committee on
Production Guidelines for Book Longevity of the
Council on Library Resources.

Most University of Georgia Press titles are
available from popular e-book vendors.

Printed in the United States of America
28 27 26 25 24 C 5 4 3 2 1

Library of Congress Cataloging-in-Publication Data

Names: Turner, John, author.
Title: Killing the Buddha on the Appalachian Trail : walking
on through self-doubt and aging / John Turner.
Identifiers: LCCN 2024011665 (print) | LCCN 2024011666
(ebook) | ISBN 9780820367736 (paperback ; alk. paper) |
ISBN 9780820367743 (epub) | ISBN 9780820367750 (pdf)
Subjects: LCSH: Turner, John. | Hikers—Appalachian
Trail—Biography. | Hiking—Appalachian Trail. | Self-
consciousness (Awareness)—Religious aspects—
Buddhism. | Self-actualization (Psychology)
Classification: LCC GV199.42.A68 T87 2024 (print) |
LCC GV199.42.A68 (ebook) | DDC 796.51092 [B]—
dc23/eng/20240515
LC record available at https://lccn.loc.gov/2024011665
LC ebook record available at https://lccn.loc
.gov/202401166649

Maps created by Liliana Vittini

For Dianne

CONTENTS

PREFACE

First things first—most accounts of hiking the Appalachian Trail, and there are many fine ones published each year, begin at the beginning of the adventure and end at the finish, usually at the summit of Katahdin in Maine, and the hikers often complete their hikes in less than the span of a single year. My story is different. I hiked the Appalachian Trail in sections, some as short as a single day covering only a few miles and others nearly a month long and more than two hundred miles in length. And although I generally traveled from the south, in Georgia, northward to Katahdin in Maine, circumstances often required me to jump around, leaving gaps that I had to go back and fill in at a later time. Thus New Hampshire came early, before Vermont, and big chunks of Virginia; I hiked North Carolina, Tennessee, Maine, the mid-South states, and Pennsylvania in pieces at different times and seasons, and Massachusetts was near the end. My final day and final mile of the Appalachian Trail ended not on the summit of Katahdin but at a nondescript trailhead near the little Maine village of Stratton.

To unspool all those miles, states, seasons, and hikes through fourteen states in chronological order would be hopelessly confusing, so I have chosen to tell the story instead mostly in geographic fashion, state by state, south from Georgia to north in Maine. This is not a perfect solution, but it will have to do because my patchwork trek of the A.T. spanned the better part of six years, and not until the final two years did I allow myself to hope that I might one day actually walk all 2,193 miles of the trail. The fact that I did, finishing on August 24, 2022, just ten days after my seventy-third birthday, seems in retrospect a little miraculous. But no miracles were involved, just a lot of stubbornness, a little luck here and there, and putting one foot in front of the other. Along the way some amazing things happened.

ACKNOWLEDGMENTS

Undertaking a successful hike of the entire Appalachian Trail, much like writing a coherent story about the journey, is an effort born of thousands of hours of solitude, but rarely is either feat accomplished truly alone. The author would like to acknowledge and thank the assistance he received from the following, both on the trail and in the process of editing this story: Carol Crawford, Ivo Fravashi, Randall Williams, Suzanne La Rosa, Bruce Johnson, Eric Graves, Jane Trentin, Margaret Treadway, Mary Hall, Carol Dorn, Don Converse, Richard Judy, Alexander Nix, Adam Stanley, Kim and Jarrod Hester, Homer Witcher, Dennis "Trail Pilgrim" Newton, Dr. Jac D. Scheiner, Jim Stauch, Miss Janet, Trail Angel Mary, Nancy Hoch, Ron Brown, and Tom Levardi. Each of them in their own way made my journey enjoyable when times were good and bearable when they weren't. Added to this list is a long anonymous roll call of hikers I met briefly on the trail who brightened my days with a smile or a cheerful hello, often when I needed it the most. To each of them, my gratitude and best wishes. And most of all, to my wife Dianne, who put up with all of it.

AUTHOR'S NOTE

Memories are often unreliable, especially when called upon to recount details of events that happened decades in the past, as is the case with a few pieces of the story I have to tell. But the events from my past that I have related are so indelible and vivid to me that I have confidence my memory of them tells the story accurately enough to put them into print and offer them in good faith as facts. Where conversations are involved, I, of course, cannot vouch for my memory's word-for-word veracity, given the decades, in some instances, that have elapsed since they happened. But I have tried to convey what was said as closely as possible and I believe I have captured the gist of them on each occasion.

More recent events are a different matter for I was and still am a habitual note-taker. Every evening of my many days of hiking the Appalachian Trail I spent a few minutes writing in a small notebook, recording the happenings, chance encounters, random thoughts, and a few pertinent facts, the where, when, who, how many and why of those particular hours on the trail. Many of the passages in my story flow directly from those notes. I have changed the names of many of the people mentioned in my story to protect their privacy, and I have condensed some of the events to smooth out the narration.

What follows, then, is a mix of memory and reporting, assembled from years past and from thousands of hours walking in solitude on the most famous hiking trail in the world.

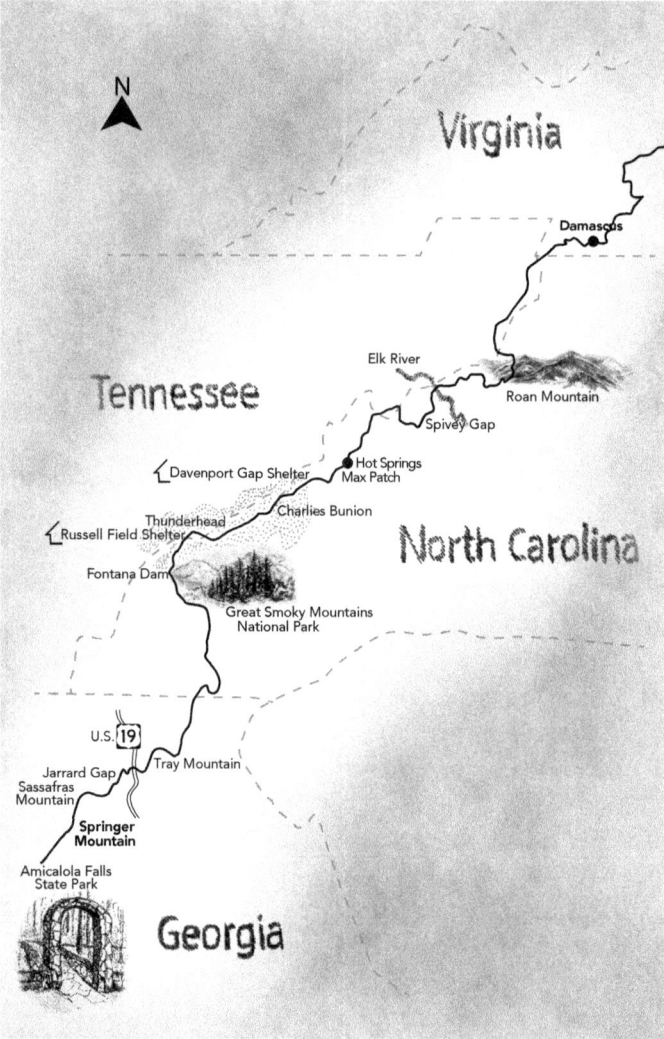

N

Virginia

Damascus

Tennessee

Elk River

Roan Mountain

Spivey Gap

Davenport Gap Shelter

Hot Springs
Max Patch

Charlies Bunion

Thunderhead

Russell Field Shelter

North Carolina

Fontana Dam

Great Smoky Mountains
National Park

U.S. 19

Tray Mountain

Jarrard Gap

Sassafras
Mountain

Springer
Mountain

Amicalola Falls
State Park

Georgia

Killing the Buddha on the Appalachian Trail

The Raven

On a nameless mountain in North Carolina, on a lovely late March afternoon, I came undone as a serious hiker of the Appalachian Trail. My mind and body simultaneously revolted, refusing to participate in this crazy, pointless exercise any longer. My rebellious mind reeled as I staggered up a forested slope that was as steep as a fire escape. What could I possibly have been thinking? That at my age and with my minimal physical preparation I could come out here and hike for five days in a row up and over these rugged mountains, miles and miles each day, days at a time? That this would be some fun adventure in North Carolina, especially after what I had already been through and learned?

The idea that at the age of sixty-eight I might, over time, in sections spread over perhaps a couple of years, successfully hike any significant length of the Appalachian Trail unraveled on the side of this mountain like a ball of yarn rolling across a floor. I trudged five or six steps up and then stopped to lean against a tree trunk and bring my breathing back to something short of gasping for air. Then five or six steps more on this narrow ledge of a trail, the steep incline ahead stretching straight and far and blocking too much of the sky to permit any hope that I was near the summit. What folly to do this. My knees ached, the hip belt of my backpack was pinching my right side, and sweat was dripping off my wrists and arms and brow, even though the day was not especially warm. My back ached from four sleepless nights on hard ground. Turning around was out of the question. Spivey Gap, where I had started climbing an hour before, offered no escape. Up was the only way out of this. Up and then up some more.

On my right twenty yards below the trail was a beautiful tumbling creek, the rapids and little waterfalls spilling over glistening rocks taunting me with the lovely sound of cold rushing water. On my left I could extend my arm and touch a wall of mountain, weathered mossy rock and thick rhododendron. Five, six, seven steps advanced me a few yards up the trail and then I stopped for more gulps of water and air in my lungs.

I was done. I would drag myself out of this forest, somehow, however long it took, drive home, and put away this foolishness about hiking. No more of this torture. No more pretending I was a long-distance backpack hiker. No more sleepless nights, no more aches and pains. No more pretending I was a twenty-something . . . or even a fifty-something. Face the facts . . . I was too old, too out of shape. Not strong enough.

As if to confirm the good sense of this decision by showing me what a *real* hiker looked like, a young man came tromping up behind me, his hiking pole tips clicking on the rocks to a steady, quick-tempo rhythm. I edged aside as much as I dared on the trail to let him pass. We exchanged hellos and I watched him climb with long, practiced strides. I both admired and hated everything about him—strength, competence, determination. The little triangular plastic tag with the A.T. symbol attached to his backpack told me he was headed for Maine. I was headed home. He was going to succeed; I had already failed. He was what I would never be, going where I would never go. And he disappeared up the trail within less than a minute, climbing at a rate I had imagined was impossible for any creature other than a mountain goat.

Every mountain has a summit, every ridge a highest point, and this one could not be an exception, though every step told me it must be for I was going nowhere. This one was not even significant enough for a name and not especially high and certainly not technically difficult, nothing compared to the long list of other named and famous big mountains that dot the 2,193-mile length of the Appalachian Trail from Georgia to Maine. A couple of them I had already hiked on previous trips to the south. Knowing this made the embarrassment and complete failure of it all the worse. If a mountain so undistinguished could bring me to such grief, what chance did I have of climbing the big ones farther north? None.

Not even reaching the summit cheered me. Well into the afternoon, after an hour of agony, I topped out onto a forest over a broad, mostly level ridge. I was able to walk again rather than stagger like a drugged animal. My breathing settled back into a normal range of respiration. But still I was done with this. The aches in my knees, the peculiar twinges in my side, and the friction I felt in my feet with each step did not go away. No, I was done.

I was so engrossed in self-pity and beating myself up for ever thinking I could hike these mountains that for the last hour I had been missing the beauty of the forest I was in. Now, at the summit, I paused and looked around. Tall hardwoods and white pines and clumps of mountain laurel. A scattering of tiny white wildflowers. Mushrooms and ferns and lichen. Blankets of moss and mold spores. A few hemlocks and the trail ahead receded into a dark green tunnel of rhododendron. And a deep silence broken only by a birdcall somewhere or the hollow rapping of a woodpecker on a tree trunk and the soft swish of my boots over the pine needles. The trail leveled out into a series of modest dips and rises. Now, finally, I could just walk, just get this over. One more sleepless night and then home. My destination for the night, I realized with a grim chuckle, was No Business Shelter, the name apparently given because it was in times past the location of a moonshine still and strangers had no business hanging around there. How appropriate, I thought.

As I walked, the trail began a pattern of loops, with the summit of the ridgeline high above me on my left and below me on my right long expanses of forested valleys and distant mountains. The trail would swing left, hugging the mountainside, and up a draw, then turn sharply right, usually at a trickle of water pouring out of the mountain, and head out toward a nose pointing to the distant ranges and open sky. Vaguely, through my discomfort and all the negative thoughts buzzing around my head like flies, I became aware of how stunningly beautiful this mountain range in the Cherokee National Forest was, how alone I was here, how quiet and remote the forest was. And how much I would miss places like this.

At the second turning two loud squawks broke my miserable reverie and a large black bird was soaring above me at treetop height parallel to the trail. I have known crows since I was a boy, and I instantly knew this bird was not a crow, neither by the size of it nor by its call. The bird had to be a raven. I remembered the squawk from seeing and hearing ravens at the Grand Canyon. This one wheeled toward the valleys and flew off, but it circled and returned as I walked. And then again, flying closer to the trail this time, close enough that when I caught a good look at it through a gap in the tree canopy, I could take in its shape and admire the shiny black of its wings held motionless on a gentle current.

I walked and the raven soared above and beside me, flew off, circled back the way we both had come, and returned. I walked and lost count of how many times the raven repeated this circling. As though the bird were curious about me. Who was this stranger alone on this high ridge? What was he doing up here? Spellbound, I lost track of time. Every appearance of the raven made me smile. The effortless soaring on the updraft along the flank of the ridge allowed the raven to appear again and again, motionless against the blue sky, for long, beautiful moments. I am sure the raven was watching me.

And then, on the last of the trail loops, the raven broke off, flew over the trail ahead, and climbed higher on the ridge toward the top of a big white pine, squawking again and answered by a croak. It landed on a limb beside a big nest. Home. Greeted by its mate.

I walked on, still smiling. In the next moments, I was aware of something new welling up inside me. My aches and pains had diminished somewhere back down the trail. I was striding along confidently at a brisk pace, my backpack riding comfortably on my hips and off my shoulders. A warm tide of memories and images overwhelmed me. Of my grandfather walking tall beside me on his farm when I was a little boy. Of my wife at home, patiently abiding this foolishness of mine about hiking the Appalachian Trail. Of my daughter and my grandchildren and of all I loved and all that was dear to me, friends I treasure and friends I have lost. Of my grandfather's gentle laughter when, as a young boy, I would call out to him when we walked together down the long, wooded path to his pastures—"I'm coming, Grandaddy, I'm coming!"

Indeed, I was. Look at me, I thought as these images flickered, memories that had not visited my mind in years and years, my mother sewing, my pretty wife when we were dating, Africa, the smell of it in the mornings the week before the rains came . . . quail flushed from the cornrows of my grandfather's farm . . . the black snake I nearly stepped on and my grandfather's gentle laughter when I jumped backward into his arms. Tears trickled down my face, mingling with the sweat. Why were all these powerful memories so suddenly reeling through my mind? Fortunately, no other hikers were around to see a grown teary-eyed man grinning like a fool out in the middle of a high mountain forest—something that would have been impossible to explain to anyone because I could not explain this sudden beautiful flush of emotions to myself. I am coming . . . I am coming. I am doing this.

Half an hour earlier, I had been determined to quit. My decision had been clinched climbing to the top of this ridge, sealed when I was out of breath and hurting all over and disgusted with myself. Now I felt something utterly unexpected: I desperately wanted to belong here on this trail. Go home, yes, because I had to for a while, but quit, give this up after less than three hundred miles of hiking this famous trail? Yes, it had been hard, and yes, my knees were sore, and my back was fragile, but hadn't I just climbed to the top of that steep nameless mountain back there? And hadn't I survived the Smokies despite all my mistakes, including a near disaster at the end?

A new realization hit me as I walked the last miles to No Business Shelter—the undeniable truth that failure had been the hallmark of most of my adult life. Twenty years of continuous, uninterrupted failures, one after the other, each one comprehensive and without the slightest glimmer of hope that the next time would be any different. Failures so complete that I had become accustomed to them. Failures that I hid from everyone but my family and a few friends, and so much of this failure had piled up that now I never spoke about it. Like it had never happened. Or it had happened to someone else, someone who did not live around here anymore.

But I still lived with it. And now, attempting something hard and wildly ambitious, something I probably had no reasonable business doing, not at my age and in my condition, here I was staring at failure yet again. Wanting to quit. Swinging for the fence again and striking out. Giving up because it was too hard. Failing. . . . The appearance of the raven and its curious circling above me broke the grip of all those negative complaints about how hard this was and tumbled all those wonderful memories out of my head. And if something so magically unexpected and energizing as that could bubble up from the pain and misery, maybe this was a hard, crazy thing that could be different. Maybe I could hike more of this trail. All I had to do was keep walking. Which, after all, was the simplest thing I had ever learned to do.

A repeated way between what is known and a desired purpose—that is what a trail really is, according to the writer Robert Moor. Older than Homo sapiens, older than mammals, even as old as the most ancient fossils of living creatures, trails are among the most ubiquitous and long-serving creations of earth-bound and mobile life. Birds and fish need know nothing of trails, but we and our mammal kin do and have for a long, long time.

Through all those eons of deep time, says Moor, trails have built themselves through use and utility. This is the best way to the waterhole. This one is the surest way to the fruit trees. This path goes over the high pass to the next valley—to Oregon. Or California. Or Nepal. That one takes you to the clan that trades us the shells for our beads or to the next village. Or the post office, or the mysterious waterfall where the water spirits lived or the picnic tables in the park.

That is the point: throughout our time on this planet trails have taken us places we needed to go. They lasted as long as people or animals needed them, and when they did not use them anymore, for whatever reason, the trails slowly disappeared, reclaimed by forest or prairie grass, tundra or sand, obliterated by earthquakes, landslides, and floods. At ten thousand years old, the Old North Trail that runs along the eastern edge of the Rocky Mountains from the Arctic to present-day Mexico City may be the oldest human-made trail in North America. The Natchez Trace and the Mohawk Trail are also very old. The Warrior's Path that spans the Appalachians, the Athiamiowee, or Path of the Armed Ones, was used for trade and raiding by the Shawnee of Ohio and the Cherokee of east Tennessee. These trails made sense, and they persisted for hundreds or thousands of years because they reduced the complexity of a landscape, a wilderness, a forest, or a prairie to a streamlined and socially coherent way to get from here to there. Accumulated wisdom was their main ingredient, and utility was what preserved them through the centuries.[1]

Until very recently, this was the single reason for trails in the long scale of Earth time. People did not hike these old trails—that usage in the English language dates back only about two hundred years—the trails were traveled for a purpose, and on foot or by pack animal or herds.[2] But something new happened. In 1819 in America, a New Englander named Abel Crawford had the idea of blazing a trail to the summit of Mount Washington in the White Mountains of New Hampshire, a place where no human being ever needed to go, and a destination utterly lacking a practical purpose.[3] Some of his New England neighbors must have thought old Abel was crazy, because the 6,288-foot summit of that mountain was and still is a dangerous place, a rock-covered peak where many people have perished in the past and still can any month of the year if the weather conditions turn nasty.

But Abel was onto something that was brewing here in America and had already taken root in Europe. Walking just for the pleasure of walking had for some time been acquiring famous adherents—the list would come to include names such as William Wordsworth, William Belloc, Fredrick Nietzsche, and Søren Kierkegaard, and, here in America, a little later would come Henry David Thoreau and, of course, John Muir. And not just Western people—the Japanese poet Bashō famously walked everywhere, writing his haiku as he went. Chinese sages, holy men in India, wanderers, even the Buddha—these were the pioneers of walking for the sake of walking. Wandering, really, with no purpose in mind. But Crawford sensed that something else was possible. Walking for pleasure was not just for poets and pilgrims, tramps and thinkers—the appeal could spread to the common man, to the shopkeeper or mill worker, to whole families who sought a few hours of freedom from their working week and the hustle and bustle of their lives. This was what became tourism, and it was born out of a combination of our natural human curiosity, free time for leisure activity, the allure of grand scenery, and the desire to escape the congestion, filth, and tumult of cities. Abel Crawford realized he could make a go out of hauling people to the top of Washington, where the air was pure and the ground was pristine, and he needed a trail to get them up there. The Crawford Trail today remains a long, thin thread marked by old stone cairns up and over the greatest mountain in New England and no one who walks it thinks in utilitarian terms.

But the real novelty, the invention no one at the time could have foreseen, the idea that took hold and grew into something amazing, very modern, and very American, is the Appalachian Trail, a footpath of 2,193 miles stretching from Springer Mountain in Georgia to Katahdin in Maine.[4] No one saw this coming when the forester Benton MacKaye dreamed it and put the thing on paper and had his article published in the October 1921 issue of the *Journal of the American Institute of Architects*. In Vermont, the Green Mountain Club had already created the Long Trail, a 172-mile progenitor of what was to come. But MacKaye's vision was truly radical, a footpath up and down the spine of the Appalachian chain, a trail not intended for hiking week after week, certainly not from Georgia to Maine, but rather to provide refuge from urban sprawl and noise for East Coast city dwellers through short stays in wilderness camps linked by his trail that climbed the biggest mountains available.

But once volunteers hacked a path through the forests and completed it in 1937, the Appalachian Trail became a thing of its own, no longer the work of its creators. Inevitably, someone decided to walk every mile of it within a single year. Trail authorities credited as the first Earl Shaffer, who completed the length of the trail south to north in 1948.[5] The Appalachian Trail Conservancy at first had to be convinced that he had walked all those miles and was worried that his hike would be seen as a "stunt." But then the navy veteran Gene Espy and two other young men hiked it in 1951, and a woman, Mildred Norma Ryder, did it in 1952, and the same year a seventy-two-year-old retired professor did it, and then another woman, Emma "Grandma" Gatewood, more famously hiked the trail in 1955, at the age of sixty-six. The publicity they generated spawned more hikers, and by the late 1960s Benton MacKaye's vision of linked mountain camps in nature giving relief from city life for a week or so was completely replaced by the idea that the Appalachian Trail existed to be hiked, in short pieces for those who could, and from end to end for those who dared. Achieving Georgia to Maine or vice versa within a single year came to be known as a thru-hike, and its appeal grew every decade as stories of grand adventures circulated and the outdoor recreation industry promoted long-distance hiking and developed lightweight specialized gear.

The Appalachian Trail, like the Crawford and the Long and all the hundreds of other "recreational" trails they have spawned, is in some respects a crazy idea. No one needs to walk the entire Appalachian Trail. There is no point to it, nothing whatsoever useful about it, in a practical sense, and it could be the worst conceivable way for a human to travel from Georgia to Maine. Grandma Gatewood might have explained it best when after completing her hike in 1955 she told a writer for Sports Illustrated, "This is no trail. This is a nightmare. For some fool reason, they always lead you right up over the biggest rock to the top of the biggest mountain they can find."[6] And yet every year for the past few decades thousands of people from across the country and many nations arrive in Georgia in the late winter and early spring bound and determined to walk every mile of the A.T. in a single year. On average, between a fifth and a quarter of them succeed. The great majority quit in Georgia after about twenty miles or less.

How I found myself walking this famous trail in spurts is still a bit of a mystery to me. I fell into it little by little, the way a first sip of fine wine can turn you into a connoisseur. The trail's southern terminus, Springer Mountain, is about an hour's drive from my home. Since I was a teenager, it has been a place and an idea I was vaguely aware of and attracted to. I had even walked a very short piece of the trail several times without understanding that I was on it and that if I kept going, I would eventually end up in Maine. Not until I retired in 2015 did I ever intentionally set foot on the Appalachian Trail to discover what it is. I did this one day purely on a whim, to get some exercise out in the woods. After a few leisurely miles I turned around and walked back to my car and drove home. I thought nothing of it at the time because I had returned to the short section of the trail that I knew, starting at a place called Three Forks and walking north toward a pretty waterfall my wife and daughter and I had visited a few times years before on weekend camping trips. The walk was relaxing and the scenery pretty but nothing really special.

But on this short, pleasant walk after my retirement something unexpected happened. I encountered a young man headed for Maine. We stopped to chat. He was from New York, taking a year off between jobs, between careers actually, and hoping to figure out some things about himself on his anticipated six-month journey. He had never been in Georgia before and was amazed at the beauty of these mountains just now leafing out with green in the early spring. We walked on in opposite directions, and I paid attention for the first time to the small rectangular white blaze painted at eye level on a tree trunk beside the trail. Those white blazes stretched from here all the way to Maine. That was about the extent of my knowledge of the Appalachian Trail. Newly retired from an important, stressful, all-consuming job at which I had been successful beyond anything I had imagined possible, I realized I now had time on my hands. As I drove home the thought occurred to me—next time why not walk some more of the trail and see what was over the next hill? Hiking is just a fancy name for walking—it takes no athletic skill or talent or special qualifications. A good thing, too, because I possessed none of that. I enjoyed walking to pass the time. How hard could walking a trail in the woods be?

Bears

A desire has to come from somewhere. It does not just appear out of thin air. I did not just wake up one day and say to myself "I think I would like to hike the Appalachian Trail." In my case, the A.T. revived and reconfigured an attraction to the outdoors that had been lying dormant in me for a long time. James Baldwin, writing about the broad sweep of history, observed that history "does not refer merely, or even principally, to the past. On the contrary, the great force of history comes from the fact that we carry it within us, are unconsciously controlled by it in many ways, and history is literally present in all that we do."[1] Baldwin was thinking of big things, of course, when he wrote this, things like race and injustice and guilt. But what he said applies to less important things just as well. At the age of sixty-six I was carrying within me something that began around the age of five or six. None of what happened to me on the Appalachian Trail after I retired made sense until I came to remember that little boy and reflect on how he grew up.

My first steps as a wanderer and a walker in the woods began on my grandfather's one-hundred-acre farm. Every Sunday when I was a boy the routine was the same. After church my family drove thirty minutes west of town to my grandfather's farm not far from the Georgia-Alabama line, where we gathered in his small clapboard house for lunch. The meal was long and simple but ample. Afterward, the women of our family attended to the mountain of dishes, and the men, my grandfather and my father and my uncle and cousin and me, took a long walk. This was 1955, and life was unfair.

First we walked along an old wagon road through the woods and across a shallow creek, then to the barn, and then along a lane dividing the pastures where we observed and counted the cattle, then along another lane dividing the rich bottomland fields to the riverbank where Cedar Creek emptied into the muddy, fast-flowing Coosa River. To a child of six and then seven and eight, this walk had the feel of a great adventure, a long and difficult trek through a dark forest, across a shallow stream where I could throw rocks and make the water splash, across wide-open expanses in the hot sun or cold winter wind, and ending at a forbidden, dangerous place—the river the adults instructed me not to get too close to. And then, after making sure we had closed the pasture gates and the corncrib door was secured and the other little tasks my grandfather always remembered to complete, there was the long return to his house up a gradual slope through the woods.

Year after year as I grew up this Sunday ritual played out. By the age of ten sometimes it was only once a month but always it was the same. And when I was deemed old enough, each summer I spent a week with my grandfather and grandmother on that farm, sleeping on a pallet they made for me on the floor. By the time I was a teenager I had covered every corner and odd turn of the creek, knew by heart the lay of the land and had discovered most of its mysteries—the black flint Indian arrowheads from the highest of the bottomland fields every spring when they were plowed, the black snake that hid in the corncrib, the fallow corn fields where quail always startled me with their sudden rush of wings, the crows warning of my approach when I emerged from the woods.

This was my initiation as a hiker, although I did not know it and would not pursue hiking as a young man. I pursued a career instead, a family, a house, and the possessions that accompany modern life. And then I went chasing after a chimera, a huge and unlikely dream, and the pursuit went poorly from the start and never got better. But when the time was right, those wonderous days of my boyhood on my grandfather's farm returned to me as an unexpected gift from my past. Like Baldwin said, I had been carrying them with me all that time.[1]

The wrong place to first experience multiday backpacking on the Appalachian Trail in the South is through the Great Smoky Mountains. I should have known this because my two previous weekend backpacking trips years before in lesser mountain ranges than the Smokies had not gone to plan, with considerable embarrassment involved both times. Nonetheless, when a friend called me in July 2017 with the invitation to join him and hike the Appalachian Trail through the Smokies, I jumped at the chance. I had already passed up opportunities to backpack the A.T. with him through Georgia and the Nantahalas in North Carolina, and I was not going to let this one slip by me.

Like so many of the rookie hikers I had met in Georgia, I was woefully unprepared to backpack anywhere, much less the seventy-two miles of the Appalachian Trail in the Smokies. The A.T. enters the southern edge of the Great Smoky Mountains National Park at Fontana Dam, climbs Shuckstack Mountain on a mostly northern compass bearing, and then takes a ninety-degree turn to the east along the spine of the Smokies, climbing Rocky Top and Thunderhead Mountains and reaching 6,000 feet just before Mount Buckley, and then goes up Clingman's Dome to 6,643 feet. A brief dip below 6,000 feet brings the trail to the tourist-infested road and parking lot at Newfound Gap. But as the trail continues east along the narrow spine of the Smokies, hikers bounce between 5,500 and 6,000 feet over some of the most spectacular scenery and remote mountains in the southeastern United States before diving at a sharp angle into a long descent to Davenport Gap.

The weather on those ridges is different from the weather down either the northwestern or southeastern slopes into the valleys of Tennessee and North Carolina. Clear blue sky is rare any season of the year. Snow and ice are a threat except in the depth of summer, when sudden and violent thunderstorms replace that risk. Many thru-hikers I subsequently met talked about their experiences hiking the A.T. through the Smokies in the late winter or early spring with a shudder of awful memory. Days of drenching cold rain, rain that just will not end, deep layers of dark clouds and fog that roll and swirl over you endlessly, long shivering nights with temperatures in the low teens, howling winds and the danger of frostbite, treacherous patches of ice on narrow, difficult trails where a fall is going to send you to a hospital—if you are lucky enough to reach one. And the only place to get off the trail is Newfound Gap, but only if the U.S. Park Service has not closed the road due to dangerous conditions, which they do routinely.

Which is too bad, because the Smokies, as millions upon millions of American tourists would gladly affirm, are glorious beyond description. Having been one of those tourists on several occasions since I was a boy, I had no idea what was waiting for me when I stood at Fontana Dam on a bright sunny August morning to have my picture taken with my friend before we set out to climb Shuckstack. Retired like me, my friend was already experienced at backpacking and had good gear and was good at the planning necessary for a hike like this. He even had a trail name, Quicktime. But I was terribly naïve about hiking. Make a list of all the rookie mistakes an Appalachian Trail hiker could make and I would have checked the boxes of at least three-quarters of them. Wrong backpack was the worst one, a little thirty-liter day pack crammed with thirty-six pounds of stuff, most of which was the wrong stuff. Wrong shoes, heavy, clunky hiking boots. Wrong rain gear. And most ominously, the wrong sleeping gear, a thin foam roll-up pad and a too-heavy, not-low-enough-rated sleeping bag. On top of that, I was so excited about the grand adventure awaiting me that I forgot to power off my cell phone before we started.

The plan was to hike from the southwestern end at Fontana to the northeastern end at Davenport over a week. The first day was wonderful. I made it up the long climb to the top of Shuckstack mostly on enthusiasm. At Doe Knob the view to the west was a fantastic panorama of mountain ranges glowing in varying shades of green from olive to lime all the way to the limit of the horizon, a sight taken in by only a tiny fraction of those millions of Smoky Mountain visitors because of the remoteness of the place and the rarity of clear skies. We pushed on over Devil's Tater Patch and walked to Russell Field Shelter in good order after nine hours of hiking under a sky of puffy white clouds, a hike of 14.5 miles. I was very tired but happy. This was just fine, I thought. Just fine.

In the Smokies backcountry hikers must have a park permit to stay at the three-sided shelters. Section hikers cannot use tents; they have to sleep inside the shelter. The Park Service requires a permit for a specific shelter each night, which means a backpack trip has to be well planned. On day two our plan began to fall apart. Despite my fatigue, I was unable to sleep a single minute in the shelter, and I tumbled out into the cold dark about 4:00 a.m. I wrapped up in my sleeping bag and sat on a log to keep from disturbing the row of hikers on the wooden platform slumbering away to a Looney Tunes-style melody of snores, grunts, groans, whistles, and the high notes of crinkling air mattresses.

Okay, I thought, it was a bad night, but so what? A little breakfast and I would be fine. Quicktime and I set out on another clear morning into a forest with a dense understory of rhododendron. After twenty-five minutes we were both feeling good, warm and loose, I was in the lead, hiking with a good pace, and we topped a rise and I pulled up suddenly with a bear in the trail twenty yards or so ahead of us.

"Good morning, mister bear!" I shouted with Quicktime walking up my back. He was a juvenile male, a fine-looking bear, his black fur shiny and smooth and his snout busily nuzzling into some roots or grubs he had found that must have been quite tasty. The bear glanced at us but was in no hurry to finish his breakfast. After a few moments he reluctantly moved off the trail into a patch of ferns, turned around after about five or ten yards, and plopped down on his haunches to look at us. He obviously did not intend to move.

I had practiced beforehand what to do if I saw a bear—make a loud noise and do not run—but this bear was not following my script, which called for the bear to run away from us. He seemed content to sit there the rest of the morning. What to do? Walk past him seemed the best choice. The bear watched us silently and we both tried not to look him in the eye, just kept moving, not too fast, just walking on like we were passing a homeless person sitting on a sidewalk, resisting the temptation to look back. And that was it—our first encounter with a bear on the Appalachian Trail. We behaved ourselves, and the bear behaved like a bear should, and everything was fine. The good fortune of seeing a bear at close range and without trouble was exhilarating but also a reminder that we were the visitors here in the Smokies. The hiking here was serious business and we needed to be alert to our surroundings.

Three hours later the seriousness of what I was doing hit me hard. Quicktime had pushed on, hiking much faster and better than I was. Rocky Top loomed up ahead and the morning was unexpectedly warm now, hot even when I occasionally emerged from the trees into patches of sun and wildflowers. The final few hundred yards of the climb were steeper than anything I had encountered so far on my short day hikes in Georgia. I was gasping for breath at the open summit, bent over and sweaty and too slammed by the climb to notice that I was standing on bare rock with a sweeping 360-degree view of nothing but mountains and sky in every direction. Once I recovered a little and gulped down some water and looked around me, I was dumbfounded by the view on this clear, bright day. Miles and miles of forested mountains glowing in a color wheel of greens and pale blues, and with this came the sense of being very far away from anyone else except my friend standing beside me, a remoteness I had earned by sweat and burning leg muscles.

Up the trail was Thunderhead, slightly higher than Rocky Top. After taking some pictures with our phone cameras and drinking plenty of water, we resumed hiking. Very quickly the heat, my lack of sleep, and the exhausting climb began to drag me into a stupor and slow my walk to a crawl. And now my lack of preparation hit with full force, the straps of my heavy pack digging into my shoulders, my feet like two cinder blocks in those dreadful boots, and my legs no longer driving me forward with any force. The trail did not help, for although the bulk of the climbing was behind me, the rocks and the ups and downs on the ridge past Thunderhead were hard to walk. Then came another shock, a very steep descent to Starkey Gap, and on every step of it my toes jammed into the ends of those boots and my knees wavered with pains I had never felt before.

All those mistakes piled up with every mile, not helped by the irony that I was hiking through some of the most beautiful country I had ever seen. The ridge past Starkey Gap was wild and varied, with evergreens and hardwoods and ferns and exotic wildflowers I could not identify because I had never seen anything like them before. In a better physical and mental state, I would have enjoyed every minute. Instead, I dragged myself into Derrick Knob Shelter in midafternoon hot, hungry, and exhausted. Quicktime was already there and was pondering the trail map. While in much better shape than I was, he was also very tired. We had another five and a half miles to go to reach our permitted shelter for the night at Siler Bald.

"I don't know," I said between slugs of water. "If we have to, I think I can make it there . . . but it's gonna be tough."

At the pace I was now reduced to, I might just arrive before sundown. And that was if everything went well. We quickly agreed to a change in the plan. Permit notwithstanding, we were going to stay at Derrick Knob for the night.

What followed was a series of hard lessons about hiking. A second night of zero sleep. Problems with my toes. A backache that now was a permanent fixture. Climbing toward Clingman's Dome, a phalanx of thunderstorms drove at the Smokies out of the northwest, separate cells visible and arranged in ragged rows, the underbellies of the clouds dark and ominous. Alone because Quicktime had walked to the observation tower to try to get cellphone service, thunderclaps close by abruptly surrounded me, and I struggled to wrestle on the rain cover for my pack and pull on my heavy raincoat. I was soon sweltering and disoriented by the loud thunder all around me. Big heavy raindrops splattered the ground but did not intensify, as if I was right under the edge of the cloud producing them. Somehow, I walked the wrong way at a trail junction. After ten minutes or so I realized something was wrong, but I could make no sense of my map or surroundings, so I sat down on a rock in the middle of the trail and let the storm sweep past me. In the midst of that I discovered that my cellphone battery was dead.

Sitting down was the best decision I made all day. Quicktime found me, and we pushed on in the correct direction, but I was now a wreck, and we still had Mount Collins to climb and several miles between us and the next shelter. Then another sleepless night, this one worse because of the pains in my back and hips and the soreness of my legs. And the temperatures plunged after midnight because we were at nearly six thousand

feet. By 3:00 a.m. I was shivering in my bag. The next day I dragged myself over the five and a half miles to Newfound Gap, a bedraggled, filthy,
and exhausted mess of a hiker.

Arriving at Newfound Gap was like stepping through an *Alice in Wonderland* mirror, going in one instant from a National Geographic nature
film to the Disney World parking lot. Cars jammed the asphalt, tourists
milled around, dressed in shorts and flowery shirts or T-shirts blaring
messages, flip-flops and sandals and sunglasses, people from every state
except Hawaii. Children ran loose and loud and having the time of their
lives, cameras snapped pictures of the blue haze beyond the rock parapet, and people posed in front of that haze for pictures destined for their
refrigerator doors.

I crossed in between the lines of cars in a haze of my own making. At
the stone parapet I unbuckled my pack and let it fall to the sidewalk with
a thump. I carefully tugged my feet out of my shoes so as not to set off
the fire alarms in my toes and stood there in stinking socks grateful beyond words that our hike was at an end, for I knew I could not go on. And
yet that is exactly what I wanted to do—hike on, to the next shelter, the
next ridge, climb the next mountain, whatever was out there beyond the
white blaze I was staring at where the Appalachian Trail left the parking
lot and began the climb toward Mount Kephart. Our plan for this day had
been to reach Pecks Shelter, a hike of fifteen miles. Impossible, and we
both knew it. Instead, a shuttle was on the way to pick us up and then we
would drive home.

As I leaned against the rock wall in a fog of recrimination and defeat,
a woman tourist walked by and smiled.

"Are you an Appalachian Trail thru-hiker?" she asked hopefully.

Aghast, I quickly set her straight. Oh no . . . just out for three days . . .
thru-hikers are a very different class, and the great majority of them who
leave Georgia never make it this far. Those who do are the elite, the very
few who have a chance to make it all the way to Maine. I was . . . well, I
was none of that and to be misidentified as belonging to the elite was
embarrassing. I was not even a respectable section hiker. I was a wreck,
headed home. I tried to explain all of this, hoping no *real* thru-hikers
were around to hear it.

To my surprise, the lady was not disappointed. Instead, she was impressed that I had walked here from Fontana Dam.

"That's pretty cool," she said.

In that moment, hot and so sleep-deprived I could barely string together coherent sentences, I was not impressed with what I had done. This was another failure. Not as consequential as the larger failures that always tromped behind me like little demons living in the cobwebs of my memory, the one that started in Africa and the rest strung out in a twenty-year line like the painful miles I had just hiked. Still, it was a failure I could not deny. But one thing I knew—I would come back to the Smokies. And next time would be different.

⌒⌒

The novelist John Wray by chance discovered an obscure book titled *Bear Attacks: Their Causes and Avoidance.* From this mostly technical book by a well-known authority on bears, Steven Herrero, Wray learned the story of a man who played dead in an encounter with a grizzly bear and was not harmed. That turned upside down a conception Wray had long held. Playing dead, Wray said, does not play well at the macho end of our modern American culture. There is something weak about it, more than a little whiff of cowardice in the idea that you would not fight back if you were attacked.[2] Indeed, that is the "expert" advice often given: fight the bear and hope it goes away.

But there is another side to this idea, he said. In an extreme moment of great danger, fighting back against a force much greater than yourself might be the worst thing to do. Wray discovered that "playing dead" could at times in fact be the only means of "remaining alive," and thereby a creative act requiring great discipline and courage. The fear, he said, is inescapable, and therefore fighting it is worse than futile. And this fear relates to doing something both solitary and difficult, like writing or any form of concentrated thinking that requires being alone in complete silence—which can be terrifying, much like facing a real bear can be. That kind of bear, the cold numbing terror, is one you can never run away from because it is in your head, and you are all by yourself when you encounter it. You can't run away from it, and no one can help you face it. But you can learn to do this hard thing. And with practice and a little bravery, you can learn that the silence in your own head is actually the sound of remaining alive to all sorts of new and wonderful possibilities.

The temptation is to run away from a bear. But the correct thing to do is stand still, make yourself big, make some noise, and watch. A grizzly bear and a black bear are two entirely different species of danger, as anyone who has ever faced both of them at close range will tell you. But the principle is the same for either species. Escape is rarely an option. Standing your ground against the fear works best but is, of course, no guarantee that you will walk away unscathed. Or even at all. Sometimes a bear goes rogue and attacks, and sometimes, very rarely, but sometimes, bears kill people. If a bear attacks, you have to decide whether to fight back or play dead. Either choice might be wrong. You can never be sure.

Hiking for just three days in the Smokies had taught me lessons about the proper gear to take, better hiking techniques to use, and things to avoid. But mostly I learned to stand still in the presence of the bear, both the one I met on the trail and the one I carried around in my head. The most amazing and surprising thing that happened to me on my first Smokies hike was the calmness I felt in the bears' presence. Both of them, the actual bear and being alone for long stretches of time. I wanted to go back and finish what I had started and do it better the next time.

A Different
Kind of Bear

The philosopher Martin Hägglund has written that how we should spend our time is the most important question humans can ask. What should we care about? What do we owe each other? And he says that capitalism helped give us the idea that we have a right to freedom and equality. We own our time, each of us, but we either gladly or unhappily or mindlessly allow others to buy most of our time from us, and unequally so. We are free to sell our time on this earth, but usually we do so to make a living, to pay the bills, to have a roof over our heads. Therefore, neither the worker nor the capitalist, the seller nor the buyer, is actually free because profit dictates how each of us spends our time. Profit calls the tune, and we dance profit's dance, oblivious to the price we are paying.[1]

And our time runs out. After essentially wasting the productivity of two decades of my middle age, I was acutely aware of the truth of this, painfully aware that I had sold a big chunk of my best years for exactly no return. From that perspective, walking in the woods on a trail no one needs to walk for six months or more seemed like a colossal waste of time. Hägglund argues that what truly matters in life is how we treat one another in this life and that the highest good is the communities we build and the way we recognize and take care of one another. Our responsibility, he says, should be horizontal instead of vertical.[2] And hiking a pointless trail for weeks at a time, not to mention half a year, falls unquestionably in the vertical category.

I had determined that my retirement would be horizontal, devoted to making up the time I had lost with my family due to work, and doing what I could to help build my community. I became a mentor at our local high school. I was appointed to the local library board and then became a trustee of the district library system. And I launched into a long list of projects around the house that I had neglected for so long. I stayed busy, my weeks mostly filled with responsibilities. An occasional walk in the woods on the Appalachian Trail provided exercise that I allowed myself after years of office meetings, sitting at a desk, attending more meetings, telephone calls, travel to conferences, and always, always, more meetings. My stressed-out body needed the exercise, and my mind needed the solitude.

Over the next months in increments of four or five miles, six or seven hours at a time, I had explored new stretches of the Appalachian Trail in Georgia, carrying a few items with me in a twenty-dollar pack. I had no idea what I was doing. Worse, I was blissfully unaware that the world's most famous hiking trail was seducing me. And, of course, this ignorance could not last.

The enticement, I realized only much later, after hundreds of miles of hiking, was in my head. When you walk alone, your mind does not have much to do. Most of the time in those hours of walking in the woods up and down the mountains and ridgelines in Georgia, my mind raced along faster than my feet, constantly thinking. Most of those hours I walked with thoughts and ideas and monologues swirling around in my head. I was used to this, after all, for my former job required me to think through problems and plan out my time down to the quarter hour. I had developed the discipline to squeeze work out of whatever loose time I could find—while driving, while eating lunch, while riding to the airport, even on Saturday mornings and Sunday evenings. I need to do this and this and this, in that order. Next, I need to attend to that and finish this and then there will be meetings and then I will go to the tiny apartment near my office, eat a cold supper, call my wife to catch up on our family, read a little, and then roll out of bed at 5:00 a.m. the next morning and do it all over again. But on my walks odd little moments found me not

thinking of anything in particular. Not enough was going on in my retired life to fill all these hours of walking, so occasionally I simply walked
and noticed what was all around me. A bizarre, twisted tree that looked
like something that should illustrate a Grimm fairy tale. A scattering of
tiny yellow flowers. An amazing number of spider webs across the trail
that I kept walking into. The sound of a creek splashing over rocks well
before I came to cross it. The labor of my breathing as the trail climbed
steeply and switched back right and left to reach a summit. The beams of
sunlight through the tree canopy refracting and playing patterns of light
and shade over the green forest floor.

These "empty" moments were the best waste of time I had ever known.

⤳

For an unprepared beginner, walking into the unknown on the Appalachian Trail can be painful, or even dangerous. Every year in Georgia this
happens when thousands of hikers arrive from all over the country and
many other nations to attempt to hike all the way to Maine. Eager, excited, maybe a little bit scared, many of them are oblivious to the seriousness of what they are about to encounter during the first few days of
their great adventure. The North Georgia mountains can contain some
nasty surprises for those hikers who are not properly equipped or well informed about what awaits them. The weather, for one thing, is not what
many hikers expect. Georgia is in the South, so they assume it must be
mild there, even in February. And plenty of relatively mild, even balmy,
winter days in the Georgia mountains can reinforce that illusion. But
then a cold front sweeps down from the plains or even Canada, and the
North Georgia mountains bear the brunt of freezing cold, high winds,
snow, sleet, and heavy downpours. Hiking the Appalachian Trail at three
thousand feet or higher in those conditions is miserable under any circumstances, and downright dangerous for hikers who are not prepared
for the awful weather. Hypothermia is a real threat, and every season
some unfortunate hikers feel its sting. Occasionally the sting can be fatal.

And then the mountains themselves provide another shock. The plan-
ners who routed the Appalachian Trail through North Georgia brought

the treadway down out of the Nantahalas in North Carolina and followed the ridgeline of the Blue Ridge range first south and then in a sharp swing to the southwest, which took the path over a series of peaks— Kelly Knob, Tray Mountain, Rocky Mountain, Blue Mountain, and Blood Mountain, all of them more than four thousand feet high. In between are peaks only slightly less tall and a series of gaps, all the way to Springer Mountain, the southern terminus. For a hiker on the Georgia A.T., the word "gap" means a big descent immediately followed by a big climb, and thirty-two of them are waiting for a hiker between Springer and the North Carolina state line.

All this elevation change while carrying thirty pounds or so in a backpack can have some unpleasant effects on someone not accustomed to the toil of hiking ten or twelve miles each day in Georgia. An athletic, slender young woman thru-hiker I met on the trail in North Carolina in early spring, upon learning I was from Georgia, blew out a deep breath and shook her head with a scowl on her face.

"Georgia kicked my butt!" she said. "I couldn't believe how hard it was."

She looked to be an exceptionally fit young lady. "Did you train for your hike?" I asked.

"I run marathons and 10Ks! I play tennis! I'm in great shape . . . and Georgia kicked my butt anyway."

This did not quite add up, so I paused a moment, smiling awkwardly, as if I, a native Georgian, might somehow be to blame for this. Then I noticed the deep brown tan of her face and hands.

"Where are you from?" I asked.

"Miami."

"Ah, well. . . ."

"Yeah, Miami's flat. Dumb me. . . ."

No, the Appalachian Trail through Georgia is not flat, and the elevation changes are hard on knees unaccustomed to climbing and descending. And the weather accentuates the physical difficulty. In the late winter and early spring, when most thru-hikers arrive at Springer to begin walking north, the weather swings abruptly from mild, even warm, to wet and bitter cold to even violent with high wind, ice-covered trees, limbs that break and crash to the ground without warning, and sheets of ice on steep exposed rock.

And it was on one of those relatively mild but gray gloomy days in late winter that I encountered Thomas, who would have to deal with all those hazards plus another difficulty imposed by southern Appalachia, one the large majority of other hikers never have to consider.

Thomas towered over my six-foot height. He came walking toward me, a Black man wearing blue jeans and a cotton sweatshirt, with a smile that lit up the forest, like he was meeting an old friend on a city sidewalk. He was wearing heavy work boots, and had a tree branch for a walking stick in one hand and a plastic bottle of water, half consumed, in the other. Around his left shoulder was a rolled-up plastic tarp that he had tied with cord, and on his head was a give-away baseball cap. From a distance he gave the appearance of a Civil War soldier dressed in half blue and half gray, emerging like a ghost out of the gloom. And he had just climbed up and over the first truly difficult mountain on the Georgia section of the Appalachian Trail, 3,350-foot Sassafras Mountain, difficult because of the steep ascent out of Horse Gap.

I was out for a day hike with a light backpack, still a novice at this hiking business myself, and I had already heard about Thomas. Two Georgia Appalachian Trail Club trail ambassadors had met him at Hawk Mountain Shelter earlier in the day.[3] They had reported that Thomas was alone, that he had hitchhiked to Georgia from Texas, that someone had given him a ride from Atlanta up to Springer and let him out to begin walking the Appalachian Trail to Maine. And there were two other important details—Thomas was homeless. And he had next to no money.

He had gotten this far, nearly twelve miles from Springer, on food given to him by other thru-hikers. (Most rookie thru-hikers pack far too much food and are more than happy to give some of it away once they realize what the extra weight is doing to their knees.) But at this juncture Thomas was in trouble, and worse, he did not have a clue why. A storm was coming. Within twenty-four hours the mild midfifties and overcast sky would turn into sheets of rain, forty-mile-an-hour gusts of wind, and temperatures in the low forties—perfect hypothermia conditions for a man wearing all cotton, who had no tent or jacket or rain gear except for the plastic tarp over his shoulder.

Thomas was happy to stop and chat. I introduced myself as a local native, which he evidently took to mean that I knew what I was doing out here on the A.T. I asked politely how are you, and he replied in a beautiful baritone voice that he was having a fine day and enjoying the experience of hiking the Appalachian Trail. I motioned to his half-empty water bottle and mentioned that the next water source was another two miles north. I had an extra unopened bottle of water in my pack that I offered him, and Thomas thanked me. I handed him a snack bar and his reaction was like I had just given him a winning lottery ticket.

"How was climbing Sassafras?" I asked.

"Pretty hard, but I made it okay. Kinda hurt my feet some."

"How are you making out in those boots?"

"Not so good. I think I've got some blisters."

I had a moleskin kit in my backpack that I pulled out and gave him, explaining that from my own limited experience I knew blisters would only get worse the farther he walked and could lead to real trouble. Again, Thomas thanked me over and over.

Then I mentioned the weather forecast. Thomas had heard from other hikers that bad weather was coming but he figured he would just keep walking. Or maybe get to a road and hitchhike somewhere if it was really rough. He said this nonchalantly, as though he had done this plenty of times before. But Thomas was now in southern Appalachia. Not so long ago, a Black man hitchhiking on one of the few roads that wind up through the gaps and cross the Appalachian Trail in Georgia would have been both an anomaly and a man at risk. Now . . . well, times had changed, but how much was difficult to measure.

In fact, a Black man anywhere on the A.T. was still an uncommon sight. The first Black person known to have thru-hiked the Appalachian Trail was Lori "Tenderfoot" Pierce, who hiked in 1987.[4] The first Black man known to have thru-hiked the Appalachian Trail was Robert Taylor, who completed the journey in the 1990s. Taylor encountered racism and discrimination in every one of the fourteen states between Springer and Katahdin. He reported that southwestern Virginia was the worst, but he had persevered. In towns he was yelled at, called the N-word, told by a postmaster "Boy, get outta here!" when he stopped at a post office for a mail drop. Even on the trail itself other thru-hikers wondered what he was doing out there and acted like he was going to steal their gear. "I remember thinking," Taylor said, "I'm not going to steal your stuff. I'm having a hard enough time carrying mine."

Racism burrowed deep into the mountains of southern Appalachia long ago, even though the mountain ranges, valleys, and coves were mostly populated by poor Whites who could not afford slaves and made a hardscrabble living off land ill-suited for large-scale farming that demanded slave labor. The region was infamous for its suspicion or outright hostility toward strangers of any kind, all the more so toward Blacks, and streaks of that sad legacy remain today in isolated pockets. The characterization of Appalachian Whites depicted by poet and novelist James Dickey in his novel *Deliverance* and especially in the movie of the same name starring Burt Reynolds, was a warped literary exaggeration, but those scenes of degradation were drawn from Southern stereotypes that lived in the popular imagination of suburban America and are, as the saying goes, "old as the hills."

And the Appalachian Trail that traverses those mountain ranges was thus long known as a place where Blacks were not welcome. Many of the hiking clubs that built the trail had exclusionary membership policies that discriminated against Blacks and Jews. The Smoky Mountains Hiking Club, to point to one example, was founded in the 1920s and was open to "any reputable White person," according to the club's handbook. In 1960 a club member raised an objection to the policy, writing to the president, "I think the time is ripe to amend our constitution to eliminate the racial discrimination clause."[5] Three years later the Whites-only policy was gone, but you have to wonder if the attitude that put it there went with it.

Even the esteemed chief builder of the Appalachian Trail, Myron Avery, expressed unabashed racism about the trail and who it was built for.

Writing an essay in 1940, when he was president of what was then called the Appalachian Trail Conference, Avery extolled the virtue of a section of the route near Roanoke, Virginia, that, he said, had a "definite charm" and some "outstanding features," one of which was that the area's "racial stock was reputed to be perhaps the purest Anglo-Saxon in the eastern United States."[6]

A generation has passed since Robert Taylor hiked through Georgia and entered the history of the Appalachian Trail as the first Black man to make it all the way to Katahdin. Much of the overt and aggressive racism of the region has boiled away since then, but Confederate flags are still easy to find on the pickup trucks and front porches and flagpoles that dot the southern mountain valleys. They send a not-so-subtle message that times may have changed but plenty of people have not. So the idea that Thomas would hitchhike into one of those little crossroads like Suches seeking shelter and help was almost as alarming to me as the thought of him shivering in wet blue jeans and a sweatshirt on top of a mountain with windchills down in the twenties and nothing to protect him but that rolled-up tarp.

But as we chatted and I explained to Thomas what lay ahead on the trail and how far he would have to walk to reach a road, another thru-hiker came tumbling down off Sassafras Mountain and stopped. They knew each other from a night together at Hawk Mountain Shelter and their greeting was like two lost friends reuniting after decades apart. The new hiker was well equipped with the latest lightweight gear, a heavy down jacket, hiking shoes, and trekking poles. He knew about the bad weather approaching and had already made plans to get off the trail at the next road crossing. And he insisted on Thomas coming with him to spend the night in a motel. Everything was arranged, he said.

I left the two of them hiking down toward Cooper Gap, chatting away like old friends even though they had known each other less than twenty-four hours. Six days later I heard again about Thomas from one of the GATC trail ambassadors who patrol the Georgia section of the trail during thru-hiker season. He had met Thomas on the A.T. a few miles below the North Carolina line. Thomas was hiking alone, but now he had a backpack and a good jacket and proper hiking pants and shoes. He was well supplied with water and some food. He had acquired his new equipment from hiker boxes at hostels and from the generosity of other thru-hikers.

The trail ambassador had asked Thomas what his experience had been like hiking through Georgia and reported that his beautiful baritone voice had replied that it had all been good. People had been generous and helpful to him, he said. He was having the time of his life and looking forward to crossing the Smokies in a week or two. He had made lots of friends among the thru-hikers he had met, but he couldn't keep up with most of the young ones.

The Appalachian Trail has become over the decades not just a footpath through the woods and over mountains. It is something much more, something Benton MacKaye and Myron Avery and all the other trail pioneers could never have imagined. It is a catalyst for friendship and generosity, and a solvent that dissolves meanness and suspicion. Not always, of course, because the A.T. is American in every sense, and no part of the trail is immune from America's tragedies of violence and hatred. I would learn that indirectly later when I was in Virginia. But one of the defining characteristics of the Appalachian Trail is change. Walking it indelibly changes people, and change is just as much woven into the fabric of America as any of the ideals the nation was founded on. By the time I began hiking the Appalachian Trail, that change in attitude about race was evident everywhere I looked. Meeting a Black man or woman hiking the trail was still not a common thing, but it was no big deal, and no A.T. hiker I ever met would have eyed a Black person with the suspicion that they were up to no good. Thomas was lucky, no doubt, and his story could have turned out differently, maybe even tragically. Like any hiker, he should have been better prepared, and there was the issue of trying to undertake such a huge journey with no money or means of support. But his good fortune in Georgia was not a surprise. As I hiked farther north, I saw and encountered similar happy endings often enough to judge them a feature of the Appalachian Trail, not a bug.

Also, there was one more thing the trail ambassador reported about

Thomas, and it was one thing that had not changed since I met him—Thomas's broad smile still lit up the forest. He was indeed having the time of his life.

⤢

A few weeks after my aborted first hike through the Smokies, Quicktime and I were back at Newfound Gap, determined to finish the Appalachian Trail through the park. I was better prepared, carrying less gear, and most of all now fully aware of the challenge of hiking these high mountains. We had our permits, but the Park Service threw up a last-minute hitch by closing Cosby Shelter due to "bear activity," which meant that an aggressive bear had been reported in that vicinity. The closed shelter would require us to hike 14.8 miles from Tri-Corner Shelter all the way to Davenport Shelter near the northeastern end of the park.

This time was better. Our first night at Icewater Springs Shelter was enjoyable because we were in good company, a friendly group of young men, a young woman from Korea, and, most intriguing, a middle-aged man who was thru-hiking southbound, heading for Springer Mountain and now only 223 miles from finishing. One final occupant arriving for the night was a ridge runner, a young man employed for the summer by the Park Service to hike back and forth on the Appalachian Trail checking on hikers and reporting any problems. He did a cursory check of our permits and settled in for the night beside us in the shelter. And he had news. Cosby Shelter was closed, he said, because it was fairly close to a large campground. Garbage was a problem there. A few weeks earlier, a Park Service crew had hiked up to the A.T. to do some maintenance work and had stopped at Cosby Shelter for lunch. One of them, a young woman, had walked down to the spring to collect water. While she was bent down at the stream, a large male bear suddenly appeared and pushed her to the ground. Unhurt, she then did everything right, yelling for her companions, scrambling back away from the bear as best she could, and waving her arms. Her fellow workers ran down the slope yelling, and the bear disappeared. But this bear was habituated both to humans and to human food. And very clever. The bear circled behind them in the woods and reached the shelter before they did. They had arrayed their backpacks on the table, their lunches an easy free meal for the bear, who promptly ripped the packs to shreds to get at the sandwiches.

The lesson here applies broadly to nearly every backcountry national park in America. Bears are not the problem—people and their smelly garbage are. Take food with any kind of aroma into bear country and you should expect a bear to come around to investigate. Hikers therefore have a responsibility to safeguard their food supplies, especially at night. Hikers and trail clubs endlessly debate the best methods of doing this, and the solutions they have devised range from simply asking hikers to hang a food bag in a tree out of the reach of bears to providing heavy steel boxes with bear-proof latches at shelters. In the Smokies, strong steel cables are strung between trees and arranged so hikers can hoist their food bags well out of reach.

At Icewater Shelter I was the first one awake and out of a sleeping bag in the predawn cold and badly in need of a cup of coffee, so I stumbled out to the cable system, lowered my cable, and retrieved my food and little stove. While I waited for the water to boil, I stared in amazement at the Milky Way above pitch-black mountains off to the southeast. I'd gotten maybe two hours of sleep on this night. Which meant another day walking in a mental fog. If I could not solve this sleep problem, how would I ever hike anywhere on the Appalachian Trail or any other one? Years of habit dating back to my days as a reporter for an afternoon newspaper had rigidly formed me into an early riser, but I had never before had such difficulty falling asleep. Instead, I tossed and squirmed and rolled back and forth in my sleeping bag, trying to get comfortable while my companions in the shelter snored away. Such a simple thing, falling asleep, but it was proving to be beyond me. How do you command yourself to go to sleep? You don't. I sipped a cup of hot coffee while the first dim light creased the eastern sky and I wondered how I would manage this day, when we had about 12.5 miles of hiking to reach Tri-Corner Shelter.

The answer was a day unlike any I had experienced so far on the Appalachian Trail. Quicktime and I were the first out of the shelter and looking forward to one of the Smokies' great wonders, Charlies Bunion, a rock promontory often visited and photographed for its fine view. On a clear day, that is, and as we hiked through the dark forest at around 5,500 feet, the prospect of a clear dawn was not good. A morning mist had seeped in over the highest ridges, not a deep cloud cover, but enough to obscure any view. Low shafts of sun would occasionally break through the tree canopy and then quickly blink out, so we walked on with a little hope we might see something.

The short trail off the A.T. took us to the big rock formation jutting out the side of the mountain. The thin cloud deck looked low enough for us to reach up and touch, and thick gray mist obscured the valleys below us, but Quicktime climbed the rock and I pulled out my cellphone camera anyway. As he stood there posed for a picture and I fumbled with turning the power on, the cloud deck and the mist peeled aside like stage curtains being drawn open and the sun burst through and there was blue sky and half of the Tennessee Valley spread out below us glowing green in golden light.

Two hours later the young fellows who had shared the shelter with us caught me. I asked if they had stopped at Charlies Bunion. Of course, they said, but the spot was socked in by thick fog. No view whatsoever, so they left. This was no more than thirty or forty minutes after Quicktime and I had been there, both of us dazzled by one of the finest mountain panoramas on the Eastern Seaboard. Such is the luck of the draw in the Smokies. Right place at the right time or nothing.

Our luck held all day on the high narrow ridge. Often the ridgeline would curve in such a way that I could look back where I had been walking an hour before, or even more, and discern the bend of the ridge and the folds of the mountainside and marvel at the distance I had covered. Another grand view opened out to the southeast around midday: miles of forest and lower mountains and distant pale blue ranges at the limit of the horizon. Then, as if that were not enough, in the early afternoon I walked over a rise where the ridge broadened out into dense evergreen forest, and to my right I heard a whimpering noise and scratching on tree bark, and sliding down a hemlock came two bear cubs. They hit the ground one after another, tumbled head over heels into each other, and took off down the slope into the forest, wailing for their momma, who undoubtedly was nearby. The scene lasted no more than five seconds and was so comical and cute that I bent over laughing. But I did not hang around. I walked down to Tri-Corner Shelter before 5:00 p.m. after a day like no other, a day when everything went right, and I hiked without pain and felt strong and like maybe I was getting somewhere as a hiker.

Early in the morning, well before daylight, I groped my way out of my sleeping bag, trying to be quiet so as not to disturb the row of sleepers on the high raised platform of the shelter. Another sleepless night and I could take no more of the aches lying down. I had to get up and move. As I shoved off from a sitting position, unable to see what I was doing, I misjudged the distance and landed hard and wrong on the uneven ground, wrenching my right knee. Dazed by the pain, I reached for the support of a wooden beam to keep myself upright and hobbled a few steps out into the night, under twinkling stars.

How bad was it? I wondered, testing the knee with a little of my weight, then a little more. Neither horrible nor okay. Each tentative step squeezed a twinge of pain out of my right knee. I knew to get off of it and prop up my leg and wait for the swelling to come. Then I would know. By first light, wrapped tight in my sleeping bag against the cold air, I had something of an answer. Not much swelling. I would be able to walk, but only with deliberate movements. Today was going to be an entirely different kind of challenge—14.5 miles on a gimpy knee. A different kind of bear.

First was a gradual climb to 6,215 feet and then a two-mile section of ridge. This was glorious in the early morning sunshine, and my knee responded well as long as I was careful. At Deer Creek Gap the Appalachian Trail begins one of the longest continuous descents of its entire fourteen-state length, a drop of 3,472 feet over not quite twelve miles, with three modest shelves of ridgeline to break the long incline down to Davenport Gap. Cosby Knob Shelter was located about halfway and would have been a good resting spot for lunch except for the reports of the aggressive bear.

I hiked alone in near total silence. The day was warm, clear, and still, an oddity in the Smokies. I had plenty of water, and I reminded myself to drink often. As long as I did not twist or overstride or step up too high, my knee was okay. Any deviation, however, gave me a quick needle of pain. What was required of me, then, was near total concentration on every footstep, and this turned out to be a good thing. I had never hiked like this before. Usually, my mind wandered all over a slew of random, unimportant thoughts, but today I had to lock in my focus on what I was doing with my feet. This was not as easy as it sounds because on any trail you must look where you are going to avoid clunking your head on a low tree branch or missing a blaze or, here in the Smokies, walking up on a bear. And then there was the temptation of all the glorious scenery to look at. So I developed the practice of looking up ahead quickly and then back down at where my feet were going, over a protruding root or around a rock obstacle, or stepping high over a downed tree limb across the trail. And stopping occasionally to admire the mountain views. To my amazement, this disciplined way of hiking worked. I was able to sustain a decent pace, not tweak my tender knee, and also enjoy the fabulous scenery around me, some of the wildest, most remote terrain in the entire Southeast. I passed the trail down to Cosby Shelter midmorning, stopped to rest at a trail intersection leading to Mount Cammerer early in the afternoon, and then plunged off the eastern shoulder of the Smokies on the long, steep descent to Davenport Gap. When I arrived at the shelter, Quicktime was there waiting for me. My knee was very sore but seemed okay. Only a few miles remained to walk the next morning to reach the Pigeon River, where a shuttle would meet us, and we would have completed the Appalachian Trail through the Smokies.

I was exhausted but also riding a wave of exhilaration from my long day, the magnificent views, the solitude, and most of all that I had hiked more than fourteen miles on a gimpy knee without further damage. I dared to wonder if this meant I had learned something about hiking and about myself, that maybe I had pushed through the worst of what the trail had to throw at a hiker, and I was ready to move on to new challenges.

The next morning my swollen right knee buckled underneath me less than a hundred yards after leaving the shelter. Only my trekking poles saved me from collapsing in a heap face down on the trail. For a horrible moment I wondered if I would be able to walk at all. I limped the last two miles in pain with each step, leaning heavily on my poles to take some of the stress off my knee. The little hills between Davenport Gap and Pigeon River felt like reclimbing Rocky Top, Thunderhead, or Collins, each step up or down another stab of hurt, until I was barely walking at all. I straggled out of the forest and onto a gravel road where the shuttle driver was waiting, dropped my pack and trekking poles into the back, and eased myself into the car, my knee throbbing and my head swimming from three nights of next to no sleep. I still had a lot to learn and overcome if I was to ever walk another mile of the Appalachian Trail.

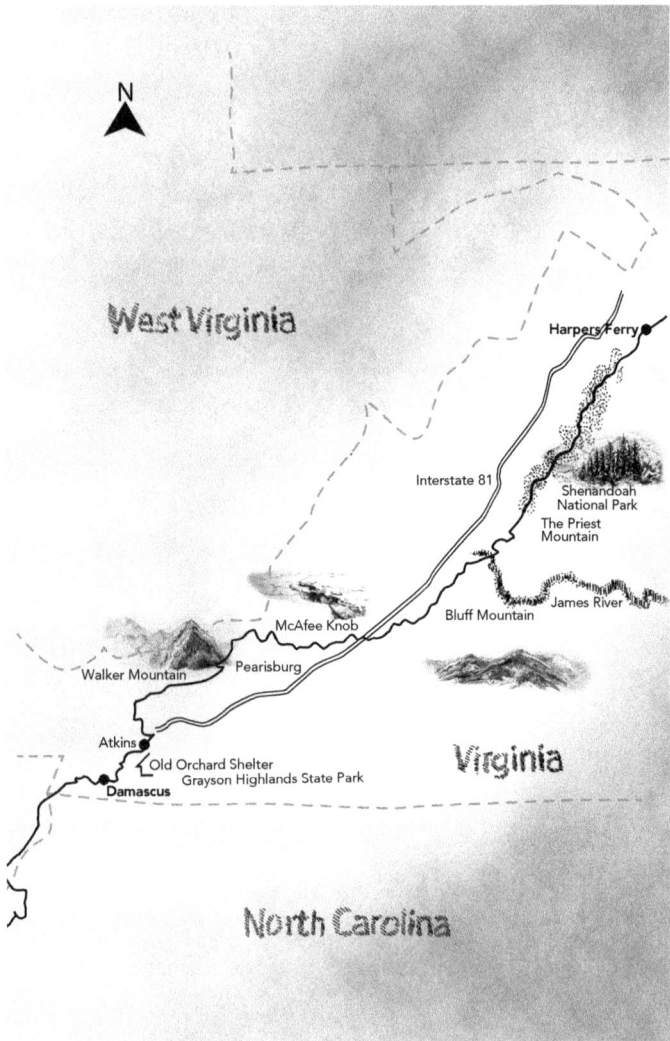

N

West Virginia

Harpers Ferry

Interstate 81

Shenandoah
National Park

The Priest
Mountain

McAfee Knob

Bluff Mountain

James River

Walker Mountain

Pearisburg

Atkins

Old Orchard Shelter
Grayson Highlands State Park

Virginia

Damascus

North Carolina

Maniacs

The shuttle driver glanced at the sky through the windshield, turned his head to me in a quizzical way, and tossed out an opinion like he was commenting on the price of pork bellies in Chicago—"You might get some snow later today."

Snow? Nothing in the weather forecast had mentioned anything about snow or even much chance of rain. Partly cloudy, temperatures in the high fifties. The day was April 20, and this was southwestern Virginia. I was heading north, and I would reach a fairly high elevation, but I would bypass Virginia's tallest peak, Mount Rogers. And these mountains were not the huge ones of the Appalachian Range, like the Smokies or the Whites, that make their own weather through sheer altitude and mass. Or so I thought. The all-night soft rain had stopped. The cool breeze was no concern.

I thanked the shuttle driver and paid him, hauled my still-new backpack and trekking poles out of the rear of his little SUV, and faced up to what I was about to do, my first extended backpack hike on the Appalachian Trail alone. My previous A.T. hikes had been with Quicktime and some Georgia friends. The planning and the big decisions were made for me by more experienced and younger hikers, how far to go each day, where to camp, where to find water, even how much food to carry. This time it was only me. I felt good about it, too. I was surely ready for this, the misgivings of my wife notwithstanding. I had a new fifty-eight-liter backpack, a decent sleeping bag and a blowup mattress, a one-man tent,

and a respectable supply of food. I had the experience behind me of hiking almost four hundred miles of the A.T., with many lessons learned,
some of them painful, all of them important.

The possibility of snow in late April had never entered into my planning. But the high clouds and comfortable temperature seemed to hold
no threat. I even spotted patches of blue sky. I said goodbye to the shuttle driver who had driven me to this remote trailhead, acknowledged his
wish for good luck for me, hefted on my backpack, checked one last time
to make sure I had everything, and set off north, passing through a pasture gate and closing it firmly behind me. As I did, a memory came tumbling back through my mind, a picture of the boyhood me doing this
same thing a hundred times with my grandfather on his farm. The famil-
iarity of it and the warm memory made me smile. I knew pastures, and
this was a lovely one, the trail an eight-inch-wide rut bending through
the new spring green grass and heading toward a distant tree line. The
newness of hiking across pastures meant my Appalachian Trail journey
had now brought me to a very different place from where I began. All
through Georgia and most of North Carolina and Tennessee, the A.T.
traverses forests, only rarely emerging onto a bald, treeless mountaintop, such as Max Patch or the Big Bald or the Southern Highlands. Until
now, with only two minor small-town exceptions, the trail had inhabited
a wildness, a feeling of remote isolation from the world of houses and
farms, roads and cars. Now it was crossing a farmer's pasture that was
well-manured with cow pies.

Ahead was a large red barn, the familiar white A.T. symbol painted on
the side and posted below a small sign asking hikers not to camp inside.
A rusting tractor of 1950s vintage looked not to have moved for a decade
or more. I warmed rapidly as the trail gradually climbed toward the trees
and a shaft of morning sun lit up the pasture. This was fine, I thought.
Just fine.

Once across the pasture and through the gate at the fence, I began a
long, slow, gradual climb through a mature hardwood forest. I had two
options for a destination for this first day. I could hike 9.3 miles to Wise
Shelter or 12.5 miles to a good camping spot called The Scales. Quick-

time had stayed at The Scales recently on his section hike of this same stretch of trail and had recommended the nice grassy flat spot for tents and a cinder-block bathroom adjacent to a fenced area for horses. That was my preference, and twelve miles was a good first-day length, especially with my late start due to a long shuttle drive.

As I climbed and the morning wore on, the temperature did not warm up, nor did the cloud cover break. Instead, the ceiling steadily dropped as I gained altitude. A light rain began falling. I was approaching Grayson Highlands, a Virginia state park well known to hikers for its fantastic views, weathered rock outcrops, and, most of all, the small herd of wild ponies that roam free there. The ponies had long been accustomed to people and sometimes approached hikers to be fed. No views today, but I was looking forward to seeing the ponies. I reached the intersection of a spur trail to Mount Rogers after an hour of steady climbing. I had now climbed to 5,400 feet and the clouds had descended to ground level and become swirls of fog that would envelop me, thicken until I could see no more than twenty or thirty feet ahead, but occasionally lift enough and thin out to reveal a bizarre world of rock outcrops.

Then, just before I reached the Fatman's Squeeze, where the trail required stooping low between two enormous boulder outcrops, the rain switched over to sleet and the wind abruptly went from breezes to gusts. Sleet pellets attacked me sideways. I reached the fence marking the southern boundary of Grayson Highlands State Park and expected the trail to improve. Instead, new trails appeared intersecting with the A.T. and I had to search for the white blazes in the fog and sleet to make sure I was on the right course. Within thirty minutes of this I was wet. My rain gear did a pretty good job of keeping me dry when the rain was not hard and fell straight down. Not so when a sleet-and-snow mix blew at me like sand thrown in front of a turbine. Worst of all, the melt and the previous night of rain had turned the trail into a water-filled ditch wherever it was not routed over the rock outcrops. Keeping my feet dry was impossible, and I soon stopped trying.

This was all new to me. Hiking in cold rain and tough conditions is the standard fare for thru-hikers who leave Georgia in the late winter or early spring bound for Maine. "No rain, no pain, no Maine," is their motto that nicely sums up their fate. But to this point I had been only a section hiker and I had tried and mostly succeeded in avoiding rough weather. Now I was in the teeth of a storm and the shock of it sobered me. Worse was to come—at Wise Shelter, which I had been considering as a good place to stop and get out of the snow and sleet, I encountered two hikers who were loading their backpacks and preparing to depart. A bear, they warned me, was hanging around the shelter. They had tried to drive it off, but it kept coming back. The bear had approached pretty close to the shelter while they were cooking their lunch. They had promptly abandoned any idea of lunch and were heading north. I soon joined them, sloshing awkwardly through water and mud that seeped over the top of my boots, and they quickly left me far behind.

I had crossed Grayson Highlands without seeing any ponies. In fact, I saw next to nothing but fog and sleet and snow and an occasional hazy white blaze painted on a rock or a post. Now my feet were soaked, my socks squishing out water with every step. And cold. The wind came in pulses that tore at my rain jacket and threatened to rip my hat off my head despite the lanyard around my neck. But the idea of an aggressive bear kept me going. The trail held steady at about five thousand feet and every mile of it seemed either water or mud. As the afternoon wore on and the wind and snow and sleet did not abate, I realized I had to get off this mountain before dark. I reached The Scales about 5:00 p.m. and immediately ruled it out. The grassy tent area was under two inches of water and there was no shelter from the screaming wind. I plunged on, crossing yet another fenced pasture, and was grateful for the tree line beyond that gave me a little relief from the slanted driven sleet that now covered the ground. The trail began to wind down through a darkening forest of hemlocks. I hiked with a grim determination, knowing it was the only option available to me, no matter how long it took. I pulled into Old Orchard Shelter well before sundown, but the clouds had followed me down off the mountain and settled thickly around the shelter and around the forest enclave where it was set into the mountainside.

Two men were there. They had a weak, smoky fire sputtering in the fire ring in front of the shelter. One of them was jabbering wildly about something but I did not pay attention. I ripped off my muddy boots, tugged my feet out of the wet socks, spread out and inflated my mattress on a far end of the shelter platform, rolled out my sleeping bag, and crawled in. I had hiked sixteen miles and I was cold and exhausted, I had seen no ponies or grand views, and worst of all, though I was only dimly aware of it as I closed my eyes, I would be trying to sleep that night next to a maniac.

❦

He was a small, wiry middle-aged man with a thin, pointy nose and dressed like a medieval court jester and he hopped, leaped, and flapped around the smoldering fire ring like a flamingo on drugs. He was wearing dirty red tights, a top of several different clashing colors, and a conical purple toboggan with a bouncing white tassel. He never stopped moving, never stopped talking, and every third or fourth word was "fuck." He sprayed the "fuck"-laden sentences like machine gun fire aimed at no one in particular. I thought of King Lear's fool—except this wild, vulgar little man commandeered the stage and allowed no other players to speak any lines. I thought of packing up and leaving but I was too tired and cold and wet, and the drizzling rain was still falling, and the daylight was almost gone. I was stuck.

His obscene monologue could not be ignored. The other fellow at the shelter was a normal and polite young man who seemed transfixed by this guy. The wild man introduced himself to me with his trail name—Skeedaddle—and he gladly, mischievously, and too eagerly confessed that other thru-hikers had pasted the name on him because that was what they wanted to do when they met him—run away as fast as possible. I scrunched down into my sleeping bag and pretended to be asleep. While the gray light faded to black, I heard Skeedaddle blast through a long monologue aimed at the other poor fellow about all the actresses he had bedded in Hollywood and the fast, expensive cars he had borrowed from celebrities and the money and the drugs and the fast living he had enjoyed at other people's expense.

Dawn found me alone with this man. The other hiker was evidently long gone. I had no choice but to wiggle out of my bag and face the prospect of wet socks and shoes and enduring his running "fuck"-laced monologue. How a man could be so wired so early was one mystery; how his brain could churn out so much babble before the sun rose was another. I wanted to be away from him as fast as possible.

I was not yet well-practiced at breaking down my new gear and loading it into my backpack. I fumbled with the air mattress, mashing and rolling and mashing it some more to get enough air out of the cells to cram it into its little bag. It refused to cooperate. If I had possessed a gun at that moment, I would have used bullets to let the air out. I even briefly thought of just leaving it—which is heretical behavior for any self-respecting hiker.

Through all this noisy mayhem something odd came to my attention—two large black plastic garbage bags beyond the fire I had not noticed before. And somewhere in his rambling speech Skeedaddle dropped the hint that he had picked up all the fucking garbage around this fucking shelter and he planned to fucking haul it out with him to a fucking trailhead a short distance up the trail. Which led to a long aside about fucking campers who had fucking trashed this beautiful place with their fucking garbage, which he proceeded to itemize—a fucking Styrofoam cooler, a fucking burned pan with fucking food still in it, fucking empty beer bottles, a fucking cigarette lighter that doesn't fucking work anymore. . . .

I started chuckling. Skeedaddle was dead serious about this crime against nature, flapping his arms and hopping around the fire as he sputtered out his string of curses, the tassel on his pointy toboggan flapping up and down, but I could not repress the humor of it. This little man was not a maniac; he was a cuss-word comic. And he really meant to haul out two big garbage bags of trash that he had picked up the evening before in a cold rain. Which, I realized a moment later, meant he carried garbage bags with him, probably for this very reason.

There was more. Before I could finish packing, he spun off into a fretful monologue about his friend, a fellow thru-hiker. They had met about a month ago, having left Springer Mountain just a few days apart, and they had hiked together off and on ever since, sometimes splitting up but always meeting again at a predetermined spot. Old Orchard Shelter was where they had agreed to rendezvous, and Skeedaddle had expected him to come in late last night. But there was no sign of him. He was not answering his cell phone. He was having problems with his feet and Skeedaddle was worried that something was wrong.

Then Skeedaddle told me what had happened to him the previous day. He had stopped early in the morning at Wise Shelter. A bear had appeared while he was eating breakfast. The bear would not leave, so Skeedaddle did the sensible thing: stuffed his gear in his backpack and headed back to the trail. But the bear followed him. Skeedaddle claimed the ability to hike pretty fast, but the bear had no trouble staying behind him.

"How close?" I asked.

"Too fucking close! I was scared shitless!" The fucking bear had followed him for almost a fucking mile before disappearing, he said, shaking his whole body violently so that the white tassel swung back and forth.

I mentioned that I had stopped at Wise Shelter a few hours after he had, and two hikers had told me about an aggressive bear. Obviously the same one. That sent Skeedaddle into paroxysms of worry about his friend. He would have stopped at Wise Shelter, maybe for the night if it was getting dark.

I left Old Orchard Shelter with Skeedaddle babbling to himself around the fire, trying to decide what to do.

Experienced hikers live by a motto—hike your own hike. The root of this dictum is the simple truth that rarely do two individual hikers share exactly the same pace, the same endurance level, or the same preferences and needs. Go out for a hike for an afternoon with someone or with a small group and this does not manifest itself as a problem. Hike for day after day, week after week, and the individual quirks and abilities of hikers are magnified a hundred times. Unless hiking companions acknowledge and properly manage this, it can lead to problems. And if there is one characteristic the Appalachian Trail never fails to exhibit, it is the capacity for little problems left unattended to explode into trouble.

I knew about this long before I ever began to hike the Appalachian Trail. It was one of the threads running through Southern writer Paul Hemphill's book *Me and the Boy*, published in 1986.[1] I was acquainted with Paul in two ways. When I was a teenager, Paul was a columnist for the *Atlanta Journal*. Every afternoon after school I helped a neighborhood friend roll up and rubber-band the *Journal* for his paper route, but the first order of business as soon as the stack of newspapers was delivered to the curb was to open one and read Paul's column. He wrote about anything and everything, strange people, the down-and-out of the city, the subcultures beneath Atlanta's shiny veneer of progress, and its boast about being "The City Too Busy to Hate." Paul found and wrote about the gritty parts of Southern life, both in the city and in the rural countryside, with a grace and humanity and intelligence that sparked something inside me. I wanted to be like him. I wanted to be a writer.

Later, after my own stint as a reporter at the *Atlanta Journal*, I met Paul several times at the locally famous Manuel's Tavern in Atlanta. We talked about writing and newspapers and politics and the South. In his book, Paul related how he and his estranged son had attempted to hike the Appalachian Trail in 1984. The idea had been for father and son to get to know each other after years apart, years of divorce and alcoholism and words that would better have been unsaid. Their hike did not go as they had planned, or as Paul had wished. His nineteen-year-old son was strong and quickly adapted to the rigors of hiking twenty miles or more each day up and over the southern mountains. Paul did not adapt. The years of hard living and alcohol had taken too much out of him. The pain in his knees was unrelenting, and finally, in Hanover, New Hampshire, with the notoriously hard White Mountains and Maine still to come, he could bear it no longer. A doctor told him it was impossible. Paul's book was a long lesson in "hike your own hike." His son was capable of walking on but enrolled in college that fall. Paul had no choice but to go home.

And now that I was hiking the Appalachian Trail, albeit in sections rather than in a single go, I was learning this same lesson, that sooner or later every hiker must hike their own hike and not try to hike someone else's hike. The lessons had been painful at times. At my age and in my physical condition, I was a slow hiker. The group of friends I hiked with were younger and much stronger. My plodding pace never matched theirs, and if I tried to keep up with them, I quickly paid a steep, painful price. On multiday hikes with Quicktime, I always left camp early, often just before first light, because I was awake anyway, having been unable to sleep much. Within an hour or two Quicktime would catch me on the trail. We would speak briefly, then he would stride out in front and soon disappear. I would usually not see him again until I reached our mutually agreed upon destination for the night. Some days I was two hours or more behind him.

At first, this bothered me. I did not mind hiking alone, but it just did not seem right. I felt like I was holding my friend back, that he could easily crank out many more miles each day if he did not have to wait on me. I fretted about time and distance, recording what time I left camp, how long I needed to reach a milestone such as a creek or road, how far I had come in a specific time. All these calculations had a vague and unpleasant echo of my former life in an office, of meetings and deadlines. I found it hard to let all of this go and just hike my own hike.

Now I was truly on my own, making my own decisions. The decision the day before to push on to Old Orchard Shelter had been a good one because a night spent high on that mountain in the sleet and howling wind would have been miserable, maybe even dangerous if the temperatures had plunged into the teens. And then there was the aggressive bear. So I felt good when I set off that morning into a hemlock forest, leaving Skeedaddle muttering to himself around the smoky fire he was tending to dry out his boots and socks, which he had propped up on sticks. It felt good to leave all that obscenity behind, all his rambling noise, and enter the quiet and solitude of the forest. Within a few hundred yards I came to a country road and a muddy pull-off for cars. That explained all the garbage at Old Orchard Shelter. Thru-hikers and even day-hikers do not carry coolers of beer and pots and pans and loads of junk. Local folks sometimes do, and occasionally use easily accessed shelters along the Appalachian Trail for campsites. Thru-hikers quickly learn to avoid these places when they can. I made a mental note of it and pushed on, hoping to put some distance between myself and Skeedaddle. I entertained myself humming the old Del Shannon rock and roll song "Runaway."

A day later, and twenty or so miles up the trail, I ran out of gas. Two sleepless nights in a row and not eating enough food had brought me to such a low energy level that I was trudging along the trail in a stupor. Another mystery of hiking that I had yet to untangle was why, after a day of climbing mountains and pounding out a dozen or more miles, I was not hungry. This made no sense, but other hikers had mentioned the same first-week phenomenon. The experienced thru-hikers I discussed this with assured me the lack of appetite would soon flip over into an insatiable hunger. All I had to do was keep walking.

And now, in the early afternoon, I knew I was walking into trouble if I did not change my plans. I had decided to push on past the next shelter because it was adjacent to a parking lot and a road and a state park building, which meant it might be crowded and noisy. But that idea was out of the window. I needed to stop and rest and eat, even if I was not hungry.

Partnership Shelter came into view midafternoon. It was a nice, two-story structure set on the edge of the forest beside a generous patch of green grass with a fire ring and picnic table out front. Beyond and within plain sight was a parking lot, a trash dumpster, and the roof of the park building. People were milling around several cars in the parking lot. I did not care. This was home for the night. I was too exhausted to put up my tent, and besides a snarky sign said no camping on the grass was allowed. I said hello to a couple of hikers who were already there, dumped off my backpack, spread out my mattress and sleeping bag, pulled off my wet boots and socks, and pondered my choices for dinner: dry granola or a dehydrated pouch of powder that purported to be chili.

As I was mulling this dreary prospect, my empty stomach suddenly grumbling, a man pulling a child's wagon approached the shelter from the parking lot. And one of the hikers from the shelter came behind him, dragging a grill on wheels and toting a sack of charcoal over his shoulder.

They rolled up to the picnic table, set up the grill, made a couple more trips to the parking lot for coolers and boxes, and unloaded a feast onto the picnic table. Out came hamburgers, hot dogs, chicken, bratwurst, buns, potato salad, chips, five kinds of fruit, mustard, ketchup, pickles, relish, lettuce, onions, cookies, a red-checkered tablecloth, paper plates, napkins, and hand sanitizer. An ice chest appeared loaded with soft drinks, and then another one exclusively for beer. And lawn chairs to sit in. Within minutes the aroma of meat sizzling on the grill sent me into a state of advanced hunger I had never known before.

The man who had brought all of this was Eric, the middle-aged father of the tall young hiker who was helping him. Eric had attempted a thru-hike in 1979 but a broken leg on the trail had ended it. Now he was hopscotching along the trail ahead of his son in a camper van, providing these feasts for hikers. He owned a chain of restaurants and had the time and money to do this. He asked for nothing in return and insisted that we all dig into the food and eat as much as we wanted. I needed no encouragement to do just that. The comfort of a lawn chair and a paper plate loaded with fabulous food hot off the grill washed down by ice cold beverages after three days of hiking, sleep deprivation, and eating little but granola and peanut butter crackers was wonderful. The total surprise of this made the food and cold drinks delicious beyond any meal I can remember. My fellow hikers and I were in rapture as we wolfed down hamburgers and hot dogs and a bratwurst on the side, the potato salad and slaw and chips and whatever else we could cram on our plates.

Eric took great pleasure in this. As we ate, he talked a little about his failed thru-hike attempt, the disappointment of his injury after a bad fall in Pennsylvania, and his abandonment of the dream of reaching Katahdin. He said his trail name had been Darth Vader, assigned because of his blunt manner, but we promptly overrode that and named him Angel Vader. And as I basked in the glow of a satiated stomach and the relaxation of sitting in a lawn chair with my aching feet propped up and the sun settling into the treetops, a small man strode down the trail toward us. Skeedaddle, in those ridiculous red tights, walking fast like he was late for an appointment, the white tassel on his toboggan bouncing furiously up and down. I was too tired and full and happy to care. This might even be fun to watch, I thought, for Angel Vader appeared to be no man to mess around with. Angel Vader invited Skeedaddle to join us, and his eyes lit up like sparklers at the sight of the food. He ripped off his backpack and piled on as much food as a doubled paper plate could hold, talking nonstop.

But without the obscenity. This little man was no dummy, I realized. He knew how to "read the room," and must have understood that the situation called for better manners. An occasional fucking something or another escaped into the cool evening air, but no one seemed to care. And when it was time for Eric to pack the food, Skeedaddle was the first to leap to his feet and help, thanking everyone profusely. Even me, and I had done nothing for him but sit there in a warm, happy, stuffed-stomach daze. To return the kindness, I asked Skeedaddle if he had heard from his missing friend. That touched off a torrent of run-together sentences that something terrible must have happened because Skeedaddle, after hauling the two garbage bags to the trailhead, had backtracked south on the A.T. all the way to Wise Shelter and then well beyond looking for his friend, half expecting to find bloody scraps of his clothing or other signs of mayhem and disaster. Instead, he had found nothing. Not even the bear.

This took a moment to fully register with me. Thru-hikers *never* willingly go backward over trail they have already hiked. And Skeedaddle's fruitless search had taken him back up the mountain, a climb of about a thousand feet and several miles, to a place where an aggressive bear had followed him the day before, then back down to Old Orchard Shelter where he had started and where he waited for the night, expecting his friend to appear at any moment. This was staggering, for it was anything but hiking your own hike. It was genuine concern for a fellow human being, as horizontal a way of living as you could find out here on the trail. And it meant that Skeedaddle had hiked nineteen miles today, nearly the same as my pitiful distance over two days.

This humbled me. We sat on logs around a fire while the sun sank low toward the western ridge. We talked about the trail, told stories of bad weather, snow reported in the Smokies, and the exploits and accidents that had happened to other hikers. I heard from my new friends the grapevine gossip that travels up and down the Appalachian Trail each spring, advice and warnings, tips and who was hooking up with whom, hostels, bargains, food, and places where hitchhiking into town was okay and places to avoid. Skeedaddle kept glancing toward the dark woods where the trail met the shelter clearing. And after a short time, well before dark, a new hiker arrived, a young woman, and since we were all men around the fire and three of the others were young, she immediately attracted everyone's attention.

Her trail name was Moonrise and something about that vaguely rang a bell with me from talk I had heard in Georgia months before. She slipped off her backpack, eagerly dove into some of the leftover food, and then came to join us. But I had noticed that strapped to the rear of her backpack was a long white plastic tube, with a diameter and a shape that suggested a mortar but obviously was meant to carry something. And then it hit me—Moonrise was a musician. I asked and she confirmed this. She was an orchestra violinist taking six months off to hike the Appalachian Trail. But she had to keep practicing so the tube contained a narrow-style violin.

And so it was that on this lovely evening around a campfire I and my fellow hikers listened to the clear, sweet and precise notes of Moonrise's violin playing a Brazilian melody that rose and fell in a rhythm that had each of us swooning. And then another piece, one she had written, simple and yet haunting, the notes slow and sustained, the violin's sound so soft we each strained to catch every note, every tremolo and slide up and down the scale she played with a gentle swaying of her body as she sat on the log beside us. I thought I saw a tear in Skeedaddle's eye.

That night I slept ten hours straight.

⤳

Hiking for long stretches of time, for most people, is essentially a selfish endeavor. An extended absence for a series of weeks or months imposes an inconvenience on loved ones. Such an absence for military service or humanitarian reasons, or to fulfill a commitment or simply pay the bills, is certainly justifiable from an ethical standpoint, but hiking a long trail just for the sake of having walked it does not qualify for such an exemption. Even with just a few sections of trail behind me, and the ambition of hiking the entire A.T. still an amorphous, unspoken idea, I was already feeling a twinge of guilt every time I left home for a new extended section hike. My wife did not complain or object, but I knew my absence was hard on her.

Even if a person has no family commitments, no spouse left behind, the principle still applies because the rest of us have to keep the lights on, keep the beasts of modern life fed so that the civilized world continues to hum, and the grocery shelves remain stocked. And how far would any hiker go without those grocery shelves brimming with candy bars, tuna fish, and ramen noodles?

So long-distance hiking is a form of social deficit spending, an unequal equation. That does not make it wrong, but it is something important to know, to constantly remember, and ultimately something that calls for some action on the part of the hiking community, if not every individual hiker, if we seek to balance the equation, if we choose to live in such a way that we are contributing to the common good. Or at least doing no harm. It is part of living horizontally at least some of the time.

Skeedaddle had found a way to do this on the trail, by picking up garbage at campsites and looking out for a friend in trouble. Every hiker who ponders this imbalance between life on the trail and life everywhere else—a minority, I fear—has to solve the equation for themselves, to un-hike their own hike when they return to the world of clean clothes, warm beds, and daily routines. But when the horizontal and the vertical clash in such a personal way, we should know what we have to do. I was hiking alone on this trip only because I had made the decision to stay home and help my wife handle a difficult situation; Quicktime and our hiking group of Georgians had pushed on deep into Virginia without me. Our family dog had developed a disease that had left her unable to walk. The veterinarian had told us the dog might recover if we gave her a little time, and so every day for weeks of beautiful spring weather, I hefted this thirty-pound pooch and lugged her outside and up the driveway so she could relieve herself. The dog and I were both embarrassed by this chore, the dog looking away from me in shame when I gently placed her on a suitable patch of ground where she could go about her businesss.

The dog slowly recovered enough to walk a few tentative, trembling steps at a time. I built a doggy ramp up the three sidewalk steps she had to climb to reach the driveway. After another month of rehabilitation and a mountain of vet bills, my wife was able to care for the dog by herself and I was free to resume hiking the Appalachian Trail.

My friends were hundreds of miles farther north by then. "Just be careful," was the last thing my wife said to me as she waved goodbye.

Being careful was indeed part of my responsibility to her. But I had already sought out other ways to balance my hiking account. I had learned that volunteers maintain the Appalachian Trail for its entire length. Every log or stone step, every footbridge, every shelter and privy along the trail, all of this and much more was either installed long ago or is now maintained by volunteers. From Georgia to Maine thirty-one different nonprofit clubs and organizations are responsible for this gargantuan task and have been dutifully and skillfully doing it since the trail was completed in 1937, mostly behind the scenes, unrecognized, unrewarded, and without much government help. Some of the work, such as cutting back the weeds in summer, picking up trash, or raking out the water bars that divert rainwater off the trail on steep sections, required next to no skill. Other tasks, such as cutting and removing a big tree blown down across the trail by a storm, were hazardous and required training and certification and careful planning. Small cadres of men and women in each of the fourteen states the A.T. touches are devoted to these tasks. Many of them have spent most of their adult lives doing it purely out of love for the trail and the experience of hiking it.

I had joined the Georgia Appalachian Trail Club to find people to hike with, but I was drawn to the club's mission of trail maintenance as a way to pay back the hours I had spent hiking the trail. I helped on a couple of trail work projects and learned how to handle a Pulaski and the basics of trail construction and maintenance.[2] In due time, the club assigned me a seven-tenths-of-a-mile piece of the Appalachian Trail in Georgia to maintain along with my hiking buddy Quicktime. From Jarrard Gap to Horsebone Gap and up and around the knob of Gaddis Mountain was my little stretch of the Appalachian Trail that I soon came to know and treasure like it was in my backyard.

Now I was farther up the Appalachian Trail from Horsebone Gap than I had ever been, hiking over totally new landscapes in southwestern Virginia. Big open pastures with knee-high grass that was still and limp down at the foot of a valley and stirred by a breeze once I climbed to the top of a hill. Then down again and through a fence at the bottom and up another hill toward a distant tree line, and above the hardwoods the looming mass of a big mountain. On this hot afternoon I longed for the shade of the forest I had left behind earlier in the day. The trail had entered the small town of Atkins and for a few hundred yards paralleled a busy four-lane interstate. At the top of a hill at an intersection with Interstate 81 stood a restaurant famous among hikers for their giant hamburgers and fried onion rings. I had treated myself to both and was now hiking sluggishly in the midday heat out in the open. I thought of the hikers I had met and enjoyed talking to two evenings earlier at Partnership Shelter—Moonrise and Ninja Mouse and Boomerang and even Skeedaddle—and I wondered if they had stopped for a big hamburger. Probably so, for they were at the stage of their thru-hikes when the prospect of prepared food was irresistible. They were all far ahead of me now. Skeedaddle had caught me within an hour after I left Partnership at the beginning of a long climb up Glade Mountain. His friend was still missing, and he was still worried out of his mind about it, but he had decided he had to push on. Skeedaddle wished me good luck and I said I hoped his friend was okay, and he bounded up the mountain in a double-time march and disappeared. I never saw him again and never learned what happened to his friend. "Hike your own hike" will always ultimately prevail on the Appalachian Trail.

My hike was approaching a decision point I had not expected. I had planned to stop for the night at a designated campsite at Davis Hollow a little more than two miles out of Atkins. Already I was running low on water after drinking a liter and a half in the heat out in the open pastures.

But I never saw the cutoff trail to Davis Hollow and did not realize I had missed it until I came to a little ledge of flat ground set into the mountainside where there was room for a couple of tents. But there was no water source nearby, and I was down to half a liter. I could camp there for the night and conserve my remaining water until the morning, or I could push on over Little Brushy Mountain and camp beside a stream. It was only 4:00 p.m., plenty of daylight left, and I did not like the idea of being so low on water. I decided to hike on.

Little Brushy Mountain proved to be more of a challenge than I had expected. On the profile maps it is barely a bump, and the summit is only 2,900 feet. But the trail went straight up a steep incline—no switchbacks to ease the ascent. And now I was tired and hot and thirsty. I parceled out my remaining water over fifteen-minute increments and leaned into the climb with the energy I had left from my big lunch. I remembered on one of my day hikes in Georgia following behind a middle-aged, overweight thru-hiker climbing one of our big mountains and muttering to himself "No mountain is gonna beat me . . . no mountain is gonna beat me," over and over, all the way to the top.

Little Brushy Mountain was not going to beat me. I climbed it with all I had left and then began a long winding descent. *Now* there were switchbacks! Why not on the other side? Down I went into a lovely mixed forest of hardwoods and white pines and a few hemlocks, the trail looping and dropping very steeply toward a gap. As the sun was lowering into the treetops, I heard water splashing and soon there was a rushing creek beside the trail and rhododendron and mountain laurel and deep shade from tall white pines. I heard the voices of campers ahead and smelled smoke from a campfire, but I chose an isolated flat spot amid the rhododendron for a single tent. I had hiked 18.3 miles. I now had all the water I wanted, filtered from the creek, cold and refreshing. I ate a decent dinner of granola and dried fruit and a couple of protein bars, crawled into my tent, and settled into my sleeping bag feeling good about the day. The next day I had less than six miles to hike, up and over Walker Mountain and then down to a road and back to the hostel where my car was parked. Then home. And with stories to tell my wife and friends.

Two days later I was sitting on my couch reading the news with my first cup of coffee in hand when I came upon a headline that bolted me awake. A man had been murdered on the Appalachian Trail. An army veteran from Oklahoma. He had been attacked in his tent while he slept and hacked to death with a machete. A young woman hiker camping nearby had been severely wounded and had survived only because she had heroically staggered out to a road crossing and gotten help. A manhunt was underway for the murderer.[3]

Where was this? Southwestern Virginia. Beside a creek between Little Brushy Mountain and Walker Mountain. Fifty yards or less from where I had camped two days before. The murderer was mentally disturbed and was quickly found and arrested. Thru-hikers who had encountered him prior to the attack described him as a maniac.

We Have to Wait

Among the thru-hikers I have met there is a common saying: "The Appalachian Trail is the best teacher for those who are willing to listen." Of course, the experience of hiking the trail is the teacher, not the soil and rocks, mountains, and forests themselves. But the distinction hardly matters; hike the trail long enough and you will inevitably learn some things. About hiking, obviously, but also about yourself and about others.

Skeedaddle had reminded me of something important I had absorbed over years of study, something that coalesced into coherence in the long miles after I last saw him while climbing Glade Mountain. Regarding human beings, there are two important truths:[1] one, that all human beings are essentially the same; and two, that all human beings are uniquely different. Both of these statements have elements of literal truth, but the point is much broader. Discovering how and why they are true, and all the subtleties, facets, and implications of this truth, is a life's work and the basis upon which maturity and wisdom grow and flourish within us. Balancing the two truths is the ongoing, perpetual, and evolving foundation of a life well lived and human happiness.

There is more to say about these two truths. Neither one should stand alone. They are dependent upon each other. And since each truth, when taken separately, contradicts the other, the result is a paradox when they are set beside each other. The paradoxical aspect of these two truths is what makes them so valuable and useful to us. Neither truth should be believed. We should only live them. If we live in such a way that we regard all human beings as essentially the same, we naturally avoid sorting people into them and us. We regard the grouping of people into races, tribes, clans, or nations skeptically, and we see past the superficial differences. And if we live in such a way that we regard every individual we meet as uniquely different—one of a kind—and therefore uniquely worthy, then we are equipped to avoid the trap of thinking in terms of superior or inferior, good or evil. This is by no means easy—human history is chock-full of individuals who test this idea to the breaking point—and therefore it works only if we embrace the paradox. It is seeing both the sameness and the difference in one instant, neither one first nor second, that brings the two truths alive.

This came back to me from a lifetime of reading about Buddhist teachings and reflecting on my recent hikes while I was lying in a hospital bed. My plans for hiking the Appalachian Trail had screeched to a halt against a wall of abdominal pain from a failing appendix. I was one week from leaving home for Virginia and resuming my trek north with Quicktime and my friends. Instead, I spent a week in a hospital recovering from complications following the appendectomy. In the hospital all I could do was pace the twenty-seven steps down the hall, rolling the stand carrying the IV bag hooked into my arm through a tube, turn around, and pace twenty-seven steps back to the pale green exit sign over the heavy double doors of the ward. At the age of sixty-nine, I glumly wondered if my serious hiking was over. At the very least, I would be starting from near zero physically as a hiker.

The forced inactivity of lying in a hospital bed gave me time to ponder some things I had put off or avoided altogether. What was it about hiking the Appalachian Trail that was so appealing? Why does anyone set out to hike the entire trail? And, most important, why was I doing this? These are not easy questions. In fact, the great majority of hikers I have met and discussed this subject with do not have good answers. At this stage of my hike, I certainly did not have a complete or satisfactory answer either.

But some sort of an answer is important given that long-distance hiking is such a self-centered endeavor. I have heard many reasons from thru-hikers. Combat veterans sometimes hike to reintroduce themselves to civilian life and spend time dealing with the demons they have to fight. That was Earl Shaffer's motivation after World War II, and it is one I have heard from many Iraq and Afghanistan veterans. The loss of a loved one or managing other forms of trauma such as a divorce or recovery from an illness are fairly common reasons. A career change or gap year between schools often offers the time and space for a thru-hike and is like a forced reset, a reassessment or needed adjustment in a life's direction. Reconnecting with his estranged son was Paul Hemphill's reason. The list goes on and on. "It's just something I have always wanted to do" is a standard answer that is handy when no other explanation is available. The uniqueness of every individual and the commonality of our humanity just about guarantee that the question will pop up over and over but never land on a hard-and-fast encompassing answer.

None of these motivations applied to me, nor are they really answers. In my case, the short answer for curious friends and family members was that hiking the Appalachian Trail made me happy. This was next to no answer, for all it does is pose the next question: why does hiking for days at a time over mountains make anyone happy? A starting place is because it is hard and humans have an age-old affinity for doing hard things, especially things that only a small percentage of the population can do. Climb the Matterhorn. Climb Everest. Reach the North Pole or the South Pole, swim the English Channel, run a four-minute mile or a marathon or race a bicycle across a continent. Walk on the moon. Put into that context, hiking the 2,193 miles of the Appalachian Trail is on the lower end of the scale of difficulty. Still, it is hard. The proof is in the high failure rate.

Accomplishing something hard brings a measure of satisfaction but it cannot be the end of the story. What is it that drives us? Is it something missing in our lives, some unformed yearning or mental hole we have to fill? And if so, where does that come from? To dig around below the surface and approach the deeper truth hiding under these questions, we have to explore the idea of how our lives change from moment to moment doing that hard thing, and what that change ultimately means in our lives. And if there is one thing hiking the Appalachian Trail for any

significant distance indisputably does, it is change human beings. After hiking only a few hundred miles of the trail I could sense this in my
own life. I was becoming something new and unexpected, not arrived at
or completed, certainly, but on my way to a new sense of confidence and
authenticity. The trail had humbled me again and again, but those hum-
bling moments and the moments that came after them had also opened
up new perspectives, unimagined possibilities. I was at peace with the
bear that John Wray says we can never escape. The trail was slowly but
steadily drilling into me a harder stamina after the high-stress softness
of my years working in an office.

Along with the pains, aching muscles, and creaking joints from the
pounding my body was enduring out on the trail had come a new and
very welcome physical toughness. I was still prone to mistakes, still fumbling and uncertain on the trail at times, yet more willing to dare, to push
myself into new zones of difficult terrain, both physically and mentally.
Some of that new terrain was glorious, all of it was fascinating, and some
of it was a bit risky. And exploring all of it made me happy, even if at times
these new places were distinctly uncomfortable, even painful. None of
this new stuff brought on by all those miles really got at the core of an
answer, however. To better understand this emerging change, I needed
to zoom backward in time and find moments in my life where this fumbling uncertainty mixed with dreaming of doing something hard and important might have begun. I could have found no better place to search
through my memory files to find and examine those moments than lying
in a hospital bed with a tube in my arm dripping morphine into my veins.

In the fall of 1971, I found myself in eastern Nigeria, armed only with a
recently conferred bachelor's degree in English and philosophy and the
naïveté of a young American abroad for the first time, staring through the
dust-streaked windshield of a Peugeot station wagon at the muzzle of an
FN assault rifle held by a teenage boy-soldier standing in front of a line
of oil drums. The boy wore the rags of what had once been a shirt and

shorts, both nearly the color of his dark skin. Beside him stood a younger boy wearing only greasy olive drab shorts. The barrel of the heavy assault rifle was aimed at me, but the weight kept pulling the muzzle toward the ground, and the teenager would have to draw it back level to my approximate direction, whereupon it would begin to slowly sink again. The boys said nothing and stared at me with an unearthly indifference and the absence of any emotion or expression. After the boy with the rifle had raised the barrel toward me a few times, a real soldier appeared in front of the boys, though his uniform was not much better, the patches and insignia too faded to mean anything. He wore a web belt with a British revolver in a holster.

Beside me in the front seat, my guide Matthew took the brunt of a sudden flurry of loud commands from the soldier while the boys stood still, utterly expressionless. I was not certain what language the soldier was speaking. My attention was fixed on the boy with the FN, and slowly it dawned on me that the rifle's ammunition box was missing. Maybe there was a round in the chamber, maybe not. Matthew remained calm and replied to the soldier in an even, steady voice, firm but not aggressive.

"What's going on?" I asked during a lull. The soldier had turned his berating toward the two boys.

"He wants us to dash him something."

"What?"

"Bribe. Dash him a little something. Don't worry."

As we spoke, I realized the soldier had disappeared and the two boys were still standing in front of us but now the butt of the assault rifle was resting on the ground. The tip of the rifle's flash suppressor at the end of the barrel came up to the chest of the boy.

"What should we do?" I asked.

"Don't worry. I told him you are a very important man. A big man. . . . They will let us pass but we have to wait."

"But I'm not . . . what did you tell him I am? I'm not important. If he thinks I am somebody else . . . what if he. . . ."

Matthew's answer was indirect—"Yes, very much. We have to wait."

Matthew was about my age, slightly built, his skin very dark, his face round and handsome but somehow older than he should have been. He was a ministerial student at the Baptist mission school, and he had volunteered for this work with a naïve young American to drive miles from the town of Owerri out into the bush on barely passable roads in a station wagon loaded beyond carrying capacity with burlap bales of dried stockfish and large cylindrical tins of casein vitamin supplements. This was my first day on the job as a relief worker, and I became immediately lost from turning and twisting through a maze of paths and roads in the forest. I was helpless without Matthew.

"We have to wait," Matthew repeated firmly. Somewhere off to our right in a cluster of thatch-and-mud huts the soldier was arguing with someone. The two boys had lost interest in us but were still at their post. I do not know how long we waited. I just knew I was not an important man. In fact, I had never felt smaller or more unimportant in my life.

❦

In Nigeria that fall the rainy season was approaching and within two or three weeks these dirt tracks would be impassable. The Ibo people called it "the hungry season." In Owerri, where I was staying with a Baptist missionary family, a corner of a concrete-block and tin-roof warehouse was stacked to the rafters with relief supplies provided by world charities and churches in the United States. The missionary in Owerri was new to Africa and was not much older than I was. His job, he explained to me, was to teach his ministerial students, not to distribute relief supplies. But if I agreed to help him, I could use his Peugeot and he would loan me his brightest student, Matthew, and we could see how much we could get out of the warehouse before the rains began.

I had not traveled to Africa to be a relief worker. I had made the journey at great expense to attempt to write about the civil war and the effort by churches and volunteers, many of them heroic missionaries, to prevent mass starvation. But here, as I listened to the missionary I was staying with asking me to help, was the vertical and the horizontal clashing with deadly implications. People were already starving out there in the remote bush villages beyond the towns such as Owerri, and the situation would soon get much worse. I said yes, of course, I would help. My research could wait. And that was how I became an impromptu volunteer relief worker in eastern Nigeria eighteen months after the end of a horrible civil war in which between half a million and two million Ibos died of starvation. The exact number will never be known.

The night before my first trip out into the bush, around the dinner table the missionary had warned me in his soft Southern drawl not to trust his workers. "They lie to me sometimes," he said. "I don't know why. We love them, of course, they are wonderful, but you can't trust them." The four of us around his table, the missionary, his wife, their young daughter, and me, were the only White people in Owerri, he said. The nearest other White person was probably up north in Enugu. "You have to be careful all the time," he said with a sad shake of his head. "Tell them there will be no more food coming. This is all we have. Be sure you tell them that."

But he had said nothing about roadblocks made of oil drums or kids with assault rifles. He had not often ventured very far out of Owerri. Too busy, he said.

Already I knew something this earnest young American from Mississippi had not learned in his few months of living here. I knew because Matthew had patiently explained it to me as we had lurched and bumped and swerved around the worst holes in the dirt tracks in the rising early morning heat, bearing right when Matthew indicated, or left or straight. In Ibo culture it was then considered very rude to tell an important man bad news. Especially so for a young man to tell an elder or a White man bad news. There were other ways to get the truth across, and to bluntly blurt it out was a breach of every standard of politeness. A sin, in effect. No respectable person would do such a thing. And in this war-ravaged country bad news was a daily occurrence. To state bad news, no matter how true, plainly over and over to a man of importance in these times was an unbearable violation of what was right. Even if that meant lying. The person being lied to was supposed to figure it out.

I deserved no credit for learning this within a day of my arrival while the missionary still had not learned it. I knew this only because I had learned to ask questions, and out of curiosity I had brought the subject up with Matthew as we were getting acquainted. Epistemology is trying to understand what you do not know and always testing what you think you know. My young missionary host had studied altogether different subjects, and the Southern Baptist denomination had sent him to Africa for a single purpose, which did not require learning about other cultures. And now, when we stopped the car beside a mud wall and thatched-roof hut and stepped out into a little clearing crowded by the surrounding bush, Matthew was teaching me a lesson in philosophy, this one in the branch of ethical and cultural relativity, which, ironically, I had recently studied during a summer at Emory University in Atlanta. "We have to wait," he said as we got out of the car. "The chief will come, but we have to wait."

Our arrival at this nameless village had brought a few people from the paths around the hut but no one from inside it. They crowded around me, talking excitedly with Matthew, and bowing to me and shaking my hand with both of theirs. More people arrived. Most of them were women, and all of them were between the ages of sixteen and twenty-five or thirty. No one young or old. A man slightly older than the rest gestured with a sweep of his arm and his pleading eyes for me to go inside the hut. Matthew said I should, so I ducked my head under the thatch and went in. My eyes slowly adjusted to the darkness and what I saw took some time for me to comprehend. These were the dying people. The villagers had arranged them in a row on the mud floor, some of them wrapped in cloth and a few lying on makeshift beds. I could not count them. There were no more than ten. Some were old, and two were children. They made no sound or movement and were too weak to even look at me. I was grateful for the dim light. I registered the skeletal thinness, the ribs, the protruding pelvic bones, but not much else. I stood there not knowing what to do or say for as long as I thought was right and then stepped back out into the sunshine, my eyes blinking and watery.

"They say you are a doctor," Matthew said, to explain why the people crowded around me.

His words nearly knocked me down.

"*Why?* How could they. . . ."

"They think any White man who comes must be a doctor."

I stammered something to protest this but stopped in midsentence.

"There's nothing I can do," I said.

"They know. We have to wait. The chief will come."

The village chief was an elder with a thin ring of white hair and a regal bearing, but he was dressed the same as the others, no shirt, dirty ragged shorts, and sandals made from rubber tires. He greeted me warmly, grinning through a mouth of gapped white teeth. He moved very deliberately, in no hurry whatsoever, a man used to the deference of others. He took my hand with both of his but did not bow as the others had done. Improbable as this sounds, I had the overwhelming sense of having met him before, maybe when I was a boy, not this man, of course, but someone who looked very much like him. A man who had suffered much and still bore himself with dignity and hope.

Without explanation from Matthew, I understood why we had to wait to distribute the food and supplements from the back of the Peugeot. That was the chief's job and prerogative, not ours. The missionary had explicitly warned me not to let this happen, to make sure I distributed the supplies evenly. But that was not a wise thing to do without first deferring to the chief. Matthew translated my instructions on how to parcel out the food, the chief nodded his head repeatedly and smiled, and everyone pressed around the back of the car in anticipation. As they did, I noticed for the first time that two of the women had babies in their arms. They were not up front, and this bothered me enough that I asked Matthew to tell the chief to please make sure the mothers received a good share of the food.

"Yes, yes, yes," the chief said, using one of the few English words he knew. Something about his broad smile worried me, but there was nothing I could do. The back of the Peugeot was already empty.

Hours later, back in Owerri, the missionary wanted an account of our trip. "Did you make sure?" he asked. "Like I told you?"

"Of course," I said.

But the truth is I would never know. Not then nor the next day nor the

day after that. Truth can be an elusive thing. Sometimes trust is the best
you can do.

⊱

Released from the hospital, I returned home pathetically weak. A week of
random thoughts, of morphine-induced memories and shuffling up and
down the hospital wing in a flimsy gown, had upended my plans but left
me more determined than ever to return to the Appalachian Trail as soon
as I recovered enough strength. If nothing else, a week in a hospital is a
reminder of human frailty and mortality. The closed doors of the rooms
I passed on my unsteady walks up and down the hall concealed patients
much worse off than I was. Their pain and suffering sometimes drifted
into the hall as moaning or mumbled words, their fates unknown to me
and to each other.

  I spent some of my recovery and recuperation time learning more
about the Appalachian Trail and the people who have hiked it. I learned
that according to one source, over its full course from Georgia to Maine
the A.T. gains approximately 464,464 feet of altitude, which is the equivalent of climbing Mount Everest sixteen times. And another source pegs
the total altitude gain and loss at 917,760 feet, or an average of 420 feet
up or down per mile. That hikers who walk the full length of the trail in
between five to seven months lose an average of thirty pounds. That there
are approximately 16,500 white blazes and exactly 262 shelters along the
way. That the oldest man known at that time to have thru-hiked the A.T.
was Dale "Greybeard" Sanders at the age of eighty-two in 2017. (Sanders' record was broken in 2021 by M. J. Eberhardt, trail name Nimblewill
Nomad, who finished his hike in Dalton, Massachusetts, at the age of
eighty-three.) That the Appalachian Trail Conservancy estimated that as
of 2018, 14,485 people had thru-hiked the A.T. (an estimate that is surely
too low, but by how much is impossible to determine). That Jennifer
Pharr Davis ran the thing in 2011, taking forty-six days, eleven hours, and
twenty minutes to complete the distance, and that Scott Jurek and then
Joe McConaughy set and then broke the records for the fastest thru-hike.
That only about fifty hikers older than seventy were known at that time
to have completed a thru-hike. And that Bill Irwin, who is blind, thru-

hiked the A.T. in 1991 with the help of a guide dog, and that Bob Barker, who suffers from multiple sclerosis, thru-hiked the A.T. three times on crutches.

But reading and learning about the trail and talking to people who had hiked the trail, while interesting, certainly was not satisfying. As soon as I felt I was strong enough, I tested myself on short day hikes in Georgia, slowly building back my strength. When the time came to hike serious miles again, I wanted to be ready.

But why? What was pulling me back to the Appalachian Trail, to the climbs and the exhaustion and the sleep problems and aches and pains? That was a question I had yet to fully answer. My wife listened patiently to my musing about the trail, put up with my obsessing over my hiking gear spread out over the floor, and the maps and logistics of travel and shuttles and hostels. I think she may have glimpsed more of the answer before I did.

"Are you sure you're ready?" she asked on the way back home from the doctor's office after he cleared me to resume hiking.

"No," I said. "It feels a little bit like starting all over."

"Well, just be careful."

She knew I was impatient to go back to the trail. And she didn't say don't go, even though my absences were stressful for her, especially since I would be alone again, and she would worry about me all the more. She had never said it was silly or foolish or crazy for an old man to be hiking such distances, had never complained about being left alone for weeks, much less asked why I was doing this. She knew the question would not go away and I could find an answer only out there, on the Appalachian Trail, where the vertical rises over the horizontal. I knew that, too, which was why I wanted to go.

"Just be careful," was the last thing she said as I hauled my backpack out the front door.

⤳

I came to know George by accident. We shared a shuttle while riding to two different trailheads, his five or six miles farther south than mine. We were about the same age, and this sunny day we were both going to finish at the same place, a nice hostel in Tennessee just down the hill from the trailhead at U.S. 19. The shuttle driver dropped George off at a U.S. Forest Service gravel road crossing, we said goodbye, and I did not expect to see him again since his southbound hike would be much shorter than mine. The shuttle driver drove me farther up the road to my drop-off place.

The morning was lovely and this section of the trail in Tennessee was not difficult, just rolling hills through hardwood forest and occasional dips down into rhododendron and laurel thickets. I was hiking with a light pack since I would not be camping for the night, and I was feeling stronger than I had any right to feel after my long lay-off from the trail. Within an hour I met a couple of well-dressed day-hikers crossing a pretty mountain stream, chatted briefly with them, and pushed on. I had a long day in front of me to reach the hostel and felt the need to not tarry too much. Sometime later I was deep in a rhododendron tunnel clipping along nicely and I looked up and a few yards in front of me was a middle-aged woman coming my way. She wore spotless white slacks and a red-and-white polka-dot blouse, her blond hair fixed as if she had just stepped out of a salon, and she was wearing expensive hiking boots that had never seen mud or rocks. Around her neck was a pricey Nikon with a zoom lens and on her fingers were a couple of rings that caught the sunlight. She smiled at me, and I had to stop because there was no room to pass her in the rhododendron, and besides, she obviously was delighted to see someone.

"Hello," she said in a cheery voice, as though we were met at her country club. "Can you tell me where I am?"

I should have resisted the temptation, but just then I noticed that the orange Osprey backpack she was wearing still had the price tag dangling from a strap, and I could not help myself, an image of Minnie Pearl and the Grand Ole Opry drifted through my mind at this inopportune moment.

"The Appalachian Trail," I said.

"Oh, I know that. I mean where?"

Feeling ashamed for my smart-aleck answer, I pulled out my map profile and pointed with my finger to the approximate spot, about mile 408 on the trail northbound from Springer Mountain.

"Oh," she said with an embarrassed smile. "I guess I mean where am I going?"

I was beginning to feel like I had fallen into a scene from *Alice in Wonderland*.

"Well," I said, "here's the next trailhead. That's about two miles. Are you hiking with some friends?"

"Yes! They're supposed to wait on me."

"I met them at this creek."

Satisfied, the lady smiled at me again and began fiddling with her camera. "You must be a thru-hiker. Let me take your picture."

Not again, I thought, shaking my head vigorously. I agreed to the photo but straightened her out about being a thru-hiker. She did not much care, and I stood in an awkward, embarrassed pose while she snapped away. I badly wanted to ask her some questions—like what she was doing out here in this forest separated from her friends—but I let it go and walked on after she wished me well and I responded with "Take care."

By midmorning I had crossed the gravel Forest Service road where the shuttle had dropped off George, and at noon I ate lunch alone at Mountaineer Shelter, enjoying the shade and the deep silence and the occasional twitter of birds high above in the tree limbs. Then I hoisted on my backpack and pushed on, mindful of the time and the miles yet to be hiked.

Within a few minutes I rounded a bend and coming toward me was George, struggling against what did not seem much of a climb. We were both startled to see each other.

"Hey . . . you're going . . . the wrong way!" he said between gasps for breath.

"No, I'm afraid not. You are."

An argument ensued. Actually, it was not much of an argument because I knew I was right and I had both a compass and a map to prove it, but he was stubborn and at first refused to concede. Finally, I told him if he kept going north, he had better have some camping gear in his backpack because he was going to be out here all night. That seemed to walk him down off the ledge where he had been stuck.

"I don't understand it," he said, shaking his head and we both started hiking down the slope.

"It's happened to me. Up in the Smokies."

"Yeah, but I can't figure out how . . . well, anyway, I'm glad I ran into you. I might have walked all the way to Hampton."

"No, you would have realized your mistake pretty fast." The moment I said that I was not so sure. George seemed genuinely befuddled.

"Do you hike often?" I asked to make conversation as we walked together.

My question seemed to turn on a switch inside George. "Oh, all the time. Almost every day. Except when it snows. I've got a bad foot and the cold makes it hurt. And not so much when it rains. But yeah, I hike all the time."

"Just around here or. . . ."

"Oh, mostly here in Tennessee. Some in North Carolina."

"How about down in Georgia? Have you ever been—"

"Oh no! Never that far. I stay pretty close to home."

I was about to ask George if he had walked this particular stretch of the trail, since it had to be fairly close to where he lived, but something about the blank look on his face made me decide to let the paradox go.

We walked on and George struggled with the conundrum of having become turned around on the Appalachian Trail, as it was his favorite trail because he met so many interesting people to talk to, but as he went on about his hikes, I began to suspect George had gotten himself turned around out here before. Maybe several times. At Elk River we came to a grassy hill and stopped for a break and George swung slowly around in a circle with a dizzy expression and admitted that here was where he had eaten lunch and he must have headed the wrong way. Given the beautiful river, and the current flowing over gentle rapids to point the direction to go, and the mountain we had just descended looming over us, and a post with a white blaze painted on it for good measure, I doubted that was possible for an experienced hiker. But George obviously was an exception.

We hiked together single file for most of the afternoon. George talked continuously. He was a Vietnam veteran and I thought he might have some interesting stories about his experiences in the war but all he wanted to talk about from his Vietnam days was his pet spider. The spider had taken up with him in his hut and George had looked after it and fed it bugs and made sure its web was protected. They became big buddies, he said. The spider had helped him a lot.

"George, that's the wrong way!" I yelled to him when he missed the double white blaze up ahead.

"Oh yeah. . . ."

But he barely missed a beat telling me about his spider. As the miles rolled on George began to tire and fall behind me. At a side trail to Jones Falls I halted and told George I wanted to go see the waterfall and take some pictures. He wanted to push on, so we said goodbye for the second time that day. But I caught him within thirty minutes, and we climbed together up Buck Mountain. I suspected he had been waiting for me. He finished telling me about his spider, how he couldn't find it one day right before his unit pulled out and how he missed that spider. I listened and when he was evidently finished, I told him I understood. But, of course, that was not true. I suspect no one understood because George had probably seen and experienced things in Vietnam he could not describe, and only a fellow veteran could understand.

At the summit we crossed a road where there was a plain country church and George fell behind me again. The trail paralleled a fenced cemetery, the grass recently mowed between the old gray headstones. A chipped concrete Jesus painted in garish colors stood guard, his back to the chain-link fence and one extended arm and hand blessing the dead. Someone had recently painted Jesus' robe bright purple. At the end of the fence the trail turned hard right and climbed into the woods. I walked a short way up to get back into the shade and watched as George hiked along the fence, head down. George passed Jesus, passed the end of the fence, and kept going straight.

"Hey George! Up here!"

"Oh yeah. . . ."

George backtracked a few yards and found where the trail entered the woods. We climbed together and emerged onto a grassy mountaintop with stunning views to the west, where the sun was now low. Staring into the sun I knew pictures with my cell phone camera would not do the scene justice, so I pushed on. George stopped to take pictures of the distant mountains and valleys glowing in the late afternoon sun, then hurried to catch me.

Our descent off Buck Mountain took us over pastures and past ancient apple trees and a massive maple and then onto an old farm road. This time both of us missed the trail cutoff. At a gap I realized the road ended and I had not seen a white blaze in a while. Four options were available, a very bad jeep track to the right, a faint trail straight ahead into the woods and up the next mountain, a trail to the left steeply down into a meadow, or back the way we had come. George wanted to try the woods straight ahead.

"No, we better backtrack to the last white blaze and find the trail."

That meant going back uphill, which George did not want to do, but he followed me and within a hundred yards we were back on the Appalachian Trail and heading down through an old, abandoned orchard. Once again George fell behind, but now in the late afternoon light, I was sure we were close to Highway 19 and the hostel, so I pressed on. When I looked back up the trail, I did not see George. Surely not, I thought, briefly considering going back to find him because we had crossed a country lane and an intersecting trail. But now I could hear traffic on the highway, big trucks gearing down as they climbed through the gap where the Appalachian Trail crossed U.S. 19. I walked on, emerged onto the highway, crossed to the spot where months before I had sat on a rock after finishing a long, hard hike, just to be able to say I had not skipped a single foot of this section. I waited a few minutes, expecting to see George emerge from the woods. But no George. I headed down the hill toward the hostel where I had parked my car, happy and hungry after a fine day on the trail. I'll wait ten minutes, I thought as the driveway to the hostel came into view. If he's not here in ten minutes, I'll walk back up to the trailhead and go look for him.

At the hostel there was my car and another car parked beside it, the driver's side door open and George standing there about to climb in, his pack already stowed in his trunk, George proud of himself and grinning at me like the Cheshire Cat.

"Been waiting on you," he said, that grin nearly busting his face wide open. "Where you been?"

Kissing the Earth

An often quoted saying attributed to the ninth-century Buddhist master Lin Chi sounds shockingly wrong—"If you meet the Buddha on the road, kill him!" In typical Zen fashion the master intended to zap his acolytes out of their complacency, but the Buddha himself was long dead, and murder was not what Lin Chi had in mind. What the master urged his students to "kill" was their entirely wrong-headed ideas about themselves, the illusions they carried in their heads. The writer Daniel Levin understands the expression to mean that when we find ourselves acting holy, we must kill the holy man, and just be ourselves.[1] Another Zen proverb takes this thought further and gives it a different twist: "The mind is a tool. The question is, do you use the tool or does the tool use you?" Wishing, pretending, desiring, fretting, and all the other busy and unsettled states of mind we could list are nothing more than the tool using the person instead of the other way around.

The concept is related to, but not quite the same as, John Wray's idea about trying to run away from the bear on your shoulders—which you can never do. Face the bear, Wray says, embrace the fear, the deep, silent, hollow emptiness of being alone with the bear, and accept the consequences. Then you can obey Lin Chi's command and kill the Buddha because you don't need the Buddha anymore. You are free of all those illusions, desires, and misgivings. The Buddha (or any other conceptual construction) actually stands in the way of that freedom, and thus you must kill him out there on the road, on the trail, in your head or however you meet him.

A day came long before I set foot on the Appalachian Trail as a hiker when I decided to kill all the illusions of the holy man I had been pretending to be, to stop letting the tool use me and to free myself from an ambition that had become crippling and destructive. The end came very suddenly. On the way home from taking my daughter to Berry College's sprawling campus in northwest Georgia, where she would begin her freshman year, I knew it was over. All the other dads of the freshmen girls moving into the dormitory that day had jobs, careers, titles, various degrees of importance. All I had was the humiliation of constant failure and amid all the introductions and swapping of business cards and "my little girl is all grown up" photos, I was too embarrassed to say anything. This could not go on. I could no longer face the depression of all this failure. Twenty years of being alone with the "terrifying silence" John Wray described and all writers know was enough. The American ethos of success worship is that if you try hard and work hard and dream big, keep fighting, never say never, you will make it to the big time, whatever that is—a corner window office or a place on the first team roster, or, at the minimum, a list of accomplishments that will pad out your obituary. Or maybe even a career as a writer.

I now knew that was a lie, for I had done all of the trying and the hard work and the dreaming and starting over, head down, nose to the grindstone, and all that, and I had exactly nothing to show for it. Actually, that too is wrong—I was way behind by most American measures of success. I had a house foreclosure in my past, a failed stint as a weekly newspaper editor, years of unemployment sprinkled with odd jobs—hanging wallpaper, construction, sign painting, even several off-and-on years as an archeology field technician and a technical editor. The pay was never much, and each job was a dead end. All while I chased the dream that had sent me to Africa right out of college in pursuit of a story I thought I could tell. A story, it turned out, no editor wanted to read, much less publish. The world had moved on from that tragedy in Africa, the rejection letters said. And there was the religious thing, the missionaries . . . that religious stuff does not sell. But I had to come to grips with what the terse letters did not say. I had not sufficiently researched the story, and the writing was not sufficiently polished and compelling. So it failed. And worse, I gave up on it far too soon—rationalizing that there were bills to pay and that a newspaper career might be an acceptable alternative. And when that career died abruptly the day the weekly newspaper closed, I tried again at writing—fiction, this time. And it failed again. As did the successive stories, each for a different set of articulated and sympathetic reasons contained in the rejection letters, but each a failure, nonetheless.

The morning after taking our daughter to college, after my wife drove to her job as a schoolteacher, I went down to my closet-sized office that I had built myself, turned on the light, and began boxing the manuscripts up, one by one. First the one set in Africa and then the rest, in order, and finishing with the screenplay. The cast of characters was already dead, the heroic Southern missionary, the tragic Atlanta lawyer, the small-town Southern sheriff, the Charleston concert pianist, and all the rest; I just needed to give them their final rites. Then another box for the rejection letters, and more boxes for the notebooks and the phone contacts of editors and literary agents and the notes and letters from the writers' workshops. All this paper went into boxes, like miniature coffins, and the boxes went into a large storage tub, a Rubbermaid crypt, and I sealed it with tape, turned off the light, and went upstairs to find the classified ads in the local newspaper and start calling. That was the end. Very simple and final. As John Wray said, not only can you never run away from the bear, sometimes you have to decide whether to play dead and accept the consequences. And sometimes, no matter what you decide, the bear kills.

Virginia, thru-hikers like to say, goes on forever. At 556 miles, it is the state with by far the longest stretch of the Appalachian Trail and the most variety: ridgelines and valleys; farmland; dense forest; the so-called Triple Crown of famous features: McAfee Knob, Tinker Cliffs, and the Dragon's Tooth; plus the glory of Shenandoah National Park and finally the Roller Coaster.[2] The trail begins south of the trail town of Damascus and ends at Loudoun Heights and the West Virginia line near Harpers Ferry. Make it through Virginia and you have 1,023 miles of the A.T. behind you and 1,167 miles to go to Katahdin. A little celebration is usually in order.

My hike through Virginia was a patchwork of starts and busted plans and interrupted trips, a two-year journey chopped into pieces and nothing worthy of celebration. Just as I was recovering well from my appendectomy, I endured another surgery, this one for removal of a skin cancer that left a skin graft the size of a large slice of salami on the back of my left hand and an eight-inch scar down the left side of my chest. The recovery from that was not as long or difficult as the appendectomy had been, but the timing was terrible, spoiling my plans to travel back to Virginia to resume my hiking. When I did get back, the beautiful spring weather was past and midday temperatures were rising well into the eighties. But when my hand sufficiently healed, I was eager to load my backpack and head out on the A.T.

In Virginia I met a buddha several times on the Appalachian Trail but failed to kill him at each opportunity. That would have to wait. But I did begin to learn some things that made me a better hiker. I learned how to sleep at night in a tent or even a shelter—no small thing for me. The solution was embarrassingly simple—good ear plugs, a headband pulled down over my eyes, and investment in a high-quality sleep pad with a good R-value to keep the cold that radiates from the ground from direct contact with my sleeping bag. My loaded backpack was lighter now because I had a new tent that weighed only 2.1 pounds, half the weight of my first one. My experience on the trail had at last taught me something thru-hikers learn very early, a formula that applies universally—extra weight plus distance times elevation gain or loss equals pain. Successful long-distance hikers learn to listen to the daily aches and pains of their bodies and distinguish between what is normal and will go away and what is perpetual and indicates trouble. Normal pain can be managed, something a determined hiker can push through and endure. Perpetual pain in the knees, ankles, feet, or back multiplied times weeks and months of hiking up and down the mountains and ridges of the Appalachian Trail can result in an injury or physical infirmity that can end a thru-hike. That is what happened to Paul Hemphill—his knees simply broke down from the stress. That is also why long-distance hikers obsess over the weight they are carrying, and by the time I was one hundred miles into Virginia the trail had schooled me well in this lesson—carry on the trail only what you absolutely need, and you need a lot less than you think.

Virginia also taught me some valuable lessons about water. I left Pearisburg in southwestern Virginia under a gray sky with two liters of water and the twinge of anxious happiness I always felt when starting out on a section hike alone. This hike was to be the completion of a hike I had made with Quicktime and friends months earlier that was supposed to have ended in Daleville some ninety-four miles farther north on the trail. But we necessarily cut it short in Pearisburg when Quicktime received news of the death of an old friend, and we had to return home. Now I was alone, and the weather was turning hot. Once I was across the New River the trail began a long, gradual climb to a very long, nearly level ridgeline. I had planned a short first day, another of the lessons I had learned on previous hikes, and I expected to camp for the night somewhere before Dickenson Gap. As I climbed the ridge, the cloud cover dissolved into a hazy sky and the temperature rose and I was sweating but maintaining a decent pace and feeling pretty good. Near the summit I met two young women coming toward me, the first hikers I had seen that day. Such a meeting of northbound and southbound hikers nearly always involves a cordial greeting and then a quick exchange of information about trail conditions to the north and the south. And these two women had news for me and anyone else heading north. First, there was no water at Rice Field Shelter. Second, and more importantly, they had decided to camp the night before at a beautiful grassy spot high on the ridge just past Dickenson Gap. They had erected their tents and arranged their gear inside and were just about to make dinner when a bear appeared. The bear slowly walked toward them and sat down about thirty yards from their tent. They did all the things you are supposed to do, yelled as loud as they could and waved their arms to try to get the bear to go away. But it just sat there, watching them. And then another bear showed up.

That was their cue to pack their gear and move on. The bears watched them but did not follow when they set off southbound to put trail miles between themselves and the grassy campsite.

I thanked the two women for the news and pushed on, revising my plans in my head as I consulted the trail guide for landmarks and options. I had about a liter and a half of water, and it would have to last me the rest of the day. Camping on the ridge with human-habituated bears in the vicinity was out of the question. That meant I would have to hike all the way to the end of the ridge, descend, and try to reach a water source either that evening or first thing the next day. I had not planned on a twenty-mile hike my first day out. I had never gone that far in a single day. I pressed on, wishing I had gotten an earlier start and calculating the daylight hours left and the pace I would need to sustain. It was going to be close. Fortunately, the trail on the high ridge was not difficult and was nearly level, as advertised by my profile map.

But the Appalachian Trail is a constant source of surprise. In the late afternoon what had been a smooth dirt path turned into a tumbled bed of rocks in a few places that slowed me down. I came to the grassy spot where the two women had encountered the bears. It was an old apple orchard, the few surviving trees gnarled and barren but still hanging on to life. No bears in sight, but thick scraggly bushes ringing the orchard made me pick up my tempo. Then came more rocky trail and the next surprise, a steep but short climb, and then the second one, even steeper and up into rock outcrops. Plus, a thunderstorm was building to the northwest. Thunder rolled toward me, and I stopped to stretch the rain cover over my backpack and judge where I was and how much daylight was left. Not enough to reach the next shelter but enough to get me off the ridge if I pressed on. I was down to less than half a liter of water and almost wished for a good rain to cool me off. Instead, the five minutes of rain just sent the humidity soaring into steam bath range.

Twilight caught me in a thicket of rhododendron, and I found a flat spot where I could pitch my tent for the night and hang my food bag safely in a tree. With eighteen miles behind me, exhausted and now completely out of water, I settled on top of my sleeping bag and sensed the coming coolness of the evening with a feeling of having done well for that first day. To heck with those bears, I thought. Both the ones up on the ridge that I never saw and the one on my shoulder that travels with me.

Arriving at a place on the trail where the guidebooks indicate that water is available and finding none to be had is a bad omen for the first day of a long hike. The next morning, I was out of water and my situation was just short of critical. Nearly every shelter located along the Appalachian Trail has a reliable water source nearby—that is a major reason for putting them there—but the spring at Pine Swamp Branch Shelter was dry. A thru-hiker packing up at the shelter told me I could find water farther down the trail but not to expect much.

He was right. The trail crossed a stream, but the drought had reduced the water flow to a thin trickle in a maze of shallow pebbly channels. I could find no pools to dip into or spots where the water poured over rocks and would be easy to catch in the one-liter-capacity bag that screws on to a water filter. Instead, I spent thirty frustrating minutes on my hands and knees scooping water an ounce or two at a time into the bag so I could filter enough to drink what I needed. I knew I was less than two miles from Stony Creek and decided to hike on there, where it would be easier to fill both my one-liter bottles.

Arriving at the bridge over Stony Creek, I slipped off my backpack and was bending over to pull out my filter and water bag when I noticed the small sign warning not to drink water from the creek. Stony Creek was a broad, lovely ankle-deep stream sparkling clear in the early morning sunshine, but it ran parallel and very close to a paved road. If I filtered the water, would it be safe to drink? The sign was no help. Maybe, but I decided not to take the chance. *Giardia lamblia* is a waterborne bug that can make a person seriously ill. As few as six *giardia* cysts can cause an infection, and the stomach sickness is distinctly unpleasant—especially for a hiker out in the woods. The cysts are five microns wide, and the filter I was using claimed 99 percent effectiveness at removing bacteria. That left a 1 percent chance of getting sick, which is not zero, and given the dry conditions and the low water levels, the proximity of the road and the possibilities of pollutants from the asphalt, plus that ambiguous sign, I did not like the odds. My trail guide indicated more water sources to come farther up the trail, and fortunately I soon found a tiny branch flowing out of the mountain and emptying into Stony Creek, a much safer water source. Filling up there was not easy, but I filtered and then drank half a liter of cold water and left with two full liters in my pack and the confidence that I would be okay for the hot afternoon to come.

Next came a big climb of 1,550 feet back onto a ridge, and the rising heat worked me over. I drank half my water getting up the ridge, believing I could find more at the designated water sources listed in my trail guide. The first one was a hundred yards down off the trail before I reached Bailey Gap Shelter, where I planned to rest and eat lunch. I hauled off my backpack and scrambled down the path into a deep defile that looked promising only to find the rocky stream bed so dry the moss was crinkly and brown. Back up I went, sweating now and hoping that I would find water at the shelter.

Bailey Gap Shelter was located just off the A.T. but not in a gap, and there was no water in the spring. I pulled off my backpack, sat on a bench, and ate a meager lunch and sipped gingerly at my water as I studied the trail guide. The text indicated two more water sources over the next three miles and then a nice campsite at Wind Rock at the highest point on this ridge. I decided to get water at the next spring and aim for Wind Rock for the night instead of pushing on another nine miles to the next shelter. The heat and the long hike on my first day had sapped my energy and I knew better than to go over the line.

The next spring was dry. So was the one after that. And now I was hiking in a broad boulder field along the side of the ridge, and I had about half a liter of water left. I had hiked over boulder fields before, and at first this one was not a problem. A boulder field is simply a place where gravity and rain have washed most of the soil downslope, leaving exposed rock that has been heaved up and cracked and broken into fragments ranging in size from suitcases to basketballs by freezing temperatures and tree roots until what remains is a maze of jumbled stone. The uneven surfaces and loose rock make for tricky footing. Young, athletic, and experienced hikers can hop and skip over boulder field trails at a decent hiking pace, but I was none of that, and my pace slowed to the progress of a possum up a tree. Or so it seemed in the afternoon heat that radiated off the rocks despite the shade of the forest cover. Most boulder fields I had come to in my A.T. hiking thus far were relatively short patches where the trail traversed a narrow seam of exposed mountainside. But not this one. This boulder field was the entire mountainside. It stretched up toward the summit and far down the slope. After a mile of picking my way through and over rocks, I was tired and thirsty. After two miles of it I was exhausted and parched. And after the next half mile I knew I would not make Wind Rock this day. I had to stop. This was dangerous. I was beginning to stumble unsteadily, and a fall in these rocks would be a disaster. At the first flat bare spot I found beside the trail I pulled off my pack and slowly began the work of making my camp in a patch of soil among the boulders just large enough for my tent. I had a quarter of a liter of water. I drank the last of it before I crawled into my tent and stripped off my damp clothes and lay on top of my sleeping bag, hoping the cramps in my fingers would ease a little so I could get some sleep.

I endured a painful night of leg cramps that woke me up jerking like a mad man on the half hour. The next morning, I methodically loaded my pack in the dark and as soon as I had enough light to see the trail I began slowly hiking north, and the trail climbed gradually toward Wind Rock over yet more boulders. The trail guide said the next water source was about two miles on, but it would be high on the ridge I was climbing and very probably dry. The source after that was nearly another four miles from where I had camped. What if it was dry too?

After twenty minutes of walking, I emerged onto a gravel road not quite at the top of the ridge. Across the road the trail resumed and was blissfully rock-free. But what sent me running was a beautiful sight: plastic gallon jugs of water beside a tree. Two were empty, but three had never been opened. I drank some of one and filled up my water bottles with most of the other one, and silently praised the anonymous soul who had left the jugs there for hikers while digesting the fact that another twenty minutes of walking the afternoon before would have brought me to this road and the jugs of clean water.

Now I knew something important about hiking the Appalachian

Trail—I still had a lot to learn. Be your own trail guide was one thing. And carry more water in conditions like this, the weight of it be damned.

Over the next days, water was my obsession. The ridges were bone-dry, but the trail frequently dropped down off one ridge, crossed a valley, and then climbed onto another one. In the valleys, after crossing pastures burning hot in the sun, I usually found a stream where I could get water. I learned to drink like a camel, drink some along the way and drink a lot more at every source. After a couple of days of sweating I was vaguely aware of a stink that drifted behind me through the heat waves. That smell was me. In some of the pastures, cattle were standing under the shade of whatever trees they could find, and I had to scramble up and back down the other side of wooden stiles built over the barbed wire fences. Under the shade of the forest up on the ridges the temperature was several degrees cooler, but I had steep climbs to get there and then steep descents back down to more pastures.

After several days of this, at Pickle Branch Shelter in the late afternoon, I dropped my backpack on the platform and mused about home, about a twenty-minute shower and clean clothes and my wife's home cooking and a bed to sleep in. About plates of spaghetti and garlic bread and glasses of red wine and the dry coolness of air conditioning. My left foot was acting up and my right knee ached at odd times. I was too tired to pitch my tent and besides there was no flat place around the shelter. The water was a couple of hundred yards down a steep trail. Of course, it would be down and then back up, but at least the stream was flowing strong enough to fill my bottles and the cold water felt wonderful dumped over my head and even more wonderful going down my parched throat and through my body. The trip down to the creek and back ruined the toes of my left foot and started a stinging sensation in the metatarsal bones that would not stop even after I had stripped off my shoes and propped my feet up on the picnic bench in front of the shelter. So I simply could not put off the question any longer. Why am I doing this again? Haven't I been here before? Yes, on that ridge in North Carolina, where I wanted to quit and then saw the raven. But maybe it was worse because the question demanding an answer this time was not about desire—it was, Do I know what I am doing out here? And am I even capable of doing this? Have I waited too late in life to hike the Appalachian Trail? Or am I just meeting a pretend buddha? Again. . . .

As I was boiling water for my dehydrated dinner a thru-hiker came down the trail and joined me. He was a delightful young man with a mop of unruly long blond hair and a quick smile behind a rough beard, and I was glad for his company. His trail name was Cogs. With 698 miles of his hike from Springer Mountain completed, Cogs was used to the discomforts of the Appalachian Trail and well informed about the challenges to come. Virginia was not hard, he said, although this drought was making it tougher than he had expected. Pennsylvania was where it would really get hard, he said. It began on the rocks north of Duncannon, and you got no relief until well into New Jersey. He had learned this from southbound thru-hikers he had met. And the drought was bad up there, too. But none of this seemed to trouble Cogs.

"It's all part of the deal I signed up for," he said as he began to unload his gear from his backpack. "This is *supposed* to be hard. If you're out here to have fun, you're in the wrong place. The ones who can't hack it are long gone."

"How many miles are you hiking each day?" I asked.

"Between twenty and twenty-five. Sometimes more, sometimes a little less. I did a thirty below Pearisburg before this heat got so bad, but I probably won't do a big one like that again."

On this day I had managed fifteen miles and I felt like a whipped dog. The day before had been twelve miles. I was in awe. Hiking twenty-five miles in a single day out here on these dry Virginia ridges and valleys in this heat and humidity had the feel to me of crossing Death Valley barefoot.

We swapped stories about the trail and people we had met. Back in Tennessee, hiking with Quicktime and friends more than a year ago, I had crossed Big Bald on a sparkling afternoon and camped at Bald Mountain Shelter, I told him. I was the first out of my tent the next morning, as usual, and I groped over to the table in front of the shelter to boil water for my coffee. As I stood there waiting for the water to boil, I became vaguely aware of a dark motionless lumpy shape inside the shelter. After a moment the shape said, "Good morning."

He was a thru-hiker who had just pulled into the shelter a few minutes before I woke up. This was dumbfounding to me.

"You mean you walked all night?"

"Yeah. All yesterday and then all last night. 7:00 a.m. yesterday morning back at Allen Gap to just now. About thirty-eight miles, I think."

"Why?"

"Funny . . . but I don't really know. I just got into a rhythm and didn't want to stop. I saw all kinds of things. Walked right past a bear. Just looked at me. Their eyes glow red. Never knew that. Saw deer. Almost ran into one. Racoons . . . tons of rabbits."

My new friend at Pickle Branch Shelter nodded vigorously and grinned at my story.

"I get it, man," Cogs said. "Sometimes you get into a zone. It's cool like that. Once you get your trail legs you can crush the big miles. Thirty-eight, though . . . that's crazy big. . . ."

"You ever wanted to quit?"

"Oh, hell yeah! At least four or five times. Mostly back in Georgia and then during the snowstorm in the Smokies. I had no idea Georgia would be so hard."

Hearing this was like pouring another bottle of cool water over my head.

"Really? You thought Georgia was hard?"

"Hell yeah it was! I'm from Ohio. I trained a bunch before I started, but it was all flat back home. Then I found out Georgia ain't flat. Stupid. . . ."

"I've heard that before."

"Yeah, I wanted to quit down south a couple of times. I don't know a thru-hiker who hasn't wanted to quit at one time or another."

Cogs thought about this for a minute, as though the subject needed more explanation. My dehydrated chicken and rice was ready to eat and his water was just beginning to boil.

"But you get in a zone and you just hike," he said. "You get up each morning and you hike. It's not for fun and it's not some great vacation adventure . . . it's work, and you have to get serious about it because this trail can bite you if you mess up. I found that out in the Smokies. Damn near got frostbite up there."

Cogs paused and closed the valve on his tiny stove and began crushing a bag of Ramen noodles into his pot of water.

"See, you can't fight this trail. If you do, the trail is gonna win every time. You gotta go with the flow. You can't make it not rain or not freeze your ass or make you sweat buckets."

"I've learned that the hard way. I hate to admit this, but I'm still learning it."

"Yeah, but you're still out here, man! That's the thing, you're still doing it! The ones who can't hack doing it every day go home. But you're out here . . . that's what counts. What I try to do is I get my head right and try to keep it there. Bitching and moaning just wastes calories. See, once you get your trail legs a thru-hike is 90 percent mental. I bet it is for section hikers like you, too. It's staying positive that keeps you going."

"So, you've had bad days?"

"Oh, hell yeah, lots of 'em. But you *expect* bad days. And you never, ever make a big decision on a bad day. Because the thing is, the Appalachian Trail is never the same from day to day. You get tired of whatever it is, the rain or the constant climbs or whatever, and you keep going and the trail changes and whatever was pissing you off yesterday is over and now there is something new to deal with. And it might piss you off just as much but at least it will be different, and you just deal with that. Then, when you get a couple of nice days in a row you enjoy the hell out of them because you know. . . ." Cogs' voice trailed off and he got a faraway look on his face as he tilted his head, gazed out into the forest, and stirred his ramen noodles.

"They won't last," I offered.

"Damn right! It's always something new and it's always just the same, just getting up every morning and walking."

"I think you're going to make it all the way to Katahdin."

Cogs tested his first bite of ramen and winced. "Who knows?" he said, his voice lower now as he began slurping the noodles. "Maybe . . . I really don't like to think that far out. . . . You focus on one day at a time. It's pretty damn simple but don't let anyone ever tell you it ain't hard, 'cause it is. You just keep walking . . . and who knows. . . ."

That was it. You just keep walking. That was what I would do.

✑

An oddity about hiking on the Appalachian Trail is the juxtaposition of solitude and camaraderie the trail sends your way. Strangers who suffer the same set of discomforts, share the same goals, and meet serendipitously after hours and hours spent alone in a forest start out with a natural affinity for one another when they meet on the trail. Stories abound of how A.T. hikers look after each other and form strong bonds of friendship. At one very low point, when the trail's discomforts and miseries tempted me to quit and go home, I had the good fortune to run into a hiker who inspired me and boosted my spirits enough to get me past the negativity and keep me going. The couple of hours Cogs and I spent together at Pickle Branch Shelter before we pushed on were just what I needed to restore my confidence.

But at the same time the hours and hours of solitude on the trail were beautiful. Hiking alone, if you do it right and pay attention to your body and what is around you and let go of the second-by-second whizz of thoughts, becomes a nourishing mental and physical state unlike any other. That explains a great portion of why anyone would do it day after day, and why it is so hard to explain to people who have not done it. The Buddhist monk, teacher, and writer Thich Nhat Hanh has written about this: "When we walk like we are rushing, we print anxiety and sorrow on the earth. We have to walk in a way that we only print peace and serenity on the earth. . . . Walk as if you are kissing the earth with your feet."[3]

My best walking rarely approached kissing the earth with my feet, but I know what Hanh meant. "Peace and serenity" were hard for me to achieve hiking the Appalachian Trail, at least most of the time, because the hiking was hard work and there were plenty of rough situations that were anything but serene. The peace and serenity Hanh calls for was not impossible for me, but it was a difficult state of mind to achieve and an even harder attitude to sustain for long periods. "Calmness" might work better as a description of the mental state I shot for each day. Calm, alert, and tuned in. In the zone, as Cogs said.

Robert Pirsig wrote about this in his famous book *Zen and the Art of Motorcycle Maintenance*, which I have read probably five times. Pirsig advised climbing a mountain without desiring to reach the summit. This sounds counterintuitive—why would you be climbing it if not to reach the top?—and it is much harder to do than it is to say. But it is excellent advice. Pirsig sought to climb mountains in a mental and physical state balanced between restlessness and exhaustion so that he was thinking only of each footstep. The effort expended on the climb, he said, should be aligned with the hiker's own nature and the circumstances, at a pace not too fast and not too slow, and in tune with what is all around you—*here* a loose rock, *there* a gnarled and bent tree twisted by decades of strong wind, *now* a switchback cut into the mountainside. Pirsig said to climb merely to reach a summit is a hollow goal. His observation about climbing mountains was both obvious and easy to miss. "It's the sides of the mountain which sustain life," he said, "not the top."[4]

To live merely for reaching the end of the Appalachian Trail is shallow. Cogs intuitively understood this, which is why he did not want to talk about Katahdin. To hike it moment by moment is to grow. To discover that a bear's eyes glow red in the dark. To see an old, twisted apple tree high on a ridge that fed a family half a century ago. To feel water flowing through your body when you are thirsty. To see and feel through your feet how gravity and time and physics have broken a solid stone mountainside into billions of hard pieces. This is what Virginia was teaching me. Part of the growing was learning to live with discomfort—to expect it and handle the tough parts with equanimity and calmness, if not always with serenity. And to enjoy the silence and solitude of the walking, to appreciate that I was even out here in the first place with the gift of time and health to walk day after day for no purpose whatsoever except to walk. And, as Benton MacKaye said, to see what there was to see and hear what there was to hear and not hear anything when it was only silence.

But the Appalachian Trail is not all nature, forest and mountains, remote, wild and lonely. The trail on average crosses a road of some sort every four miles. Tens of millions of Americans live at most an hour and a half drive from an A.T. trailhead, and that fact was part of MacKaye's design from the beginning. That proximity guarantees tourists and crowds at a few places. And now my Virginia hike was approaching the state's three best-known and most-visited Appalachian Trail landmarks, the so-called Triple Crown. First was The Dragon's Tooth, a thirty-five-foot spindle of quartzite just off the Appalachian Trail on the shoulder of one of the long, forested ridges near Roanoke. I arrived there on a weekend early in the day after my night at Pickle Branch Shelter, took a picture or two, grimaced at the litter on the ground and the graffiti, and made my way carefully down the rocky and very steep descent. My timing coincided with the morning tourist rush hour. Scrambling toward me were young couples in shorts and colorful T-shirts, wearing sandals and sneakers, one young fellow holding a can of beer in his hand, all of them jabbering away in earnest conversations and one of them talking on his cellphone. Then came families with children and dogs, the kids wild-eyed with the excitement of climbing a playground of rock or bored out of their minds toiling up to this bizarre place out in the woods instead of being at the pool or behind a computer screen. None of them were kissing the earth with their feet.

The next day McAfee Knob was worse, for the trail up to the rock promontory was much easier to walk and its reputation stands out not just in Virginia but along the entire trail as being one of the most photographed natural places east of the Mississippi. The view was nice, but I did not hang around. At least fifty people were enjoying a sunny day on the broad rock. This was a good thing—get out of the house or the office and enjoy nature and all that. But the collision of noise and people milling about with fancy cameras and barking dogs and playing children and those infernal cellphones with my days of deep solitude on the trail was too jarring, and I quickly hustled back into the forest and pushed on north. Tinker Cliffs an hour or so later was better, the trail bringing me above and alongside sheer rock faces with grand views of Virginia valleys and distant mountain ranges and fewer tourists.

This was a snobbish attitude of mine, to be put off by people enjoying the scenery, and I knew it and just accepted the fact. The Appalachian Trail belongs to everyone, not just hikers, certainly not just to lowly section hikers like me. Large numbers of people using the trail are not a problem. The trash and the graffiti and the wear and tear on the trails themselves, yes, those are problems trail clubs must manage, and a big effort by their armies of volunteers is required to do it. But the visitors should be welcomed, not discouraged. We live and grow at the intersection of the horizontal and the vertical aspects of our lives. The Appalachian Trail winds both ways, south to north and up and down, and anyone who walks any piece of it is entitled to marvel at its wonders.

Meeting Jesus

Malaria would end my brief career as a relief worker in Africa. Matthew knew this, but I did not, not at first, and he would not come straight out and tell me because that would have been rude by his standards of etiquette, and Matthew was an unfailingly polite young man. "The doctor must see you," was all he would say. In the mornings I felt okay, and we would drive together to places only he knew, the Peugeot groaning with its load and the suspension compressed and battered by the ruts and deep dry holes in the tracks that meandered bewilderingly through the bush. But by midday I would feel dizzy, unable to concentrate. Then, by the time we reached Owerri and the warehouse, the fever would come in waves and by twilight sweat and chills alternated so quickly I could not keep up with them, causing me to throw off a blanket and then pull it tight to me every minute or so.

But I could not have malaria, I told the missionary I was staying with. In the United States, before I left, I had been given nivaquine antimalaria pills and had taken them dutifully until they were gone, not realizing until much later that the pills had a shelf life and mine were past due. The missionary family, recently arrived in Africa themselves, had no experience with malaria. They were concerned, but because I seemed to recover each morning, they left me to my own devices. But Matthew knew. "The doctor must see you," he said to me each morning as the boys in the warehouse loaded the tins of casein and the bales of stockfish into the back of the Peugeot.

My last day was at a village called Imafor-Imerrinway. I only remember the name because of the charming sound of it—Imafor-Imerrinway—and what happened there. We drove up to a clearing, as usual, but this time there was a long tin-roofed open-air building, smaller but very like our warehouse in Owerri. When I got out of the Peugeot the place erupted. A hundred or more children, most of them nearly naked, burst from the place, crawling over the open spaces in the low mud wall and running toward me, gleefully waving their arms, and almost singing for joy. Children quickly surrounded and overwhelmed me, all of them grinning and smiling and delirious with happiness. Behind them came a tall man dressed in black pants and a once-white shirt, an anomaly that indicated his importance. He did not try to control the children—that would have been impossible—but simply smiled and shook my hand with both of his and explained that the building was his mission school, that the reason the children were pressing so close to me and rubbing my arms and gazing at me in awe was that they had never seen a White man before. The war and its aftermath had isolated this region that deeply.

And there was one more thing: "They are saying you are Jesus."

The malarial dizziness had begun, so I was already confused.

"Who is?"

"You, sir. They are saying you are Jesus come to meet them."

"Jesus . . . but that's not . . . I mean . . . *why would they think I am Jesus?*"

"Come. I will show you."

I only remember next the heat, the terrible oppressive heat as I crossed the packed-dirt clearing swarmed by the children touching and stroking me, the heat underneath the broiling tin roof, the dust, sweat, and smell of our bodies, the stifling air in the sudden darkness of the mission school, and there, down at the front, above a simple table, hung high on the thatched wall in a plastic gold frame, was a picture of a man in profile in a simple brown robe, a man I had seen in dozens of cheap paintings in Southern Baptist Sunday school rooms when I was boy. And it was me. To the children there could be no doubt. Dark long hair and thin short beard, white skin, twentysomething. That beatific look, the gaze not quite fixed on any specific object, the serene pose of the head, of this world but not of this world.

For weeks the pastor had been telling his class that one day Jesus would return. Well . . . who could argue with them? And hadn't Jesus brought them all that food . . . a miracle if ever there was one? "Tell them . . . tell them . . . I'm not . . . tell them who . . . I'm just here to. . . ."

I was now quite literally out of my head, the tumult, the heat, and the fever swirled up into a dust cloud that hung in the air and followed me back out into the sunshine. I remember nothing about how I drove the empty Peugeot back to Owerri. The hallucinations began that night, alarming the missionary family. The next morning, I staggered to the warehouse. We still had food supplies stacked in the corner and villages to reach while there was still time, plus the clock was ticking on my visa. Any day now the rains might begin; then driving out into the bush would be impossible for nearly six months. People would starve during those months.

"The doctor must see you now," Matthew said, more firmly than the day before. He knew we were done. A few days later the rains began.

☞

In Virginia, some miles before reaching Shenandoah National Park, the Appalachian Trail climbs up and over a mountain called The Priest. At 4,063 feet it is not especially tall, and there is nothing about it that is particularly difficult, but the mountain acquired its name from thru-hikers who swear that after you climb the thing you will need to confess your sins. Something about The Priest compels hiker repentance, and I approached the mountain in exactly the wrong frame of mind. I was hiking with a new companion. My friend and long-time hiking buddy Quicktime had developed health issues and had to get off the trail and return home after our first day out from the James River Bridge. Sad to have lost him, I was nonetheless determined to push on all the way to Waynesboro with our third hiking partner, Stoneheart, who had joined us for this trip.

The first two days were fine. I had managed a 2,694-foot climb the first day to Bluff Mountain's summit and then a 3,107-foot climb the next day up Bald Knob with no trouble. We were hiking northbound, and the gradual ascent of the south face of The Priest would be nothing compared to those first two climbs or the nearly 3,100-foot plunge down the other side to the Tye River.

But at Cow Camp Gap Shelter an old nemesis found me. Stoneheart and I pulled into the shelter area after a long walk on a side trail down off the mountain and a gentle rain began to fall. No good flat places for a tent were on offer, and besides, the rain seemed to be settling in for the night, so I opted for sleeping in the shelter with my friend. No one else was around. I settled into my sleeping bag and listened to the muted sound of rain on the roof and the soothing rush of a nearby creek through my earplugs and imagined I would drift off to sleep. But no . . . a flurry of thinking buzzed around in my head. Quicktime's illness was troubling. He was younger than I was, a much stronger and better hiker, fully capable of the consecutive twenty-mile days that were out of reach for me. And yet he was done. And I had this foot issue now that would not go away, a tingling sensation that appeared to be the first signs of a nerve problem. I lay uncomfortably in my sleeping bag in the dark and mulled over my infirmities, the arthritis in my lower back, the bad toes, and the stop-start way I was trying to hike the Appalachian Trail, something always seeming to knock me off my stride, and why was I doing this again? Hadn't I been over this before and come up empty?

Just as I was drifting off, a mouse ran over my legs. Mice are the bane of trail shelters—I had a friend who slept in a shelter one night in North Carolina and had a mouse try to make a nest in her hair—but I had never had a problem with them. Not until this night. Now sleep was out of the question. Deep in a funk, I crawled out of my bag and sat on the edge of the shelter platform in the dark and listened to the rain and the occasional howl of coyotes for the rest of the night and tried, unsuccessfully, not to think.

I tried not to think about the day I had boxed all those manuscripts and turned off the light in my office, believing I had killed that buddha, that I was done with him and was restarting my life. I tried not to think about the ignominious end to my newspaper career at a failed weekly newspaper. I tried not to think about two dear friends from my newspaper days, now both dead, their lives ended far too soon. I tried not to think about the hike leader back in Georgia who, on one of my earliest or-

ganized club hikes, had fallen backward and died right in front of me at
Chattahoochee Gap on the Appalachian Trail, a man young and strong,
his love of hiking and the mountains so contagious and inspiring, his
sudden death from an undiagnosed condition on a cold December day
so shocking and tragic. I tried not to think of the man I had never met,
the army veteran murdered by a mentally disturbed man just hours after
I had camped near the scene of his horrible death. I tried not to wonder
why I was out here at all. Darkness out in the woods with rain falling on
a tin roof and coyotes yowling in the distance was the ideal setting for all
these depressing memories and thoughts. A perfect gloom. I gave up trying not to think and let the thoughts come, one after the other, a skele-
tons' march, dragging their chains. Somewhere near first gray light they
bade me farewell and I drifted off into a brief sleep leaning against the
hard wall of the shelter.

That day the inevitable happened about midmorning. I crossed a
gravel road and began a long gradual climb through pastures, grassy
meadows, and an old apple orchard. The climb should have been easy
compared to the two much steeper previous climbs on this hike, but in
hiking attitude is just shy of everything and mine was a wreck. My pace
slowed and the modest hill I was climbing morphed into a monster.
Stoneheart was waiting for me at the next shelter.

"Can you make it to The Priest?" he asked after a good look at me.

"I don't know," I said. The shelter just below the summit of The Priest
was another 6.6 miles and most of it was uphill. Although I had hiked
only a little more than ten miles, this looked like a good place to spend
the night.

"I don't think I can do it," I mumbled.

I had been here before, of course, staring squarely at a buddha in the
trail, the buddha staring impassively back at me, the bearded man in the
plastic gold frame with the dazed, far-off look. In the Smokies and out
of Spivey Gap and a couple of other places. The feeling of being an im-
poster, a man out of place, sleepwalking circles in a crazy dream. Maybe
that helped a little, having smashed into that wall of fatigue and confusion and self-pity, and somehow having clawed through it to keep going.

I thought of Quicktime now back in Georgia and wondered how he was feeling. He would want me to push on if I could. I thought of Cogs and his advice never to quit on a bad day. Stoneheart was ready to head out. He was a strong man, a powerful hiker and good company, full of stories about the trail, always optimistic and calm. And he knew to leave me alone for a few more minutes. While he studied his map, I ate some snacks, drank plenty of water, and stared out into the empty forest a few moments. Then I stood up, hoisted on my backpack, gathered my trekking poles, and drew a deep breath.

"Let's go," I said. "I'll meet you there. I might be late . . . but I'll make it."

Another 6.6 miles. Up to The Priest. Up where the air is cooler, up where you can see for miles, where you can look back south and see where you have come from and peer north into the distance to where you could go if you have the will and the stamina and just a little good luck. Where things are clear, and the choices are simple. Where your feet can kiss the earth on the way up and print peace and serenity on the trail at the summit and the hallucinations fall away, where the White American Jesus stays inside the plastic golden frame, and the dead in their little cardboard boxes stay dead and I could be forgiven for putting them there.

That was where I wanted to go . . . The Priest. The journey took me the rest of the day and cost me some pain. But when I arrived, Stoneheart happily greeted me; I pitched my tent, introduced myself to friendly hikers at the shelter, ate my supper, brushed my teeth, hung my food bag, collected my water, crawled into my sleeping bag as the sun went down, and slept for eight hours the sleep of the dead.

The next day I saw a raven soaring above the trail.

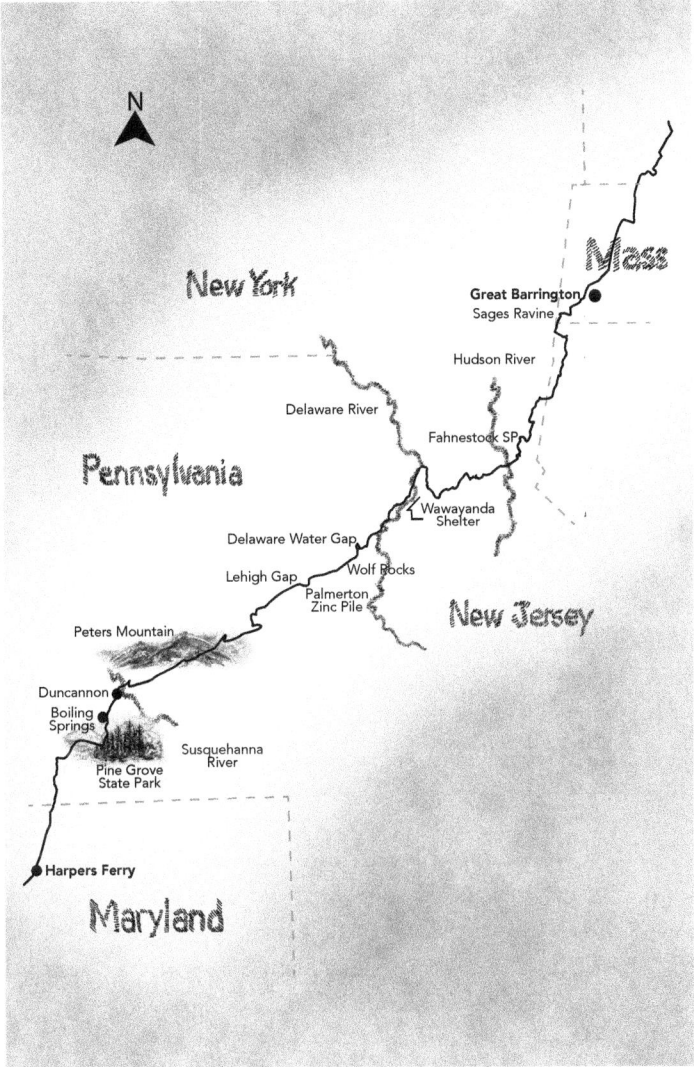

Rocks

Interstate highways run parallel to a significant portion of the Appalachian Trail and cross the trail often. The trail intersects with I-40 in North Carolina and I-81 in Virginia and Pennsylvania, even uses the I-80 bridge to cross the Delaware River into New Jersey. In New England the trail ducks under I-89 in Vermont, goes over I-91 near Hanover, and back under I-93 in New Hampshire. Travelers on I-81 west of Shenandoah National Park driving at seventy-five miles an hour or more gobble up the 102 miles that parallel the A.T. in the park, and if they look out their car windows to the east, they will see the long ridge that requires the better part of a week for an average hiker to walk.

There is a hidden irony in watching that Shenandoah ridgeline and the other A.T. ridges from a speeding vehicle on a four-lane highway. None other than Benton MacKaye was the first to suggest the interstate highway system that now laces our nation with concrete and asphalt.[1] In 1931, MacKaye and fellow forester Lewis Mumford proposed a "townless highway" to remedy the problem of traffic congestion on the country's two-lane roads. MacKaye said automobiles needed a new system specifically designed for them rather than the evolved web of paved-over footpaths, horse trails, and wagon roads they had inherited. That seems obvious now, in retrospect, but it is yet another example of MacKaye's extraordinary ability to see into the future.

American interstate highways have become synonymous with the American idea of freedom, but in a very real sense they are exactly the opposite. Hop in a car and cross a chunk of the country on an interstate and you have experienced something not so much different from flying from one place to another. Your feet do not touch the ground, and if someone else is driving you can sleep through the entire trip and not miss anything important. The "freedom" is partly an illusion. You confine yourself inside a metal box that is confined to a long thin strip of pavement. You are transported without any effort of your own from point A to point B and experience next to nothing of what is between them. In that sense, our digital world is simply a speed-of-light extension of our modern mode of traveling. We experience the land, if we do that at all, through a frame. We connect nodes of destination, as the anthropologist Tim Ingold has pointed out, but in the process, we can ignore the geography that exists between, say, Atlanta and Boston. People who fly often rarely look out the windows. It is too boring.

The wonderful writer Bill Bryson, whose popular book about his Appalachian Trail hike, A Walk in the Woods, may have doubled the number of hikers attempting a thru-hike on the A.T., aimed a passage at this idea of directly experiencing the land and missed badly.[2] Bryson viewed the forest as "one boundless singularity." Nothing but trees, hour after hour, day after day, and nothing to distinguish one mile from the last one or the next one, a featureless "same tangled mass" going nowhere.[3]

This is exactly wrong. It is what you would see and think if you viewed the Appalachian Trail through a frame. Among many thru-hikers after the publication of A Walk in the Woods, and especially the movie of the same title, Bryson is disparaged and mocked because he did not complete all the miles between Springer Mountain and Katahdin. On my trek I saw that hikers had scrawled graffiti critical of Bryson on the beams of a few of the shelters I visited. This, too, is the wrong attitude, because no hiker has the right to judge what is success for any other hiker. One hundred miles might be success. Or ten. Hiking any trail is not a contest, and completion of one does not earn you anything except what you yourself make of it. Not to mention the wrongness of the graffiti itself.

But Bryson did indeed miss the trees for the forest. Hiking the Appalachian Trail is, when hikers do it well, immersion in a continuum of geology, ecology, sociology, psychology, and history. Spirituality too, for those who are so inclined. The mix of all these characteristics on the trail tosses out constant surprises, landmarks, and fascinating places if you are alert to them. There is an exact point on the trail in the Smokies where the altitude reached is just high enough for spruce trees to appear. Dip below that altitude and the spruce go away; climb back up and they return. In Georgia, the trail in one specific place makes use of an old roadbed to nowhere cut by the New Deal's Civilian Conservation Corps in the 1930s, and in two locations the dry-stacked stone retaining walls are visible if you look carefully. In Tennessee, just above the trail, is the grave and monument to a hermit who lived and died there, Nick Grindstaff, said to have won and lost a fortune in the California gold fields. In central Virginia the A.T. winds through a forested, mossy cove that was the site of a farmstead established by Moses Richeson in 1868. The son of a slaveholder and an enslaved woman, Richeson eventually became the patron of the Brown Creek community; almost all the inhabitants were former slaves who earned enough money to buy their own land. North of Shenandoah National Park, in Virginia, hikers of the Appalachian Trail walk alongside a high but otherwise nondescript fence and have no clue that the sturdy chain link encloses rare and endangered species of animals: cheetahs, clouded leopards, Eld's deer, Przewalski's horse, and Persian onager, among others, cared for by the Smithsonian's National Zoo and Conservation Biology Institute. In Pennsylvania there is an exact spot called Wolf Rocks that was the southernmost extent of the Ice Age glaciers, and you can find and touch the smoothed rock where the ice stopped its advance. In North Carolina, I marveled at chestnut tree saplings in a deep, forested cove, rare and skinny doomed offshoots of the mighty trees that once dominated southern forests until a blight killed them early in the twentieth century. In New York, a mere twenty yards off the trail are the tumbled rock walls of a barn where George Washington set up a smallpox inoculation station for his army in the winter of 1776. In Maine the Appalachian Trail for a short distance borrows the exact path between two large lakes that Benedict Arnold used to portage his boats when he led his small detachment of the Continental Army north to invade Canada. In Massachusetts, just beside the trail is a field where the final and decisive skirmish of Shay's Rebellion was fought on February 27, 1787.

The list of such places along the Appalachian Trail could go on and on, almost every mile of it, as the subtle interplay of geology and ecology and history blend and twist amid the forests and fields and mountains. And such a list does not include the personal monuments along the trail, sometimes known only to the one who passed that spot. There are graves, memorials, and markers. Little shrines such as the one in the spruce forest in Tennessee north of Erwin where on a cold day I hiked in fresh snow on Unaka Mountain and encountered a head-high spruce tree adorned with Christmas decorations and a note remembering a young man who had died not far from there, doing what he loved to do, according to the testimonial. In Virginia, at the summit of Bluff Mountain, a marker reads, "This is the exact spot Little Ottie Cline Powell's body was found April 5, 1891, after straying from Tower Road School on Nov. 9, a distance of seven miles. Four years, 11 months old." For me, an unforgettable though unremarkable spot was in North Carolina, at mile 337 north of Springer Mountain, where I first saw a raven and was brought to tears by a rush of wonderful memories. Or the place in Georgia at Chattahoochee Gap, just a few hundred yards from the spring that becomes a creek that becomes a river that flows all the way to the Gulf of Mexico, where I helplessly watched a fellow hiker die.

As Robert Pirsig said, these are the things and the places you should notice out there. But hiking this way, so that you notice these and other things, requires an effort to stay alert, which comes only with discipline and practice. A specific disciplined attitude is necessary to achieve this mental state and even more discipline is necessary to sustain it. The more difficult the trail becomes, the more important this alert attitude is, not just to being observant but to actually surviving. What this requires is both mental and physical coordination. The philosopher of cognitive science Christopher Mole calls this "cognitive unison."[4] Basically, it is constantly paying attention to what you are doing and where you are doing it, who and what are around you, and how all of it combines moment to moment. Being in the zone, as Cogs had said.

To do this, three elements have to come together. The first is awareness of your body as you move over the trail: feet, calf, and thigh muscles; breathing; body temperature; arms and hands. Next comes awareness of what is around you, the treadway itself, first and foremost, but also the weather, the landform, the compass direction, the white blazes, the forest and types of trees, the transition from hardwoods to evergreens or from a pasture to soybean fields, the sounds of birds or wind in the trees, the smells, the scent of galax or the whiff of a skunk or the ozone-burned air after a lightning storm, and the wildlife itself. Plus, the oddities, a bizarrely twisted tree, an artisan spring bubbling up, the graffiti on rocks at a view point, a sign memorializing the World War II hero Audie Murphy near where he died in a plane crash, the giant three-hundred-year-old Kieffer Oak below a hillside pasture in Virginia or the even older Dover Oak in New York. . . .

The third element, and this is the tricky part, is bringing these two together so they work in harmony and neither takes over or is neglected. Hiking this way is hard work. I am pretty sure that every time I have wandered off the trail by missing a blaze, my mistake has been to allow the balance to become badly unsettled. One form of awareness took over and I almost forgot the other. Doing this can result in a harmless diversion costing ten or fifteen minutes, or maybe an hour or two. Or it can be fatal. In 2019 a man went missing after he wandered off a trail that connects with the Approach Trail heading up to Springer Mountain. He died of exposure. A woman hiking with her daughter in the Smokies the same year did the same thing and suffered the same fate.

This is also why when the trail comes down off a mountain and enters a town, the distractions of noise and traffic and people can be overwhelming to a hiker after days in the forest. Hiking in a state of cognitive unison in a town, for me at least, was nearly impossible. The Appalachian Trail does traverse sidewalks in towns such as Hot Springs, Damascus, Atkins, Harpers Ferry, Boiling Springs, Duncannon, Hanover, and a few others. Most thru-hikers I have met are usually glad to arrive at these towns because they offer the prospect of hamburgers or pizza and maybe a shower and soft bed, but they are equally glad to leave and return to the mountains. After miles in the woods, walking on a sidewalk just does not feel right. The concrete hurts the feet, and the busyness hurts the head. It is hard to kiss the earth when your aching feet are slapping concrete and trucks are whizzing by.

The Appalachian Trail changes in Pennsylvania. Every thru-hiker who makes it that far north knows it, and the huge majority of them are by that point hardened by the 1,067 miles they have walked to reach the modest Mason-Dixon sign beside the path. They are ready for the challenge, and they understand what is coming. Southbounders have told them, or they have read about it or seen the videos or heard the stories through the trail gossip line that runs back and forth from Georgia to Maine. To them, it is no big deal, just another state, number eight out of fourteen. Yeah, Pennsylvania has rocks but so what?

To me, a sporadic section hiker, Pennsylvania was a big deal. Until Pennsylvania I had managed pretty well. I had mostly solved the problem of sleeping at night and I had replaced my worn-down hiking shoes with new ones that featured special inserts to deal with the metatarsalgia that now was a permanent feature of my left foot. I had a good plan, and Stoneheart, who was section hiking like I was, decided to join me. I had been preparing myself with training hikes in Georgia to get my body ready. And, maybe most important, I had a large chunk of time set aside in the fall of 2019.

At first, the hiking was not hard. The Appalachian Trail exits Maryland just beyond Pen Mar State Park, and the climbs and descents are just little bumps compared to the southern mountains. Some of the hiking is through pleasant open forests of pine and mixed hardwoods, and none of the miles are difficult. At Pine Grove Furnace State Park, where hikers can enjoy a hamburger or ice cream from the park store, the old iron ore mines give a hint of the change to come. The trail passes pretty Fuller Lake, a ninety-foot-deep former ore pit where people now swim and paddle little boats and ride their bicycles around the shoreline. Pieces of slag from the long-abandoned furnace still litter the trail.

The little bumps then become a crenelated series of sharper climbs and descents called Rocky Ridge, and the first massive, rounded quartz-ite outcrops and boulder sections begin, nothing terrible, but they were enough of a challenge to require my full attention. And at the last of the hills, a knob called White Rocks that has the distinction of long ago be-ing the midpoint of the A.T., something momentous occurs. No doubt many hikers miss the much more important significance of the place than the old midpoint sign when they gaze northeast toward a broad valley. They have, in fact, arrived at the northern end of the Blue Ridge mountain range that they have been hiking since they started in Geor-gia some 1,072 miles to the south. Ahead lies the Cumberland Valley, a continent-spanning scar that stretches from Alabama to Canada. The Appalachian Trail had already crossed the valley back in Virginia at I-81 but from this point on hikers heading north have left the southern ranges behind for good.

The geologist V. Collins Chew, the unofficial authority on the geol-ogy of the Appalachian Trail, describes the Cumberland Valley as "an area where long, narrow bands of sedimentary rock determine the to-pography." He went on the explain that "the A.T. generally trends east-northeast for its remaining length in Pennsylvania, following sandstone ridges of various ages, including several that are younger than any to the south along the A.T. Some of the beds are of Pennsylvanian age and were once tree-clogged swamps that eventually were compressed to anthracite (hard) coal."[5] In other words, you are in new country. Expect changes.

The Cumberland Valley of Pennsylvania is rich farmland, countryside where the barns are fine, enormous structures and the farmhouses are old and stately. Coming down off White Rocks, I found myself hiking alongside broad soybean fields. The quaint and charming little town of Boiling Springs appeared shimmering under the heat waves in the dis-tance. In the town the trail crossed an arched stone bridge over a stream and entered a park beside a lovely lake where ducks were swimming and children were playing and couples were sitting on benches in the after-noon sun. A woman was throwing a ball into the shallows of the lake for her dog to fetch. Stoneheart was sitting on a bench under a big shade tree watching her and drinking a cold sports drink. I joined him and could have stayed there until the sun went down. Instead, we bought dinners and ice-cold drinks in a tavern overlooking the lake and caught a shuttle out of town and took it five miles across the farmland to a hostel for the night. A shower, clean clothes, a delicious sandwich, and a good night of sleep had me ready for whatever Pennsylvania wanted to throw at me. Three days later the state fired a high inside fastball and these pitches kept coming, one after another, until a particularly nasty bean ball literally sent me onto the seat of my pants.

The serious rocks begin north of Duncannon, after you cross the Juniata and Susquehanna Rivers. The trail climbs out of the Cumberland Valley onto Peters Mountain, which is actually a twelve-mile-long ridge, barely 1,100 feet high, and the top is as close to level as any mountain ridge could hope to be. The rocks on the ridge, layers of shale and sandstone, date to the Devonian and Silurian periods, about 410 million years ago. Chew describes what happened on this ridge in the intervening millions of years: "The softer shale underneath the sandstone eroded away. Water in the cracks of the sandstone expanded as it froze and wedged apart pieces of the rock. This action, called 'frost wedging,' and the force of gravity broke off the undercut sandstone, which then rolled downhill, leaving north-facing rugged cliffs. A level shelf extends several yards from the base of the cliffs, providing a smooth path for the A.T."[6]

That last part, the "smooth path for the A.T.," is dead wrong. What Chew is describing is a hiker's nightmare. There is no trail in the commonly understood sense of that word. Instead, the level shelf Chew describes is a narrow corridor of tumbled rock assorted into a chaos of shapes and sizes that goes on and on and on until you think an evil genius who hated hikers and wanted a way to be rid of some of them and to drive the rest of them mad had designed the whole mountain. To safely negotiate this rock junkyard, hikers must plan every footstep. On this ridge an occasional faded white blaze on a tree or a rock is the only discernable way forward. In some places, if the light was just right, I could see where the rubbing of thousands of shoe soles over decades of hiking had scrubbed smooth some of the surfaces and edges just enough to leave a faint sheen that stands out, and hikers can follow them like a rabbit path through a briar patch.

Here is where hiking with cognitive unison becomes a survival skill. The brain and the feet have to work as a team, with the eyes and arms supporting the effort. Step there, on that rock, the brain says, and then there, and reach for that one here, but not that next one that is loose and could wobble and turn an ankle. Don't step in that crevice. Climb up on this big one that is reasonably flat, then turn right, but no . . . that way is a dead end, so go back left and scoot down on your butt to this ledge and balance with your left hand against this boulder and ease down some more to that flat rock.

All the while watching for rattlesnakes. Peters Mountain is locally famous for them. And sure enough, I came to an exposed twenty yards of bright sunshine, stopped to plan my route across the maze of rock, determined that a thin flat boulder the approximate shape of a king-size mattress would be the best way to go, and was just about to put my foot on it when I decided to look just to the left of its edge and there was a rattlesnake sunning itself. The snake rattled at me, and I chose a detour.

Another thing about the rocks in Pennsylvania that Chew does not mention is that in places they have thin edges and are planted in the matrix in just such a way as to poke up in the air at slanted angles perfectly positioned to trip a person who is not careful. The local hikers, who take a perverse pride in their Appalachian Trail's rocks, like to say that little devils and gnomes come out at night to sharpen the edges. After several slow-motion miles of rock hops and straddles, bends and twists and near misses, that kind of dark humor can take over. To hell with cognitive unison and experiencing the trail moment by moment and immersion in nature and the rest of it—you just want to be done with the damn rocks. Just find some soil to walk on, something that resembles an actual trail instead of a boneyard of jagged sandstone.

And this is where the real danger kicks in, especially for a hiker of my age. A fall up here on Peters Mountain and its rock-strewn cousins for the next 145 miles of the A.T. will almost guarantee a serious injury. Back in

Virginia, at a hostel in Waynesboro, I had met an athletic young woman
A.T. thru-hiker with the trail name of Pepper who told me in great detail how she had broken her leg up here and had crawled, staggered, and
clawed her way for almost two hours down to a trailhead, where a motor-
ist had stopped, dragged her into the back seat, and taken her to a hospital. She had healed, and within less than a year was back on the trail. But
for many would-be A.T. hikers who are careless, accident-prone, or just
unlucky, Pennsylvania's rocks are the end of the line. Patience, concentration, and skill at reading the rocks are what get you through. I survived
Peters Mountain and Rattling Run, Second Mountain, Eagles Nest, Pulpit Rock, Blue Rocks, the Pinnacle, Hawk Mountain, Dans Pulpit, Blue
Mountain, the Knife Edge, and Bear Rocks. I even let myself think I was
getting pretty good at hiking Pennsylvania's rocks. I should have known
better, for the state's high inside fastballs were not finished with me.

The Lehigh Gap is both well-known and notorious to hikers. For northbounders, the climb out of the gap is the first serious steep rock scramble
of their hike, just a little taste of what is to come in New Hampshire and
Maine. Quicktime had recovered from his health scare and joined me to
finish Pennsylvania. I wanted to get an early start out of the gap, so we left
our camp at first light on a clear morning. I should have eaten more for
breakfast, but I was oddly not hungry, and the thought of limp oatmeal
was not appealing. First, we descended the ridge to the Lehigh River,
crossed the bridge, then crossed a busy road at a traffic light in the little
town of Walnutport. The climb began at a scruffy trailhead parking lot.
From there the Appalachian Trail would climb 939 feet to a ridge summit
and enter the Palmerton Zinc Pile Superfund site. One trail guidebook
casually states that the deforestation of the ridge was "due to zinc smelt-
ing from 1898 to 1980."[7] The guidebook advises hikers to stay on the trail
while crossing the superfund site and not to drink from the only spring
between the summit and Smith Gap, nearly seven miles up the trail to the
north, due to the high metallic content of the water. The geologist Collins Chew mentions in his geologic guide to the Appalachian Trail that fly

ash mixed with municipal sludge was applied to the mountainside in the hope that plants would grow, which tells a lot about what the mountain must have looked like before 1980. He also states that the A.T. "ascends to an extremely rugged, barren area of ledges and loose blocks of quartzite, reminiscent of the gold mining country west of Denver."[8]

I started up the Pile full of confidence. The trail immediately became steep, and about one third of the way up the trees thinned and then I was among nothing but rocks baking in the morning sun. Still, the Pile loomed over me, and I could not see the full extent of what was ahead until I rounded the last of the switchbacks and what had been a discernible trail vanished. Quickly the reality of what I was facing hit home—a wilderness of crazy-shaped stone blocks, many of them with the rough cubic dimensions of a modern bathroom or a compact SUV, all piled on top of each other in an ascending pyramid and sprinkled with smaller stones the size of sofas and desks. It was as though a battalion of Godzillas had spent a few decades piling these monster blocks on top of each other for no reason other than to see how high they could go. And when they got bored and gave the game up, some dang fools decided to route the Appalachian Trail as high over them as they could manage before gravity required the trail to angle sideways across the plane of the pyramid to keep hikers from falling off and tumbling all the way down to the Lehigh River.

I was breathing hard and grunting with each foothold and lift upward, acutely aware that I was carrying about twenty-seven pounds strapped to my back. My trekking poles were now worse than useless—they were an encumbrance because I needed both my hands to find secure crevices in the rock to pull myself up, often three feet or more each time. And these were Pennsylvania rocks, described by Chew as showing "evidence of extremely erosive moving ice, containing abrasive sand and grit. The quartzite ledges above this point are blocky and angular."[9] Another way to describe them is that the surfaces were coarse enough to scrub barnacles off a steel hull.

Within ten minutes of climbing and scrambling in this disaster zone I had to stop and rest. I needed water and something to eat, but there was very little space between the rocks to even stand comfortably. I sat down on the nearest rock available, balanced myself awkwardly, pulled out my water bottle, and tore open a snack bar. As I munched granola, I stared at the shimmering Lehigh River directly below me. Time passed. I don't know how long. I ate a few bites more, thought of taking a picture, decided not to, sipped on my water, and gazed at the Pennsylvania countryside spread out before me. It was quite lovely.

And then I slid off the rock. I do not know how, except that I was sitting on a tilted surface, and I was reaching for my trekking poles leaning beside me, and the weight of my backpack must have shifted with the angle of the rock and pulled me in that direction. I banged into a neighboring rock at shoulder height, spun around, and landed on what passed up there for ground. When I righted myself, I discovered that the backs of both my hands were bloody. I had scraped them against the rock as I was falling, and the rough surfaces had torn the skin in seven or eight places.

I knew right away the cuts were shallow and not serious. But the bleeding would not stop, and I could not use too much of my water to wash the wounds. I had to get up, rescue my trekking poles from falling off the rock pile, and push on. I could treat my hands later when I reached a safe place.

So I scrambled for the next fifteen minutes over the rocks with blood dripping down to my wrists, making the cork grips of my trekking poles sticky. *Who falls while they're sitting down?* I asked myself over and over. It was comical. I had fallen once before coming down off The Priest when I stabbed a trekking pole on a rock for balance and it slid off and went into a crevice and I followed it down, bending the pole but doing no other damage. And I fell in northern Virginia in the middle of the Roller Coaster when I slung my backpack onto my shoulder with too much force and the momentum spun me around and I fell face down onto a bed of soft pine straw, laughing at myself like a fool. *But sitting down?* And with such a bloody result, both my hands dripping blood? From barely touching those evil corrugated blocks?

By the time I caught Quicktime nearly a mile after my accident, the bleeding was mostly stopped, and I was fine. But I looked a mess, blood stains on my pants, my shirt, my trekking pole grips, and my watchband. As if I had just tangled with a bobcat or emerged from a bar fight. And the reward for climbing that gargantuan pile of tumbled stone? A long walk across a broad ridge only just beginning to regenerate with brown sedge and stunted and sparse pine trees and a few scrubs. The fly ash and municipal sludge had done the trick on the superfund site, but it had taken four decades to grow anything. Mercifully, the trail itself was a grassy level path for several miles before it climbed, and the rocks inevitably returned. As I walked, my fingers cramped, my back ached from the twisting and contorting on those blasted rocks, and my neck now hurt from constantly looking down at where I was putting each foot.

Slowly and almost imperceptibly the vegetation thickened, the trees were bigger, and the terrain less scarred, something closer to what I could describe as a normal forest. An hour later I was walking in genuine forest when I met three young men from the Pennsylvania Game and Fish Department. They carried snake poles and wore heavy snake leggings, and they announced that they were conducting a survey that afternoon. A rattlesnake survey.

We chatted briefly about their work. They seemed surprised to see a long-distance hiker like me out there. The weather had recently warmed enough for the rattlesnakes to come out, but they would not stray too far from their dens, the men told me. I should expect to see one or two of them on the trail in the next few days. They said this as though there might be three or four of them concealed within a twenty-yard radius of where we were standing in the trail. But the best place to see them was back at Peters Mountain, they said. If I didn't bother the rattlers, they wouldn't bother me, one of the men added in an earnest tone. Mindful of my Southern accent, I assured them I was not a snake handler and that any rattlesnakes I encountered would be perfectly safe. As we said goodbye, I noticed all three of the men had been staring at my skinned hands and blood-stained shirt and pants and then exchanging puzzled glances. But I did not feel like explaining. I had had enough of Pennsylvania.

Beyond Brave

One of the distinctive characteristics of hiking the Appalachian Trail in sections instead of in one long, continuous go is that Day One happens over and over again. And the first day back on the trail for me after a long layoff was always a mix of excitement, a little trepidation, and a whole lot of unknown. What would I be facing this time? I could never be sure, no matter how much planning and research I had done. Was I physically ready to hike the trail? The answer was always no, no matter how much training I had tried to put in back at home. A time-tested truism about the Appalachian Trail is that the only way to completely prepare physically for hiking it is to begin hiking it and tough out the hard days, slowly building your stamina and strength. Thru-hikers often say they do not develop what they call "trail legs" until two to three hundred miles up the A.T. As a section hiker, I knew I would never experience the joy of hiking at a three-mile-per-hour pace over rough trail for eight or nine hours, day after day. Plodding along like a turtle up and down the Appalachian Trail's many, many climbs was my fate.

The reality of this was hard for me to accept, even though I knew it down to my bones. I would look at the trail guides and map profiles of a section I intended to hike and think surely I could knock off consecutive days of fourteen to eighteen miles after a couple of days of lesser miles to condition my legs. This was an illusion. And when I set out on a pleasant mid-June evening from the little hamlet of Unionville to finish New Jersey and hike New York, Connecticut, and Massachusetts, ending in Vermont, I learned a very hard lesson about how advancing age had dimmed my physical capabilities. My second day on the trail served up a warning of what was to come, and the third day could have ended my section hike before I had even covered forty miles.

The hike started well enough to hide any hint of trouble. I crossed into New York on a low ridge of exposed smooth rock on a sunny day. At Wawayanda Shelter the evening before I had met a trio of thru-hikers: Hammer, a recently retired, hard-as-nails army ranger from Colorado; Wanderer, a dead ringer for Papa Ernest Hemingway with his white beard, except for his quiet, self-contained manner; and Merlot, a lady so named because she carried a heavy plastic bottle and enjoyed a small cup of red wine each evening. They had been hiking together since shortly after leaving Springer Mountain. I also met a fellow from Ohio, a recent immigrant from Eastern Europe, who had gotten on the trail at the Delaware Water Gap and was hoping to hike all the way to Katahdin. This was an odd arrangement—he had not even acquired a trail name yet, and from the questions about gear and other essentials he asked me around our camp that evening, it was obvious he was new to this. I gave him the trail name Coffee Bean because he proceeded to pull a one-pound bag of ground coffee from his pack and a drip coffee maker to brew a big mug to go with his evening meal.

Trail news that evening was about bears. The bear population in New Jersey is surprisingly large, and hikers of the Appalachian Trail passing through that state have a better chance of encountering one there than anywhere else on the trail except perhaps the Smokies. And the word was that hikers had frequently encountered bears on the stretch of trail we were about to hike. An aggressive bear had been reported in the vicinity some months ago, but it was unclear whether that particular bear was still a problem. Around the picnic table in front of the shelter that evening Merlot described a confrontation she had had with a bear earlier that day. A bear had appeared on the trail not ten yards in front of her and instead of moving away, it had turned toward her and approached. Merlot had stood her ground and fortunately Wanderer soon came up behind her and the two of them made enough noise and commotion to shoo the bear off into the bushes. The upshot of this was a conclusion that stealth camping for the next few days would not be a good idea. We needed to reach the shelters, where either a steel bear box or cables for suspending our food would provide a better level of safety against a hungry bear than hanging our food from trees.[1]

That meant back-to-back days where I would need to hike between twelve and fifteen miles each day. No problem, I thought as I drifted off to sleep in my tent at Wawayanda. I had hiked much longer miles on past sections, and no big mountains loomed ahead. The profile map showed an almost level trail dotted with a few bumps and no elevation above 1,300 feet until just before Fingerboard Shelter. Two days of relatively easy hiking.

Two mornings later, I was up early. I packed my gear as quietly as I could so as not to wake Hammer, Wanderer, and Merlot, who were camping nearby, and before first light I was on the trail, eager for a fourteen-mile day to Fingerboard Shelter. The air was humid, and as soon as the sun was above the horizon, I felt a new level of warmth, a stickiness that had not been present the morning before. The higher humidity seemed to have invited mosquitoes to come out for breakfast. No breeze stirred, and I was soon sweating on a steep descent. And from the bottom of the hill, near Fitzgerald Falls, this day settled into a pattern of up and down, up and down, as those "bumps" on the profile map turned out to be a never-ending series of ravines and escarpments, none of them very high but all of them steep and rugged, often involving scrambles over exposed rock and tumbled boulders. The heat and the humidity rose by the hour as I dragged myself up less than a hundred feet of climb and then picked my way back down into the next ravine. By noon I was already tired, and when I consulted my map, I was shocked to discover that I had hiked only six miles. Each climb seemed to suck more and more energy out of me. I realized I had not eaten enough for breakfast, and it was too late to make up the calorie deficit.

Early in the afternoon I came to the base of a particularly nasty-looking climb up a rock escarpment of less than sixty feet. The total height was not the problem—this one was nearly vertical in a couple of places, and the exposed rock did not have obvious or easy clefts for foot-holds. One fifteen-foot piece up to a narrow ledge looked very imposing. I scrambled up partway, reached a flat shelf, and stopped to study options for the best way to the final ledge. There was no best way—straight up on the rock was the only option. Up I went, using the few handholds I could find to pull myself higher. When my head was about even with the ledge, I realized that an overhanging tree branch the thickness of my wrist that I thought would be useful as a handhold was actually an obstacle—I would have to squeeze under it to get on top of the ledge.

I threw my trekking poles onto the ledge and grabbed a rock edge to pull against. Then I found a protruding rock for my right foot and a higher skinny cleft for my left. I took a deep breath and heaved myself toward the ledge, but as I did the top of my backpack jammed against the tree branch, stopping me cold. And as I struggled to free myself, the rock my right foot had been shoving against broke loose and clattered down the mountain. For several seconds I hung there holding on to the tree branch I had to squeeze under, listening to the rock crashing down into the ravine, my right foot uselessly dangling in the air. Now I could not go back down—up onto the ledge was my only hope. My first attempt to free my pack failed, and I knew the next one had to work or I would be in trouble. This time I managed to disengage my pack from the tree branch by flattening myself against the rock, wiggling on my stomach and at the same time pushing up on the branch with one hand and pulling hard with my other until I could get a new purchase for my right foot and shimmy up onto the ledge.

This whole episode took no more than two minutes, but it seemed like an hour that I had been stuck on the edge of the flat shelf I was now safely standing on. I recovered my breathing, raked off some of the dirt and debris from my shirt, pants, and out of my beard, and finished the climb to the top, where I turned around and peered down the escarpment where I had escaped disaster. A fall back down to the bottom would have dropped me fifteen feet or more onto rock—a guarantee of certain injury, maybe a very bad one. How much more of this? I wondered. The answer was an even longer steep climb up Arden Mountain, then a very steep descent, and finally a short road walk across a bridge and into the parking area of a New York state park.

Well past midafternoon I had to stop for a rest. A very kind man at the parking area gave me a cold drink, which I gratefully accepted. As I studied my map and calculated the remaining distance to the next shelter and the daylight left, I wondered why Hammer, Wanderer, and Merlot had not yet caught and passed me on the trail. All three were very strong hikers, capable of a much faster pace than my pitiful progress over all these climbs and descents. I expected them to come walking up behind me at any moment as I heaved my pack back on and set out for the last four miles to Fingerboard Shelter.

Immediately I faced a climb of about five hundred feet on Island Pond Mountain, and I hit a wall of exhaustion. Day-hikers were out in force at the state park on this Saturday, couples and families, children, dogs, runners. All of them passed me and scampered or strolled up a bump of a mountain that had me gasping. My legs had very little left in them. I felt old and discouraged and out of place—all the familiar negativity and doubts from previous hard days on the trail scrolled through my mind like little dancing demons. All I could do was plod along, one foot in front of the other, stopping to rest often so my breathing stayed within a range I could manage. I had been in this afflicted state of mind and body before, staring into the blazing eyes of a buddha, and I knew the next miles would be very hard.

With about two miles to go I reached a big double rock formation called the Lemon Squeezer, a narrow gap between two stone goliaths that requires hikers to take off their backpacks and slide sideways between the high slab walls. A soft rain began to fall, and I paused to take off my pack for the transit of the Lemon Squeezer and pull on the rain cover. I also turned on my cellphone to consult a trail app for the distance to the shelter. As I was fiddling with the map on the screen, I received a text message from Hammer: "Are you okay?"

An odd question, I thought. Why would he ask that? No one knew about my near disaster earlier in the day. Before I could type a reply another message came—the news from Hammer that Wanderer had fallen at one of those treacherous escarpment climbs and broken his arm. He had walked himself out to a trailhead, Hammer carrying both of their backpacks and Merlot helping him, and they were now at a hospital.

This news stunned me. Wanderer was one of the most cautious, deliberate hikers I had ever met. I had watched in admiration how methodical he was about every aspect of thru-hiking, erecting his tent, cooking, and tackling the rocks. And now, on a hike that had started at Amicalola Falls State Park in Georgia in February,[2] and after walking 1,383 miles north through freezing cold and heat and sieges of rain, Pennsylvania's rocks and everything else a thru-hiker must endure, his hike was over. Just like that, in one disastrous moment. I could easily imagine where his accident had happened and how he had fallen, because it could easily have happened to me on this very day.

I stumbled into Fingerboard Shelter in a steady rain and claimed the last place inside. A couple of thru-hikers who were as bedraggled and wet as I was greeted me. Their talk was about how hard the trail had been and how surprised they were at the ruggedness of New York. They had planned to do twenty miles this day but had pulled in here after fourteen, a very short day for thru-hikers. I had hiked fourteen hours and had covered 14.5 miles—an incredibly slow pace. But I had survived—that was the important thing. I had paid the price of being an unprepared seventy-one-year-old section hiker. As for Hammer's question, Are you okay?, my reply had been yes. But just barely.

That night I thought about Wanderer and how his dream of completing the Appalachian Trail had vanished in a single flash of pain. And at a point in his hike where he had every reason to believe he would reach Katahdin. Probably he had done nothing wrong back there on one of those escarpments—accidents happen, even to the strongest and most careful of hikers. Some are unavoidable. Just bad luck. In contrast, my dream of being a professional writer had crumbled in slow motion over two decades, and the responsibility for all that failure lived nowhere but on my shoulders. It was not bad luck or lack of application, effort, or even persistence. It had nothing to do with that damn bear, and no raven had appeared over my head to dispel my illusions. I had been utterly alone for the entire two decades, as writers always are, alone with the characters in my head and the plot lines, the voices, the climaxes, and endings, all of them filling reams of wasted paper and emptying cartridges of ink. But I ended my dream almost as suddenly as Wanderer's fall ended his hike. Not by an accident or trip to an emergency room but with a cold decision. With quitting. Admitting failure. Physical pain was not part of it, but considerable anguish was involved. I had a life to rebuild, starting pretty much from scratch. Wanderer's broken arm would heal, and maybe in time, say in a couple of years, he could come back and try the Appalachian Trail again. For me . . . well, that buddha was dead now and I did not want to face him ever again. All those boxed coffins needed to stay buried.

The next morning, I was first out of the shelter, as usual, but a bit dazed from a night of crazy dreams punctuated by the moans and groans of fellow hikers sprawled beside me and one wild, loud outburst that bolted me awake. One of my shelter mates was an army veteran recently returned from a third deployment to Afghanistan, and he had warned us the evening before that he sometimes had very bad dreams and not to worry if he went a little crazy. Somewhere around 3:00 a.m. he did, but his thrashing in his sleeping bag did not last long, and soon the shelter was quiet again. In the gray misty dawn, I shook off hearing his nightmares and my head soon cleared as I hiked over a broad, rounded ridge, the trees widely spaced and lots of smooth exposed rock underfoot. It was almost like hiking in a city park, the humid air still cool, the walking easy, and I had it all to myself for two miles. At a gravel road crossing I stopped to collect some water from gallon jugs left there for hikers by some kind local person who must have known water sources were scarce on this ridge. As I filled up, I looked across the road and saw a bear maybe forty yards away in some low shrubs.

I called out good morning to the bear, but he took no notice of me and ambled off out of sight before I could get a picture. That made two bears I had seen in three days on the trail. And I had to chuckle—my destination for the day was Bear Mountain, and then down to the Hudson River and the mom-and-pop Bear Mountain Bridge Motel in Fort Montgomery. By the time I arrived at Hessian Lake at Bear Mountain State Park, I was staggered by exhaustion and heat. Just four and a half days out on the trail and I already needed a day off. My plan to reach Vermont in the limited time I had available for this trip was looking dubious at best.

Something deep within us drives our species to walk. Of all the speculative theories about what motivated early humans to leave ancestral African homelands and spread all over the earth, the one anthropological explanation that I have never encountered is simply that we are creatures that must walk. Not only that, but we seem to enjoy walking where we have never walked before, and a world of deserts, forests, plains, mountains, swamps, and coastlines constantly beckoned until a day came when our species had touched every continent with our feet. Maybe as a theory this is too simple, too elemental. It leaves the question of why dangling out there, unanswered. Robert Moor asked the same question: "Why do we venture into places where we were not born and do not belong?"[3]

Another question is why this deep human desire has not ebbed over time, especially in the past few centuries, when for many humans day-to-day living has become more comfortable. We do not need to walk one hundred miles to find new sources of food or materials for our tools. Now, in America and a few other places, the things we need or want are often delivered to our door. The fortunate among us, billions strong, can and do stay indoors, out of the heat and the rain and the bitter cold wind for the majority of the time we spend on this planet.

And yet the drive to walk long distances over a wild landscape resides in some of us and will not let us be still for long, regardless of the heat and rain and bitter cold. On my hike through New York and Connecticut, I began to meet more and more thru-hikers who had left Georgia in the late winter and early spring. A young man from a town near my home in Georgia was cheerfully averaging about twenty-five to twenty-six miles per day, even across Pennsylvania's rocks and here on these escarpments and constant hills. One evening in a shelter I spoke with a late arrival, a heavily tattooed man of middle age who was all muscle and sinew, deeply tanned and hardened by years of foot travel into a human walking machine. His trail name was Snail, an intentional contradiction, even a joke of sorts, for this man claimed to be averaging thirty-three miles per day on a walk he had started in Key West, at the southern tip of Florida, on the first day of the year, and he intended to finish at the northern tip of Nova Scotia, replicating the epic hike done years ago by Nimblewill Nomad. His longest day so far, he said without the slightest trace of exaggeration or boast, was fifty-four miles. So far. . . .

Just as impressive as these extreme hiker-athletes were the others well down the hierarchy of thru-hikers, the young woman who left Georgia in mid-February and had lost thirty pounds walking here to Connecticut; the lady with zero previous hiking experience who was laid off from her job just as the COVID-19 pandemic was easing and said to heck with this, I'm going to hike the Appalachian Trail; the middle-aged college professor on a sabbatical; the couple from Pennsylvania thru-hiking just for the fun of it. And Coffee Bean, who got on the trail in the wrong place, was carrying way too much weight, did not have the right equipment, and was not exactly sure what he was doing from one day to the next but simply would not be deterred. He was going to walk to Katahdin, he said, and I did not doubt him for a second.

Spending time with people like this, for only an hour or so in the evening at a shelter, had a positive, encouraging effect on me. Listening to them recount their stories of hardship and wonderful moments, of overcoming problems and aches and pains, broken equipment, unexpected delays, days when they wanted to quit, and days blurred into weeks of simply walking, walking, walking north—all of it pulled me into their worlds a little deeper with each conversation. I began to feel that I was, if not one of their clan, then at least an accepted visitor.

And so I celebrated their achievements, one more state hiked, one more tough section behind them, and I grieved a little at their losses: an athletic young woman who had to end her hike to take care of an ill parent back home, an older woman whose foot problems had passed the serious stage and demanded medical treatment, a young man who was a casualty of Lyme disease. And, of course, Wanderer. His disaster weighed heavily on me. How could someone so careful, so responsible and strong and . . . *deserving* . . . how could his hike end so suddenly and unfairly? And if it could happen to him . . . of course it could happen to anyone. Which was a thought I had to keep at bay.

Late one afternoon in New York, several days after I crossed the Hudson River, I hiked down off the Appalachian Trail on a side trail to Fahnestock State Park to camp for the night in a grassy grove of trees beside a lake. A water fountain and an open bathroom where I found hot water and soap were a great luxury. A few other hikers trickled in off the A.T. in the twilight and camped in a nearby field, but I was already stretched out in my tent, and I did not take notice of them.

The next morning, I hiked back up the side trail to the A.T. And there at the trail junction adjusting their packs and preparing to set out for the day stood Hammer and Merlot, and between them, quiet and still, was Wanderer, his left arm strapped tight to his chest in a soft white cast.

"You are a brave man," was all I could fumble with for a greeting.

"Beyond brave," Hammer said with an admiring glance at his older companion.

Wanderer was a man who did not like to make a fuss about things like this. "It's just a nuisance," he said. He had one trekking pole collapsed and lashed to his pack and the other in his free hand and he used it to tap both his feet for emphasis. "At least I didn't break my legs," he said.

Merlot gave us one of those sideways looks of a woman in the company of foolish men, but I could tell she was proud of her hiking friend's bravery and determination. Wanderer admitted that hauling his backpack on and off with an arm in a cast was difficult, but beyond that he had no complaint and had nothing more to say about his accident. His focus was on pushing north.

"Good luck," I said as they turned into the trail, and we all headed north. Hammer lingered behind for a few moments to talk with me, explaining a little of what had happened. It was pretty bad, Hammer said, a big fall, a hard landing onto rocks, and it could have had a much worse result. Just bad luck. But at the emergency room Wanderer had declined the surgery the doctor said he needed and had refused the doctor's advice to quit the trail. Wanderer had some pills to help manage the pain, which had to be constant, even when he was standing still.

Amazing . . . and Hammer was a man who knew something about pain and accidents. While serving as a ranger, Hammer had suffered a training accident on a parachute jump when a soldier above him prematurely dropped his kit and it collapsed Hammer's parachute. He was lucky to have survived the fall, lucky that he was not an invalid from the resulting injuries. Hammer said goodbye and picked up his pace, caught his friends in a few dozen strong strides, and the three of them quickly disappeared up the trail at the three-mile-an-hour thru-hiker pace I could only dream about. I watched them go with a whiff of loneliness, for I had enjoyed their company and I knew I was unlikely to see them again. They were Katahdin bound. Nothing was going to stop them.

Ten days later my hike of this section of the Appalachian Trail ended abruptly in southwestern Massachusetts, ninety miles short of my target of Bennington, Vermont. A heat wave tormented the northeast, bringing heat indexes of 96 degrees and then 101 degrees on back-to-back days. These were dangerous conditions for anyone trying to hike the Appalachian Trail, much less for an old man like me. I slowed my pace to a crawl, but that was not enough to counter the effect of the heat, and finally I had to get off the trail in the little town of Kent, Connecticut. I rested in air conditioning at an inn for a full day before plodding on, the heat still hitting the midnineties each afternoon and the humidity nearly off the scale. The heat wave was then broken a few days later by tremendous thunderstorms that kept me awake half the night in my tent wondering if the rain fly would hold up against the beating torrent. Next, I hiked through three straight weirdly cool days of rain, with the temperatures each night dipping into the high forties. Battered by all this, the final straw was an infected fingernail that sent me to an emergency room for treatment and antibiotics.

But on my last day of this hike, I scrambled down off a long, rugged ridge in Massachusetts and came to a gravel road where a local man was just unloading an ice chest from the back of his car. His name was Bill, and he said he had been coming to this spot for the last few days to hand out cold drinks and snacks to hikers. The heat wave had been horrible, he said, and a few hikers he had met talked about quitting. One did and went home. As I enjoyed a cold sports drink a thought popped into my head.

"You haven't by chance seen a hiker come by who had his arm in a cast, have you?"

"Oh, you mean Wanderer? Yeah, he was here three days ago with his friends. I couldn't believe it. I mean, I've hiked up there on Everett and that ridge you just came down and I know how crazy it is—just about the roughest stretch of the A.T. in Massachusetts. I don't know how in the world he did it with one arm."

I thought back over my last few days on the trail, all that heat, then the thunderstorms and torrential rain, a tough rocky climb to the Lion's Head in Connecticut, an even tougher climb up Bear Mountain, and then a scary nearly vertical rocky descent into Sage's Ravine after another night of rain. That descent took everything I had to negotiate safely, and I often found myself sliding on my backside or clinging to tree branches and clefts in the wet rocks with both hands to lower myself to the next foothold, each foot of descent an opportunity to make a mistake and fall dozens of feet onto rocks below. Wanderer had survived all of that and more with an arm in a cast tightly strapped against his chest. And pain with every bounce or jiggle or bump.

Every hiker of the Appalachian Trail earns the right to determine what defines their success or failure. Hiking 175 miles into New England when I had planned 265 miles could fall into the category of failure, but I did not view it that way as I flew home with a heavily bandaged finger after a miniature operation to cut away part of my fingernail at an emergency room in Great Barrington. I had survived, and I would be back, and that was what counted. Meanwhile, Wanderer was defining success his own stubborn way, walking north toward Katahdin with his friends, and no heat wave or thunderstorm, rocks, stabs of pain, or anything else were going to stop him.

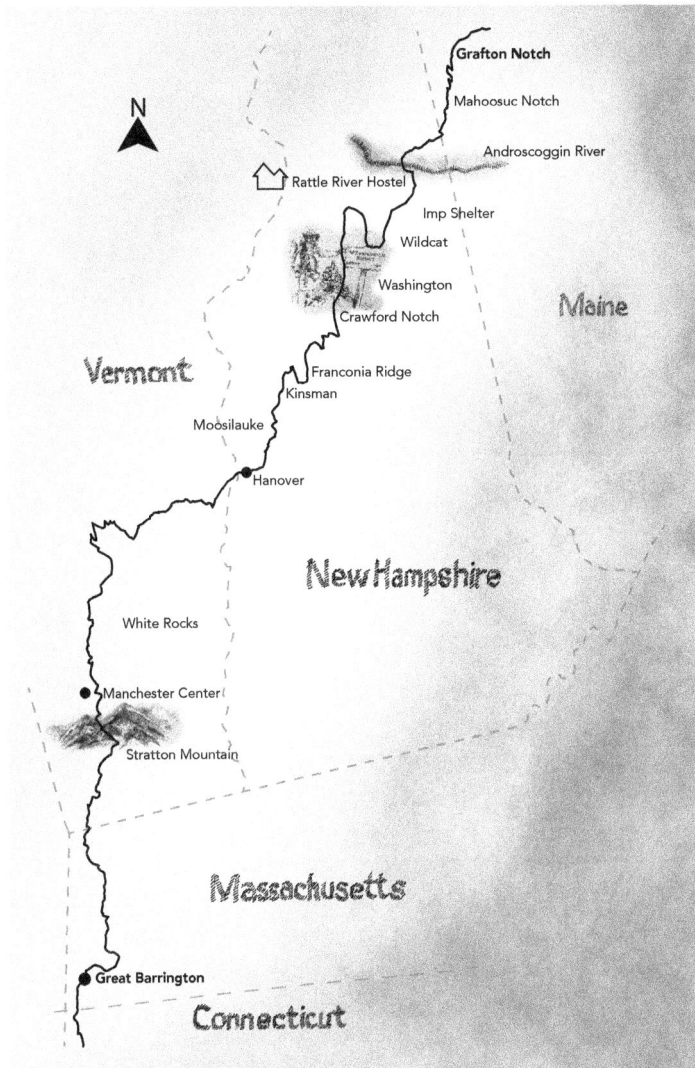

N

Grafton Notch

Mahoosuc Notch

Androscoggin River

Rattle River Hostel

Imp Shelter

Wildcat

Washington

Crawford Notch

Maine

Vermont

Franconia Ridge

Kinsman

Moosilauke

Hanover

New Hampshire

White Rocks

Manchester Center

Stratton Mountain

Massachusetts

Great Barrington

Connecticut

Mind Over Mud

Arriving at a summit after a long climb is usually cause for a modest celebration, maybe a candy bar and a nice rest to enjoy a view of the valleys below or of a distant mountain range, and at minimum a feeling of satisfied relief after the hard work of gaining so much altitude. But I reached the summit of Vermont's 3,935-foot Stratton Mountain in a downcast mood. Three continuous days of rain, gray gloomy skies, and mud, rain, and mud and then more mud had drained my ability to remain focused and positive about my hiking. My feet were wet, my shoes had tripled their weight from sloshing in water and sinking deep in thick black mud, most of my gear was damp, mud smears coated my pant legs, and my backpack had developed a rank smell that I feared was permanent.

I expected most of this. Vermont is nicknamed Vermud by thru-hikers, and the state retains that label year after year by being the second-wettest state in the nation, bowing only to Washington on the West Coast for annual precipitation. A local fellow I had met early on this section hike had told me that his community, which was not far from the Appalachian Trail and Stratton Mountain, had been saturated by twenty-two inches of rain in July alone.

Now it was early October, supposedly a much drier month on average, but the pattern of rain was only marginally loosening its grip on Vermont. The Appalachian Trail just north of Bennington was underwater in many places. Other stretches were deep and long troughs of gooey mud.

Hikers faced a choice—hop and leap from the occasional rock to a root, edge around the worst of the mud, clinging to a tree limb for balance, or simply march straight through and hope the next steps did not suck their shoes off their feet. I met a bedraggled young fellow who solved this dilemma by hiking barefoot. Mud smeared his bare legs up to just below his knees.

But the mud, rain, and gray skies were not the reason I did not celebrate at the summit of Stratton Mountain. My hiking companion, Stoneheart, had received troubling news from home the evening before. His twelve-year-old daughter had suffered an allergic food reaction at school and spent the day at a hospital. From the height of Stratton Mountain, Stoneheart had cell service and he was relieved to learn that his daughter was okay. But he had to go home to Georgia. When the vertical and the horizontal aspects of our lives collide in such an intimate way on the Appalachian Trail, the horizontal must always win. Anything else is shirking our responsibility. Stoneheart had been busy at the Stratton summit calling for reservations and researching the best way to get home as soon as possible, but it was not an easy task. We were still a long way from the nearest town, and to reach it we would need to hike sixteen miles this day and then more than seven miles before noon the next morning.

I paused at the Stratton summit for just a few minutes to eat lunch at the base of the historic fire tower and caretaker cabin. I did not bother climbing the stairs because I knew there would be nothing to see. Clouds enveloped the summit. This was a shame because the view from Stratton has some significant history. It was from this summit in 1900, before the tower was built, that a young Benton MacKaye climbed a tree, looked south over the treetops, and dreamed the idea of a trail that would cross the mountain ranges he saw and extend north to New Hampshire or beyond and all the way down the spine of the Appalachian Mountains to the south. A crazy idea . . . an impossible dream . . . two thousand miles and more of rugged forests and private land, much of it heavily logged and already despoiled. Who would build it? Who would even want such a thing? How was it possible to persuade anyone to build it, or sell the idea that such a long, winding trail would serve any purpose or might one day be a thing of value to the nation? In 1900 a trail down the length of the Appalachians was about as impractical as, say, thinking that you could fly from New York to Paris in a single day. Impossible.

Very few people can see so clearly beyond the horizon of their daily lives, beyond the vortex of the time they live in that holds them tightly in the grasp of the here and now, beyond the reality of daily life with all its demands and constraints. MacKaye was one of the very few who could see far in both space and time, could plumb the vertical and the horizontal, and understand that we need both to enrich our lives. He was truly one of a kind, and the mountain summit where I was now hauling on my backpack to resume my hike was where he had had his eureka moment. The place deserved better from me, but I had miles to walk, and the mud coating my shoes was still soaking into the frayed seams and oozing out with each step I took. I pushed on, heading down Stratton Mountain, sloshing through the mud and grateful for any firm ground I could find.

Alone again, because Stoneheart was on a bus headed for the Albany airport in New York, I left the little Vermont tourist town of Manchester Center with a heavy pack loaded with five days' worth of food. Finally, I was enjoying sun on my face and clear sky above to tackle Bromley Mountain and then Styles Peak and Peru Peak. One of the few advantages of being a section hiker was that I could sometimes choose the time of year to hike a particular stretch of the Appalachian Trail, and I had chosen October for Vermont in the hope of enjoying drier weather and spectacular autumn leaf color. The first days on the trail I had been denied both pleasures, but now conditions began to improve. As I climbed Bromley and emerged from the tree line onto a steep grassy slope that turned out to be a ski run, I came to a decision. I would chuck the plan Stoneheart and I had made for Vermont and just take each day as it came, hike as much or as little as I felt like walking, enjoy a lazy morning if I wanted to, and take as much time as I needed to reach Hanover, New Hampshire, where I would end this section and return home.

This may sound far too simple and obvious to be any kind of revelation, but for me it was a significant decision. In the past I had always meticulously planned out my hikes or had them planned for me by experienced friends. First, I would shoehorn the hike into the calendar between commitments and deadlines. Then I charted each available day and designated each shelter where I would camp, along with the miles, the resupply points, the hostels, and the end point, with shuttles, hotel reservations, and flights home all booked. Back home, those deadlines and commitments awaited me. But Stoneheart's unfortunate early departure from the trail turned me loose from that, in an odd way. As I enjoyed the view from the summit of Bromley, basking in sunshine and talking with an elderly couple who came up on the nearby ski lift, I realized that nothing had prevented me from choosing this freewheeling style of hiking in the past. I could postpone the deadlines, rearrange or even cancel the commitments. I had been stuck in an old rut, a leftover from my rigidly scheduled days at work before I retired. This new way was liberating. Why had I not thought of it before? I wondered as I set off down the trail to descend Bromley. Because I had not killed that buddha, that was why. Now that I had disposed of him, I was a free man.

This new attitude was wonderful. Not even more mud could dampen it. Nor the clouds that gathered as the day went on. I climbed the next two smaller mountains in complete silence, no wind in the trees, no birds chirping, no other hikers on the trail, just the sound of my steady breathing in my chest and my still-wet shoes rustling the leaves. Hours of silence. Whenever I stopped for a rest and a drink of water, the silence enveloped me. Occasionally a chipmunk would scamper through the leaves for the safety of a hollow log or tree hole. I saw two small striped snakes beside the path. A grouse flushed from the bushes beside the trail and flew off with a sudden flutter of wings. I heard the distant croak of a raven that I never saw. On the high ground, hemlocks and spruce and pines darkened the forest and softened the path with fallen needles. Each descent to lower elevation brought me into the birches and beech trees, and tumbling yellow leaves fell all around me and occasionally brushed my face and arms. Even lower, I encountered oak trees and acorns littering the ground. And, of course, the mud—every depression or low place was a sink of black mud churned by footsteps and treacherous to cross, sometimes twenty or more yards of it, sometimes less, but always a threat for a slip or fall.

The mud no longer bothered me so much. A nuisance, yes, but no more so than the acorns that were like trying to walk on a floor of ball bearings that rolled under my shoes. I was taking my time and being very careful, pausing when necessary to scope out the best way around or through the mud, bending to the climbs and admiring the changes in the forest, the pale-yellow leaf color of the birches and the rusty orange of the oaks, and the hours slipped by with the miles. Patches of blue sky returned, briefly pushing off the threat of more rain. Peru Peak Shelter appeared ahead as I came down a forested slope and could hear the rush of rapids in a stream. The shelter was empty, the stream just in front of it delightful, and stately tall hemlocks all around made for a pleasant setting, a fine place to stop for the night. I pulled off my backpack, spread my gear in a corner of the shelter, collected water to filter from the stream, and enjoyed a dinner alone listening to the sound of the rapids and the evening back-and-forth twittering of birds up in the hemlocks.

My pants that had been clean when I set out that morning at the trailhead after a night spent at a motel in Manchester Center were now smeared again with mud, and my shoes were soaked. As I hauled them off my feet, I noticed the seams were pulling apart and mud had seeped into the soles. So what? I thought. What was it Cogs had told me long ago in Virginia?

"All part of the deal you signed up for."

Right. Just keep walking and eventually the mud and the rain would fade and something new would replace the rain. And then something else. Could Benton MacKaye have seen that far ahead? Maybe so. What was a little mud to a man who could dream up something as outrageous as the Appalachian Trail?

On the seventh day of my Vermont hike, I loaded my backpack early at Little Rock Pond Shelter, a very popular spot with weekenders, and began a long climb under more gray skies that threatened rain at any moment. I was glad to leave behind the busyness of Little Rock Pond, campers, kids, dogs, and noise. Again, a selfish attitude, but I did not try to deny the truth of it. The solitude of the trail as I climbed was soothing, and I bent to the work of the ascent. As I gained altitude steadily, as if to compensate for all the tumult I was leaving behind, I entered a wonderland of forest.

The hardwoods and birches soon gave way to hemlocks, spruce, and pine. But this mountain was different. The trees were tall and straight, and ferns and low shrubs sprinkled the ground. A big ridge towered over me to the east, and the trail was a soft bed of needles and duff. No mud on this mountain and only an occasional outcrop of rock. The walking was easy on the modest grade as the trail gradually ascended higher and higher. The silence was incredible, deep and unbroken. An hour passed and the forest swallowed me in majestic, pine-scented silence, the tree trunks dark, straight, and thick, the branches spread high above the forest floor so I could see for a hundred yards in every direction. I walked in a reverie, occasionally stopping to marvel at the beauty of it. Mist veiled the highest tree limbs and sometimes dropped all the way down to just above my head. The ferns dripped moisture and were bright green, washed by the recent rains. If ever my feet kissed the earth, it was on this wonderful mountainside.

Walking this enchanted forest, climbing higher and higher with hardly any effort, I half expected to meet fairies or leprechauns shyly peeking around a tree trunk to see who was coming up the mountain. I laughed at the silly thought, topped a little rise, and stumbled to a halt, dumbstruck by what I was seeing. On a flat shelf of forest amid the big hemlocks and pines was a miniature village of white stones. Cairns of stone everywhere. Some almost three feet tall, others tiny, little rocks on big ones, big ones propped up on little ones, squat ones on tall ones, stacks of stones like pancakes, impossibly balanced rocks on pinnacles, crude Corinthian columns on stubby plinths, whimsical asymmetries of stones, little Stonehenge imitations, tall single rocks planted in the forest floor like sentinels, and scattered everywhere in between a loose array of more milky white rocks, the building blocks for new little towers. And all of them so delicately poised and arranged that it seemed a strong wind could wreck the whole thing in five minutes.

What was this and who had stacked all these hundreds of little columns of white stone? The mystery was not difficult to unwind, for a side trail led down the ridge, and soon I was no longer alone on the mountain. Whiterocks, as this place was known, was a popular day hiking destination, and the tradition, I quickly learned from local hikers, was to place a rock on a cairn every time one visited. Thousands of stones on hundreds of cairns told the story of how often visited and how well loved this magic forest grove was.

A few days later I encountered a trail maintainer with the Vermont Mountain Club named William and asked him about Whiterocks and how it came about. He grinned and shook his head.

"We're not exactly sure when it started," he said. "A long time ago . . . but then six years ago, someone—and lord knows who it could have been—anyway, someone went up there and knocked every one of them down. Every single cairn. So, what you saw was the work of just six years. Our local people just love that place, and every year there's more and more of 'em piled up."

A very fixed principle that governs the thinking of all thirty-one independent clubs that maintain the Appalachian Trail from Georgia to Maine is Leave No Trace. The principle asks of hikers—demands it, really—that they do exactly that, leave no trace of their presence when they walk the trail. No trace means no trace—no graffiti on the walls of the shelters, no scraps of candy wrappers on the ground, leaving the flowers alone, not disturbing the wildlife, not bushwhacking through the forest, chopping down trees or cutting new trails, and on and on with the idea that the trail and the forests and lands the trail crosses should remain as natural and pristine as humanly possible.[1] Untouched, as it were.

And here at Whiterocks was the very antithesis of Leave No Trace, almost a quarter of an acre of human intervention in an otherwise nearly pristine, wonderful forest, a work of hundreds of humans, six years and counting, that definitely had left a trace. A big one. You could not miss it.

As a trail maintainer and trail ambassador in Georgia, I both practice and preach Leave No Trace religiously, and I left Whiterocks without molesting any of the stones on the ground between the cairns.[2] But I had to laugh as I began to descend the mountain and a stream of tourist hikers heading to the enchanted grove greeted me, many of them eager to find a rock and add to the pylons of stone, leaving their own individual little trace. A way of saying "I was here." Surely, I thought, that magical stone village of human sculpture was one aspect of the Appalachian Trail the great visionary Benton MacKaye never imagined. And what mirthless knave could slink up there in the dark of night and spend hours knocking them over? Maybe MacKaye would have understood. Sometimes you have to bend a little to the popular will, especially when the result is just whimsical piles of stones. Or maybe we could just pretend the grove at Whiterocks was the work of the fairies and leprechauns.

Bite of the Wolf

Looming over every northbound Appalachian Trail thru-hiker or section hiker who makes it out of Pennsylvania intact and crosses New Jersey and New York and on into New England is the idea of the White Mountains. Not the Whites themselves, that comes two or three weeks later. No, the *idea* of the Whites is what gets insinuated into the mind and begins to grow. The idea of finally tackling the big stuff, the precipitous climbs, the wild weather, the long distances, and the sheer ruggedness of the Whites. And the idea that after the Whites comes Maine, the final state. The idea that maybe, just maybe, the hiker is going to make it all the way and stand on the summit of Katahdin.

This is all dangerous stuff, and experienced hikers know it and try to keep these ideas at bay as they stride through Connecticut and Massachusetts and north into Vermont. By this point most northbound hikers have learned to walk what is right in front of them, moment by moment, day by day, and not dwell very much on what is ahead of them. The miles from Springer Mountain have pounded into them a deep understanding of the mechanics of their bodies, the wear-and-tear price they are paying for walking twenty to twenty-five miles day after day. They have learned when to stop, when to take a day off, when a specific pain means trouble and when it is just another pain to add to the list of what they must endure. They have learned to take care of themselves mentally and physically, and it shows in how they walk, how they carry themselves, how they handle their gear, and how they size up strangers they meet on the trail, at trailheads, and in hostels and towns. By this point they have gotten very good at these things. They know exactly what they need to carry and exactly where every item is in their backpacks. All the surplus or extras they thought they had to have when they left Springer were either discarded or sent home months ago. They have a daily trail routine that rarely varies. They are experts in footwear and trail logistics. And, most important, their thighs are big as oak tree limbs, they have lost so much weight their pants no longer fit them in the waist, they have both the stamina and the stubbornness of a mule, and any of them could walk a bootcamp marine recruit into the ground. They are ready for the Whites and whatever else is coming.

That was not me. I first stepped into New Hampshire still a novice as a hiker in every way you can measure, with only a few hundred miles of A.T. hiking experience under my belt.[1] But I had already seen what merely the idea of the Whites could do to even the wariest of the northbound thru-hikers. Some of them could not disguise the excitement that crept into their voices when the subject came up, which it did with telling frequency at the shelters in the Southern states. Others would not talk about the Whites at all, as if it were a name that could not be spoken.

Later, at a shelter in New York one evening, some southbound thru-hikers who had started at Katahdin were about to launch into tales of their adventures in Maine and the Whites when a young man got up from the log that he was sitting on, shaking his head and waving his arms. "Don't tell me! I don't want to hear about it!" he said as he fled to his tent.

Why all the fuss about the Whites? Dan "Wingfoot" Bruce, a man who knows what he is talking about, has estimated that by the time a hiker walks from Springer to the New Hampshire state line he or she has completed 80 percent of the distance but only 50 percent of the work necessary to reach Katahdin.[2] Of the seventy-five steepest miles on the entire Appalachian Trail, only ten are south of the Mason-Dixon line. All twenty-five of the steepest miles are up north. New Hampshire has twelve of them, and Maine has eleven. Of the five steepest climbs, numbers one through four are in New Hampshire. The fifth is the climb from Joy Brook to Tableland on the way up to Katahdin's summit. The steepest of all is the climb out of Pinkham Notch; it ascends 2,036 feet in one and a half miles, and within that distance is a climb of one thousand feet over less than a half mile—an average slope of almost 38 percent. In several places it is perilously close to being vertical. A good rule of thumb for thru-hikers entering the Whites from the south is to take whatever their average daily mileage was and cut it in half.

And then, of course, there is the weather. Mount Washington is the eighth-deadliest mountain in the world. The reason is a combination of the number of tourists up there (because of the automobile road to the summit and a cog railroad), the altitude, and the fact that the range sits at the confluence of two major weather patterns. On Washington and its neighboring presidential peaks, Madison, Jefferson, Adams, and Eisenhower, a nice day in August can turn into a howling winter-like gale in less than an hour.

Finally, the Whites are glorious. Catch a break with the weather and what you can see is a 360-degree mural of splendor. Some New England enthusiasts claim that the great 6,288-foot summit of Washington can be seen from the Atlantic Ocean.

In December 2018 I got an unexpected phone call from a friend. Did I want to join him and Quicktime to hike the A.T. through New Hampshire next August? Yes, I said without thinking about it.

"It will be hard."

"I know."

But I did not know. You have to do it to really know.

⚯

What I did know about the Appalachian Trail through New Hampshire is that I would have to train for the challenge if I had any hope of hiking it. I would not be seasoned by walking 1,750 miles of A.T. over five months like the thru-hikers are, but at least I could knuckle down and start working to get myself into some semblance of hiking shape. The only real way to do that is to hike, and in Georgia I had the Appalachian Trail almost in my backyard, so that is where I started.

I did as much hiking as I could squeeze in during June and July, including two two-day backpack trips over 5,435-foot Standing Indian Mountain in the Nantahalas and several one-day hikes in Georgia. I pored over the maps, talked to friends who had hiked the Whites, and

learned as much as I could about what I would soon face. But I knew that
hiking in Georgia and the Nantahalas and my hours on a treadmill and
working out with weights to build my upper body strength were going
to take me only so far. When we arrived, I could only hope I was strong
enough to adapt to the rigors of the trail up there.

The chief reason I jumped at the invitation to hike the Appalachian
Trail in New Hampshire was the company I would be keeping, two fellow members of the Georgia Appalachian Trail Club, my friend Quicktime and Pilgrim. They had planned the trip in meticulous detail, and I
felt comfortable and fortunate to be hiking with them. My biggest concern was that I would not be able to keep up with them, as both were veteran hikers. My inexperience at this stage of my hiking was such that I re-
lied on Quicktime for advice, and the only big physical challenges I had
faced were in the Smokies, which had not exactly gone to plan. So I was
surprised and saddened when Pilgrim announced when we stopped for
a break around midmorning of our second day out from Hanover that
he could not continue. He had fallen far behind the day before but had
made it to our camp well before dusk and had been in good spirits as he
suspended his hammock. But his knees were giving him trouble and he
was having great difficulty with the rocky trails, and when we reached
Dorchester Road, Pilgrim decided to walk out until he could get a cell
phone signal and call for a shuttle to take him to a hiker hostel in Glencliff. Quicktime and I would push on and meet him there in a few days.

Leaving an experienced friend at a trailhead in New Hampshire on day
two of a hike planned for twenty-six days was an odd and unsettling feeling, but we choose to push on into the forest and with no guilt involved,
assuming Pilgrim would be okay to resume hiking with us after a few
days of recovery. What I could not have guessed was that this was just the
beginning of the attrition that the Appalachian Trail through New Hampshire would inflict on us.

✑

Mount Wolf is a 3,478-foot knob of little significance in New Hampshire
some 1,800 Appalachian Trail miles from Springer Mountain in Georgia,
and it is where I collapsed again before a buddha. Probably this was inev-

itable. My hiking in New Hampshire to that point had gone better than I had expected; all the training had enabled me to manage the climbs, and our distance each day had been moderate, allowing my legs and knees to adjust to the workload I was asking of them. I had climbed New Hampshire's first big test, Mount Moosilauke, without much trouble. But any Appalachian Trail hiker who has hiked the trail a significant distance will tell any novice who asks that hiking this trail is more a mental task than a physical one. I had heard that aphorism before, and that climb out of Spivey Gap in North Carolina when I had unraveled and wanted to quit had been evidence of its truth that I should have reckoned with. But not until Mount Wolf did the mental challenge of the trail rise up again and smack me so hard in the face.

My sixth full day of hiking New Hampshire had started well enough, cool and cloudy, and I had two nights of good rest and decent food at the hostel behind me to recover from the initial shock of this state's formidably steep and rugged mountains. We were down to two, Pilgrim having left for home, his knees unable to handle the stress. Moosilauke had finished him. I was eager to get back on the trail after a rest day at a hostel in Glencliff, however, and was brimming with confidence that I could climb these mountains after going over Moosilauke. But what awaited me on Mount Wolf was a nasty surprise—mud—thick, black, deep, and wide troughs of mud. Enough mud to delight an extended family of hogs. Mud that threatened to swallow a hiker whole . . . mud everywhere, even on top of a mountain. For hours, it seemed, my hike consisted of steep short climbs over rough gneiss, then immediately descending every foot I had just painfully gained, only to face another slough of mud hemmed in by green walls of impenetrable spruce, followed by, you guessed it, another utterly pointless climb. Up, down, up, down, mud . . . over and over for miles on a trail that seemed to be stuck in a repeating loop. The mud was inescapable, no matter how I tried to hop, bend, twist, or tiptoe around the worst of the wallows. The boot tracks revealed that some hikers had simply given in and sloshed straight through in places, leaving impressions with no visible bottoms—and possibly even their shoes. The mud coated my boots and smeared my pants and swallowed my trekking poles each time I foolishly tried to plumb its depths to regain my balance.

Miles of mud and rock, up and then down. Unrelenting mud. Hours of seemingly making no progress through this desolation of spruce, rock, and mud. This is New Hampshire? I wondered. Nothing about this was beautiful. In fact, it was hideous. Where were the enormous vistas, the famous mountains that northbound hikers start talking and dreaming about somewhere past the Smokies? And where the heck was the top of this infernal mountain? Again and again, I came to what seemed to be a summit and plunged down the other side of the mountain only to find a long black patch of mud that recoated my shoes, and then, inevitably, unbelievably, infuriatingly, once past the mud came another steep climb over slippery rock.

The pattern began to work on me. Waves of discouragement and doubt smothered my thinking, worsened by the thick humidity and the sweat and the mosquitoes. What the heck was I doing up here? What possessed me, still a rank beginner at this stage of my hiking, to think that I was ready for the challenge of the second-hardest state on the Appalachian Trail at my somewhat advanced age? No one had told me about the mud—that was supposed to be in Vermont. (Which at this time I still had not hiked.) All I had heard about New Hampshire was that the mountains were steep and beautiful, and the hiking was hard. Throwing miles of mud and mosquitoes into the bargain wasn't fair. The mud sucked at my shoes and the effort of pulling them out step by step, like trying to walk in just-poured concrete, sucked at my energy, and the monotony of it sucked at what was left of my confidence until I had worked myself into a state of despair. And this mountain barely rated a name, much less a mention in the guidebooks as something difficult. It was just an eight-mile stretch of bumps between Moosilauke and South Kinsman and had not looked hard on the map profile. No thru-hiker would rate it a difficult stretch of trail. The giants, the really tough stuff, were many miles farther north. And yet I was slip-sliding to nowhere. It had no end. I wanted to quit, to go home, to go back to the comfortable hostel, to be anywhere but up here on this piddly, mucky mountain going nowhere in the middle of nowhere.

And as if to reinforce and underline this misery, I came down into a dip amid thick walls of spruce and encountered a man bent over on his side at the edge of twenty yards of an especially deep, black wallow. He had just slipped and fallen in. Mud coated his legs, his right arm to his elbow, his shorts, and the lower half of his shirt. He was a hefty fellow and not a thru-hiker from the look of his huge backpack and his waistline. His left shoe was just visible on the surface of the mud lake, but his right shoe was down in there somewhere and he seemed either not ready or unable to pull it out. I stopped to help but he waved me away with tears in his eyes, I suspected just from the embarrassment of what had befallen him. I squished on past him wondering if his fate would soon be mine.

If I had not experienced something like this before, back in North Carolina early in my A.T. hiking days, I might have surrendered to Mount Wolf. This piddly muddy mountain was teaching me a hard lesson: that the Appalachian Trail is merciless and uncaring, and we walk it through stretches of what passes in our modern world for wilderness, where humans are not at home, where every comfort is stripped away and all that is left is putting one foot in front of the other and pushing on. Just keep walking.

Which is what I did. I gave up the idea of comfort on Mount Wolf. I gave up fighting the trail, the mud and the mosquitoes and the ups and downs. I surrendered any idea that I knew what I was doing and any ambition of ever completing New Hampshire, much less the whole A.T. I stopped blaming myself for being talked into this, because, of course, I had not been. I had hours before given up the idea of keeping the mud out of my shoes and socks. The rest of it was just walking and concentrating on staying upright to avoid the fate of the poor fellow I had encountered. In the afternoon I passed a pond clogged with cattails and I crossed a wide bog on a bridge of rotten boards that sank below the water under my weight, soaking my feet, and the mud became, if anything, deeper and wider and harder to navigate. The clouds eroded away, and the air became oppressive, like breathing through a wet towel. I had eaten all my snacks and I was down to barely half a liter of water. But I kept going.

Because that is what hiking extended lengths of the Appalachian Trail requires, whether you are a thru-hiker, or a section hiker like me. Every day on the trail was not wonderful. Every day in New Hampshire was hard work. I had to get used to it. I knew that not far ahead, if I could just haul myself up there, was something better, places that were spectacular, awe-inspiring, even a little frightening, the names that resound in the journals and memories of all Appalachian Trail hikers—Kinsman, Franconia Ridge, Lafayette, Washington, Madison, Adams, Thunderstorm Junction.

All of that was to come if I could outlast the miseries of Mount Wolf. On this day, I dragged myself into Eliza Brook Shelter in the late afternoon after 7.5 miles of the muddiest, hardest hiking I had experienced to this point in my Appalachian Trail journey. I had slipped three times on the slick rocks, nearly went splat into the black goo once, saved only by grabbing hold of a tree limb, muttered many a curse word, and endured sweat in my eyes and mosquitoes nipping my elbows and wrists. My pace had been a pitiful .9 mile per hour. But the trail that seemed to go nowhere had delivered me to a pretty log shelter in a nice evergreen forest beside a beautiful brook tumbling down off the mountain. The feeling of relief as I pulled off my backpack was like falling into an easy chair after running a marathon.

Twilight closed in and quickly darkened the forest as I ate dinner. I pulled out my notes and map and calculated that I had logged sixty miles in six days across southern New Hampshire—a ridiculously slow pace for hiking our southern mountains but a respectable distance up here. The next day was one of the steepest mountains in the Whites, South Kinsman, a climb of 1,972 feet nearly straight up, 900 feet of it aptly named "The Scramble." Then would come Franconia Ridge, Lincoln, the five-thousand-footers above the treeline.

But that was getting way ahead of myself again. I needed to take them as they came. And I had learned something this day—hike what the A.T. presents, one day at a time, one mile at a time, one muddy foot in front of the next. Hike without expectation or despair, with eyes wide open and a mind focused on nothing but hiking what is in front of you.

And maybe something else. . . . Maybe, just maybe, I wasn't a beginner at this hiking business anymore. Maybe the next time I met a buddha on the trail—and I knew there would be a next time and a time after that—maybe I could recognize him for what he was and kill the fellow straight away. Because just maybe New Hampshire's hard Appalachian Trail miles were making a hiker out of me.

Alone

Extended hiking over a period of more than a few days tends toward solitude. Every hiker develops his or her own rhythm, a combination of stride length and breathing and agility over rough ground that determines their pace. That rhythm becomes so natural and so comfortable over long miles that any deviation is upsetting, an irritation to avoid if possible. Some hikers seem to walk in fast bursts, walk and then stop, check out something interesting, take a picture, or eat a snack or just sit on a log and rest. Others stop only reluctantly and briefly. Quicktime was firmly in that latter category; he walked with a steady, brisk pace every day, head down, short choppy rapid-fire steps, rarely pausing to look at anything, like a man on a mission, though he loved to stop and talk with hikers, learn where they were from and all about their hikes. An elderly thru-hiker I met later on this trip, Saint Pete, was an example of a hiker in the same camp but at the other end of the dial as far as pace was concerned; he walked slowly from sunup to sundown, every day, few pauses or breaks, just plodding along with measured, languid strides. Other hikers take diversions, linger in trail towns, party at hostels, and sleep late in their tents, but when they hike, they chew up the trail at three miles an hour or more. Crushing the miles, they call it. Either way, fast or slow, in bursts or all day, those miles add up.

And that is why thru-hikers and even section hikers are usually alone out on the trail for hours at a time. Rare indeed are two hikers who have exactly the same pace over eight or ten hours of hiking. In order to stay together one of them must speed up or slow down. That is okay for a while, but invariably they separate and settle into what is more comfortable for each one. Most days the solitude is welcome. It gives a person both space and time, two extremely rare commodities in our busy lives. The long hours alone with only your breathing and footsteps and the silence of the forest around you makes the camaraderie of meeting other hikers all the better, almost a joyous occasion. After so much solitude, you are usually eager for the fellowship and grateful when it comes.

But early on this day the solitude of my hike eroded into something new and unwelcome—fear. I was staring at the forbiddingly steep bare rock slope of South Kinsman Mountain from the base of the nine-hundred-foot "Scramble," as the guidebooks labeled it. To my unpracticed eye, the climb looked dangerous. Rain during the night had wet the rocks, and the gray morning skies seemed to suggest more rain was likely. Quicktime had left me behind, and I did not like the prospect of doing this alone, but there was no alternative. Go big or go home, the saying goes, and home was a long, long way back down this trail. This was as big as it would get for many miles to come, the second-steepest climb on the entire Appalachian Trail, with a 930-foot altitude gain over half a mile. If I had already hiked through Virginia by this point and had survived Pennsylvania's Zinc Pile and the escarpments of New York and the mud in Vermont, I would probably not have peered up Kinsman with such dread. But I was still very much a rookie, still untested by near-vertical climbs, and the cool, wet rock hemmed by two walls of spruce was more daunting than anything I had expected.

The fear began as one thing, and as I started up the mountain it slowly became another. At first, I was worried about the danger, but the first ten minutes of the truly difficult part convinced me that was not a reasonable worry. This was not technical rock climbing on a sheer vertical wall. No, the fear was that here on Kinsman is where I would admit defeat because I would physically have to. What if I could not climb this mountain no matter how much I wanted to go on? There was only one way to find out.

So I kept moving up. Very slowly, very methodically, my trekking poles stowed away and gloves on my hands to protect against the rough rock.

Without thinking about it, I applied the three-point rule of climbers that I had first practiced climbing Moosilauke—three firm holds of rock crevice, root, or tree limb, and then push and pull and swing the free foot or hand up to the next hold and search for some grip or traction point. Then study the next three or four feet of rock, find the best route, plan where to put each hand and foot, and shimmy up some more. Always lean in toward the rock, caress it even if necessary, to counter the backpack's weight that if unbalanced backward for even a moment would want to pull me down the mountain. Pause and catch my breath and drink some water, then attack the next few nearly vertical feet, focusing on nothing but where to put my hands and feet, always with three secure grips and footholds.

Kinsman is two summits, South Kinsman Mountain and then a short bare rock saddle of scattered spruce and balsam trees followed by North Kinsman Mountain. From the side view their joined profile looks like the cone of a volcano. Up close the Appalachian Trail on the flank of South Kinsman is simply a scar of either smooth rock or giant blocks slashing 1,900 feet skyward through stunted spruce. And 900 feet of that climb, The Scramble, is angled at such steep incline over rocks of such crazy angles and shapes that it seems to belong somewhere else, in another part of the world, maybe the younger Alps or the Rockies, not here in the ancient Appalachians. The word "trail" does not apply. Yet here it was, and I had to negotiate it by myself.

Halfway or more up The Scramble I began to shrug off my fear of Kinsman. I could better spot the handholds and plan the routes up, across and over the rock, often because I could discern where thousands of hikers doing exactly what I was doing had buffed the rock ledges or roots smooth with their hands and feet. They had made it up this monster, so I should be able to as well. The rain was holding off. I just had to keep my concentration on the footholds and climb.

After an hour of this, the extreme slope of the mountain abruptly leveled out a bit and I could walk upright again. It was not the summit yet, but progress required less effort. And then, improbably, I heard giggling voices behind me, turned to look down the mountain, and here came two ladies, sisters, I later learned, bounding over the rocks where it was still steep and having the time of their lives. Watching them loping up the incline toward me was intensely embarrassing—they made the climb seem effortless, while here after nine hundred feet of The Scramble my legs were trembling, and my head was swimming from the exertion. They were natives of New Hampshire and they hiked mountains like Kinsman for the fun of it. I was delighted to see them, embarrassed or not, and they seemed delighted that a southerner had ventured this far north to hike in their airy playground. They said they were impressed that I had climbed Kinsman by myself, and they were so sincere I believed them and even felt a little better. They took my picture near the summit, the fog swirling around us so thick I wondered if a picture was worth taking. Then off they went, chattering merrily, wishing me a wonderful hike, bound for some destination many miles north of Lonesome Lake Hut, which was my target for the day.

I continued to feel foolish for my moments of fear at the base of Kinsman as I crossed the saddle, climbed North Kinsman, and began the painfully slow descent down a slope every bit as steep as what I had climbed on South Kinsman. Every hiker has to be responsible for him- or herself. If you cannot meet the challenge on this rugged section of the Appalachian Trail, you should not be here in the first place. It was no different here than at Spivey Gap, where I first saw a raven, or the mud on Mount Wolf. But on Kinsman I had to come to terms with that truth. There was no place to hide, no excuses available, no room for pretending. The solution to my fear turned out to be a fierce concentration and a slow, methodical, careful approach. It was heart-poundingly hard but no longer scary. At the summit I was glad I had climbed alone and in near perfect silence until the sisters arrived, a silence so deep I had heard my breaths wheezing and felt my heart thumping in my chest whenever I paused.

The rain that had threatened all morning started to fall softly around noon, but it quickly turned to stinging hail and then mysteriously petered out; the sun emerged from the clouds, and from a gap in the spruce trees I got a glimpse to the north of what I was reasonably sure, given their immense size, was the Presidential Range. Which was where I was headed, still days away. And where I knew I would hike mostly alone. But not always. The Appalachian Trail may be a lonely venture, but it constantly invents surprises, and unexpected fellowship is often one of them. Several were coming my way.

⤝

For eight days I had been hiking in a northeasterly direction through southwestern New Hampshire's isolated mountains and valleys, sleeping each night in my tent or a shelter, but now things abruptly changed. Lonesome Lake was the first of the nine huts I would stay at over the next ten days. Our group had made reservations far in advance, we had paid the fees, and the dates were locked in. That meant the distance for each day's hike was now fixed and inflexible, even more so than when I had hiked the Smokies. The huts are not true huts in any sense of that word. The Appalachian Mountain Club manages these backcountry lodges scattered at manageable intervals along the White Mountains range. Several of them are quite old, all of them are staffed by a "croo" of mostly young folks, all but one of them are impossible to reach except by hiking or helicopter, which means the food the guests eat and everything else except the big propane tanks arrive on the strong backs of the croo members hiking steep and difficult side trails. The croo cook and serve dinner and breakfast, guests have a bunk to themselves, and there are bathrooms with composting toilets and running water but no heat nor electricity in the bunkrooms.

What the huts lack in comforts they make up for in conviviality. Everyone sits at long tables and eats family style. Everyone has hiked in from somewhere and has a story to tell. A few thru-hikers receive permission to stay at each hut for a night with food in exchange for work cleaning up, sweeping floors, or handling other routine chores. They sleep on the benches or the dining room floor and none of them complain. The food is plentiful and delicious, each dinner features fresh baked bread, a soup, a salad, and a main course. The guests are ravenous. The thru-hikers wait outside so the paying guests do not have to listen to their stomachs growling. Enough food is always left for the thru-hikers, and they always clean their plates, often using a last scrap of bread to sop up the last bits of whatever they just devoured.

Lonesome Lake was not just the first hut in this chain, however. It marked a pivot of the Appalachian Trail to the east and then to the south, in the opposite direction from Katahdin. And it was also roughly the starting point of confusion. For 1,815 miles out of Georgia, the Appalachian Trail had been the white-blazed Appalachian Trail, sharing a footpath occasionally with other trails such as the Benton MacKaye in the south or the Long Trail in Vermont but always with top billing. Not so in New Hampshire. Here many of the trails are much older, and the Appalachian Mountain Club takes exception to having the upstart A.T. claim any privileges. The white blaze is often an afterthought. Instead, A.T. hikers scratch their heads and look for signs indicating Fishin' Jimmy, Gulfside, Osgood, or the venerable Crawford Path, the oldest of them all.

I had spent many an hour poring over a map of the White Mountains National Forest to learn the twists and turns and doublespeak of these paths the Appalachian Trail borrows to traverse the Whites. And after a restful night in a bunk and an enormous breakfast, I was ready for one of the longest days of our August trek, a 10.5-mile hike that would take me down to the skinny valley of Franconia Notch, underneath an interstate highway, and then, finally, up into the highlands again toward the first of the Presidential Mountains strung along the famous Franconia Ridge, high above the tree line.

Worried about the extra distance, I wanted an early start, and I was the first hiker out the door. Quicktime had scouted the trail the evening before and had advised me to go down to the lake and turn right, so that is the way I went. I was immediately bedazzled by the scenery. Below me was the shimmering Lonesome Lake, set like a blue sapphire ringed with forested mountains that towered high into the cloud deck, their summit tips just hidden by smears of gray. The trail beckoned, I was enchanted by the soft morning air, and I was soon hiking along the lake shore, enjoying the sight of ducks bobbing in the water, and wide bogs where a moose would have been a perfectly appropriate sight to see on such a fine, overcast, and misty morning. On I hiked, curving around the lake, enjoying myself, utterly oblivious to the mistake I was making. Not until the hut came back into view across the water did I realize I was circulating the lake on a trail that ended where it started.

In the past a rookie mistake like this would have destroyed my day. My error had cost me nearly an hour, and on the one day when I was worried about reaching a destination before dark. My friend's advice was correct, but I had failed to note there were *two* trails to the right, one of them hidden by the dark forest. I found the sharp turn of the one I had missed just below the hut. A white blaze on a tree twenty yards down the trail confirmed the error. Missing the trail in the Whites is a potential disaster, but I shrugged my mistake off with a few mumbled words fortunately no one was around to hear, and just got on with it.

The A.T. descended gradually beside a creek and the footpath for once resembled an actual trail. I had to negotiate plenty of rocks and mud but by now rock-hopping and mud maneuvers were not new to me, and I judged that I was managing a decent pace. After an hour or so I spotted a familiar figure ahead where the trail crossed a wide brook. My friend and fellow Georgia hiker had traveled to New Hampshire and booked reservations at all nine huts for the same days as my group with the idea of joining us through the White Mountains. I gave her the trail name Eco because she was an ecology expert, a walking Wikipedia of knowledge about plants. We had enjoyed a pleasant reunion at Lonesome Lake the evening before. Eco had left the hut later this morning, thinking she was the last of the three Georgians to set out on the trail, and so she was surprised when I walked up behind her.

We crossed the creek together, hopping from rock to rock, found a white-blazed tree on the other bank, and set out together for our destination, Greenleaf Hut. I silently resolved to make no more mistakes this day, to pay extra attention to the blazes and signs, and to not tarry too long talking to hikers or taking pictures. We had a long way to go, and previous days of slow progress over rough, steep trails had taught me not to underestimate New Hampshire distances.

The sound of traffic on a highway travels a long way in the mountains, and hearing it soon told us we were approaching Franconia Notch. This narrow valley cuts a north-south divide through New Hampshire that Interstate 93 and a local highway take advantage of. We went under the interstate beside a stream, walked briefly on a local road, and reentered the forest on the Liberty Springs Trail on a due east heading. A long climb was ahead of us but fortunately it was not straight up, and the tumbled rocks often formed convenient steps rather than an obstacle course. We climbed eagerly because we knew what awaited us at the summit. Mount Liberty is the southernmost anchor of Franconia Ridge, which runs parallel to the Notch and is the entrance ramp to the first of the Presidential Mountains. Hikers hope for a clear day to walk the ridge because Franconia is famous for its enormous vistas above the tree line. As we climbed, the clouds seemed to be lifting and little blue-sky spots appeared, disappeared, then peeked at us again from a new quarter of the horizon.

We ate lunch and rested from our climb at the intersection of the Liberty Springs Trail and the Franconia Ridge Trail at 1:00 p.m. Heading due north now on the ridge, we were well above four thousand feet and gradually climbing toward Little Haystack Mountain. The evergreens became smaller, more stunted, and scragglier, not because they were younger but because of the harsh winter climate at this altitude and the thin deposit of soil over the rock. Soon the trail climbed above the tree line, and we were in the alpine ecozone, the *Felsenmeer*.[1] The ragged cloud deck cooperated by lifting higher still, and we had amazing views of distant mountain ranges to the west, east, and south. Ahead loomed a tapered rocky massif that I knew had to be Mount Lincoln; at 5,089 feet, it is the next in line of the Presidential Range, where we would be hiking for the next seven days.

I had hiked over high mountains before in the Nantahalas and Smokies, but Lincoln was something entirely different. The open rocky terrain is completely exposed to the wind and sun. The alpine vegetation is fragile and clings low to the ground. The rock is a scree of fractured blocks ranging in size from freezers to moving vans widely scattered over bedrock scraped smooth by glaciers. Signs warn hikers to stay on the narrow trail, which has been lined in places by stacked rock and marked out at

intervals with waist-high cairns. A stray footstep onto a delicate flower
can kill a plant that has survived this harsh environment for decades, or
even centuries.

Hiking on these high mountains induces a reverie. Thoughts of time
and map distance and the world below float away. Vision is everything,
because in every direction there is an amazing sight, even at your feet, as
you pass tiny flowers and other plants that grow only here. The hiking is
still hard and requires concentration to avoid the calamity of a twisted
ankle or worse, but the views are too tempting to resist, and I found my
head bobbing up and down and sideways as I picked my way over and
around rock while trying to see it all. Attaining the summit of Lincoln
felt like a triumph. Eco and I had climbed from the depths of Franconia Notch at a mere 1,477 feet above sea level to the top of Lincoln at
5,089—a gain of 3,612 feet—and the views now were astonishing, as
though we were looking back to the south over half of New Hampshire.
But we were not done. Directly north, rising high enough to block out the
horizon in that direction, was Mount Lafayette. One more sharp climb to
go.

The afternoon was getting late. A little sun occasionally beamed
through the high cloud deck, but the wind whipping out of the southwest was so strong I had to take off my hat and tie it to my backpack and
pull on my rain jacket against the chill. The peak of Lafayette seemed to
recede from us rather than draw closer as we hiked on. And in this state,
tired but exhilarated by the altitude, I heard a familiar sound in the sky, a
croak torn away on the stiff wind, barely audible, but a sound that made
me smile and look up. Three ravens were ahead, dancing on the air cur-
rents just short of the summit. In echelon formation they tipped up their
wingtips into the wind, dove together for speed, and disappeared with a
last burst of croaks. Far below us, near the tree line, was the distinctive
shape of Greenleaf Hut. We caught our first glimpse of the hut long before we climbed the barren summit of Lafayette. It seemed impossibly far
down the mountain.

But I was beginning to learn New Hampshire's visual tricks. Down
went the trail and, of course, it was muscle-twisting and difficult and

jolted my knees and spread big wallows of mud across the path here and there just to break the monotony of the rocks. But the trail ended, as all trails must, and I pitched up at Greenleaf Hut just in time to claim a bunk, clean myself a little, and find a spot at the long tables for dinner. I had hiked 11.6 miles in nine hours and twenty minutes, a measly pace of barely 1.2 miles an hour; a mile of that distance consisted of my unconscious and foolish perambulation around Lonesome Lake rather than the Appalachian Trail. But I was happy nonetheless as I dove into the hot food. Franconia Ridge had more than lived up to its reputation, and I had enjoyed a pretty fabulous day.

⤚

That evening, in spite of my exhaustion and the good company of the hut, I spent some time alone gazing at the massive Presidential Mountain range as the sun went down. Something was happening to me that I needed to understand. Seeing the ravens near the summit of Lafayette had brought the last few days into focus, but why should that be? What was it about ravens that made me smile and feel like I was meeting old friends? Ravens are intelligent birds, capable of solving human-devised puzzles for treats, of remembering food caches and navigating errorlessly over varied landscapes.[2] But a raven is never more than a bird, and the only thing a raven can excel at is being a raven. The appearance of a raven does not portend anything. Ravens are not mysterious or mythical; they do not mean anything in human terms, and they have no powers beyond being ravens. As a staunch materialist, I have long been persuaded of the truth of this about nature and our place in the world of animals, of which we humans are but one.

When the raven had appeared above me on that midafternoon in the Cherokee National Forest in North Carolina two years earlier, I was not fooled into thinking anything metaphysical was happening. The raven did not cure me of my misery that day. I did. And that was important to know. I was the one who drove off all the negative thoughts and killed the buddha standing in the trail in front of me. A cocktail of adrenaline, endorphins, dopamine, serotonin, and anandamide undoubtedly was the catalyst that had dissolved my aches and pains, and probably accounted for the wave of wonderful emotions that had flooded over me, the tears and the pure joy, the extra strength I found in my legs. Athletes know about this, especially long-distance runners. When they push their bodies to an extreme level of exertion and bump close to the limit of their endurance, this abrupt wash of chemical compounds in their brains can take them into a state of mind and muscle pretty near ecstasy, and they can perform amazing feats. I am not an athlete, and I did not come close to ecstasy or have an out-of-body experience after I saw the raven, but I did feel a kick of new strength, and I did experience that strong tide of blissful emotions. The raven did not have anything to do with it, not in any direct way. The bird just distracted me from my discomfort for a time. And during those moments when I was marveling at the raven that kept circling back over my shoulder, my mind emptied out, and the negative thoughts melted and created space for something new and wonderful to bloom. That is all it was. And yet from that day on, every time I have seen or heard a raven while hiking the trail I have looked up and smiled. On a few occasions, when no one was around to hear me, I have even said hello to the raven. We humans plug meaning and connectivity into our lives in thousands of ways from thousands of sources, and some of our dreams and quests are harmless. Maybe even helpful. And what better source for this deeper human dimension than the natural world?[3]

But what had happened to me on Mount Wolf? And then again going up Kinsman? If I had killed the buddha once, in North Carolina, why did the buddha keep reappearing up here? Because hiking north on the Appalachian Trail is a progression of difficulties, and at this still-early stage of my journey I was far from having mentally or physically mastered what the trail here demanded. Maybe after surviving Wolf and climbing Kinsman I was no longer a beginner, but maybe that was now precisely my problem. Beginners tend to appreciate the vast extent of what they don't know. I was still learning to appreciate what the White Mountains were teaching me, my mind was still cluttered with lots of useless junk I had carried here from my past, and I had too many miles in front of me to hope I was getting anywhere close to a destination.

The maps and trail profile indicated a short, easy next day with less climbing. Our target was Galehead Hut, a mere 6.6 miles of hiking after we climbed the mile back up Lafayette to join the Appalachian Trail and head north, followed by a turn to the east. But I was suspicious. We had met and talked with several southbound thru-hikers by now, and they had told stories about the miles ahead of us, of punishing trail compounded by bad weather. One young woman vividly described to us a terrible day crossing Mount Madison in nearly eighty-mile-an-hour winds, windchills in the thirties, and driving rain. That was only four days ago—and on a day when I had enjoyed mild weather not that many straight-line miles to the south of Madison. Clearly here in the Whites a hiker needed to be prepared for extremes.

Each of the huts tuned in by radio to the Mount Washington Observatory and received very detailed daily weather forecasts, which they read to the guests at breakfast. The forecasts were segmented for the summits and the valleys and could be quite different from each other. The forecast for today on the summits was pretty good—clear skies, mild temperatures, and moderate wind speeds. I got a late start. From the front door of the hut, I could scan the massive mountain range dark and still behind the sunrise and see the high summit of Lafayette in the distance, and even the faint outline of the trail snaking to the top. A tiny fleck of red color about two-thirds of the way up was a hiker.

I warmed quickly on the climb but then cooled off in the wind near the summit. Ahead the trail dipped and then rose, dipped and rose again, like ocean swells heaving along the ridge. The trail here was hard to follow, an indistinct line over big, irregular rock, marked by cairns every few hundred yards. The hiking was a slow, strenuous scramble and required full concentration, but the morning was beautiful and the views to the east and west were tremendous under clear skies. I often stopped for a few seconds to gaze out over the expansive views, wondering what mountains I was seeing. And then at midmorning I looked ahead to find the next cairn and realized the trail suddenly vanished into the clear morning sky. The ridge simply ended, and I was staring across a mile of alpine emptiness at a new mountain in the near distance, off to the east, much smaller but ominously steep. Garfield. It was a name I would come to regard warily, the same way you would view a mean drunk in a bar.

The descent off Lafayette was the steepest and most difficult I had yet encountered in New Hampshire or anywhere else. Tilted nearly straight down, mostly rock, narrow in places, and restricted by scraggly spruce, the trail fell off the side of the mountain in big chunks of ten or even twenty feet of nearly vertical drops. Footholds had been chiseled into the bare rock in strategic places; without them I have no idea how I would have safely come down the steepest sections. An hour of this struggle to hold on to the mountainside against gravity gained me only eight-tenths of a trail mile but about 1,400 feet of descent. And then the trail began to climb, and, of course, it was nearly vertical.

This was Mount Garfield, a pinnacle of pointed rock sticking up off the mountain range between the much larger Lafayette and another, larger spire called South Twin Mountain. Later I learned from thru-hikers both northbound and southbound that they regarded the Lafayette-Garfield-South Twin complex as one of the hardest series of climbs and descents in the entire Presidential Range. Garfield is the fourth-steepest climb on the Appalachian Trail, and South Twin is the third.

The only recourse was to go slow, concentrate intensely every moment, test every hand- and foothold, and do the sweaty work of traversing these mountains. The Garfield summit was a tiny patch of bare rock no bigger than an average living room. The descent was just like the descent off Lafayette earlier in the morning. Had I been magically plopped down on this scar of broken rock without any prior experience in New Hampshire, I would probably have abandoned hope of ever seeing home and family again, but by now I had an approximate idea of how to handle going down these slopes. The key was a firm grip on something solid and strong combined with always attending to my center of gravity and never pitching forward or allowing my downward momentum to build beyond my control. It was incredibly slow, but my method worked, and I inched my way down, down, down in little stages, a few feet at a time.

I reached the hut late in the afternoon, exhausted and leg sore but vaguely pleased with myself for having survived the roughest, meanest day of hiking since I had climbed Kinsman. The 6.6 miles of Appalachian Trail down Lafayette and up and over Garfield had taken me seven and a half hours to hike. At a pace that slow, it would take a hiker ten months to hike the entire Appalachian Trail. But so what? This was the Whites at their best and their worst, and I was safely at Galehead Hut and ready to launch into a hot dinner and then fall into my bunk. So far, none of these mountains had beaten me. The next day would be more of the same going up South Twin, but I had a new measure of confidence that I would be ready for whatever the trail demanded.

❦

At Galehead Hut, since I was well into the White Mountains range now, it was time to take stock of how I was faring in New Hampshire. At dinner that evening I ate two helpings of everything the croo served and I awoke the next morning from a sound night of sleep hungry and alert. My knees were fine, I had no issues with my feet, fortunately, and the soreness in my thighs and calves was not a problem once I stretched and moved around. I was losing weight, but not too much. I had been faithfully drinking plenty of water each day to stay hydrated, and each evening when I reached a hut, I had remembered to drink more water to aid in my body's recovery. So, after eighty miles of hiking over eleven days, no damage done, and I could even speculate that I was feeling stronger and was better prepared for the rigors of these tough trails.

The same was not true, however, for my long-time hiking buddy. Quicktime had already mentioned soreness in one of his knees. I had not seen much of him as we had hiked, only reuniting in the evenings when we camped or stayed in the huts. But I could tell something was not right. Kinsman, Lafayette, and Garfield had been brutal descents on our knees and toes. I was amazed that I was still able to walk after descending Garfield. I could attribute my soundness only to the months of exercise I had done to prepare for this hike, and a massive dose of good fortune. My friend was not as lucky. And options in these high mountains were pretty

stark. A big climb up South Twin and a big descent stood between Galehead and the next hut, Zealand. The nearest road was 14.7 miles and two
hard days of hiking away.

At breakfast, I devoured everything I piled on my plate and bowl—
hearty oatmeal, scrambled eggs, bacon and potatoes, a pitcher of cran-
berry juice—and still I was vaguely hungry. I bought all the candy bars left
on the counter at the registration desk and stuffed them into the pockets of my backpack and my pants. The hike this day would tackle a steep
climb up South Twin Mountain, then a turn to the southeast and a long
walk along a ridge to Mount Guyot, where we would turn northeast up
Zealand Mountain, and, finally, a sharp turn north and a descent to Zealand Falls Hut, a distance of only 6.9 miles.

For once I had good information about what lay ahead on the trail
because of a delightful conversation we had enjoyed the evening before
with two retired New York City fire chiefs, Al and Nick. They were section hiking north, as we were, and Al had hiked this route in the past and
knew it well. These two New Yorkers seemed intrigued by three Georgians (Eco was still with us) with stories of hiking in the south to tell. We
swapped information about the southern A.T. and the northern sections.
And as we set out together, Al warned us that the ascent of South Twin
would be extra tough.

He was not exaggerating. The climb began immediately and was the
familiar challenge of steep rock. But the morning was wet from rain the
night before, cool and misty, with overcast skies. Once again, my previous experience climbing these mountains helped. The rocks and roots
were slippery, and I took my time climbing. I watched Nick climb ahead
of me. He was strong, thin, and limber, and easily could pull himself up
the steepest rock faces, but he was also careful and methodical, and he
often stopped to watch me come up behind him. I felt good in his presence. He had the alertness and technique of a fireman who has seen a lot
over a long career and survived many a tough scrape. The worst of those
scrapes—by far—was the destruction of New York City's Twin Towers on
September 11, where he and Al had both lost many fellow firemen.

The summit took a little more than an hour to attain. The rain had held off as I climbed but remained a possibility. Let it come, I thought, now that I was on top of South Twin. By midmorning I had put two breath-sucking miles between me and Galehead Hut, pitifully slow progress by normal standards but not bad for an old man attempting the Presidentials. The trail emerged onto the side of a high ridge, rocky and exposed, and the clouds mostly obscured what would have been outstanding views.

I met Nick and Al several more times on the trail. They did not have the same pace as each other, but they liked to stop often, and sit and stretch or just rest, so they were often together, and each time they stopped I soon caught them. It was nice to be greeted in these wild mountains like an old friend.

In the early afternoon, the trail became a jumbled maze of rock stacked and strewn over the path. Walking in a normal way was impossible; instead, I had to step from one rock to the next, planning each footfall just right to land on a solid, reasonably flat surface. The rock was like debris from a landslide, fractured and haphazard, sometimes loose enough to move under my feet. My trekking pole tips seemed to find more crevices than firm purchase, which often threw me sideways or caught me unawares when a tip would not turn loose and I had to wrench it free.

So it was inevitable that I would fall, and when it happened, I was barely moving forward. My right foot came down on a rounded, smooth rock with too much inward slope, and my shoe slid sideways down into a curved space, and down I went, backward, onto my backpack. The damage was minimal, a purple bruise and scraped skin on the side of my ankle, but nothing serious. I muttered a few choice words, vowed to be more careful, and pushed on.

Only to fall again not fifteen minutes later. The circumstances were nearly the same except this time a muddy root was the culprit. Three more times I slipped badly, but now I was growing wise to the tricks of these rocks and mud, and I caught myself against tree trunks or limbs each time and did not hit the ground. Still, it was sobering. Two falls and three near misses in one day—any of them could have been a hike-ending disaster. Nick and Al were having the same difficulty and had slowed their pace to account for the wet rocks. Al even dropped behind us as we began a steep descent toward the end of the day. He admitted to struggling over the rough terrain and wanted to rest a bit before the last push down to Zealand Falls.

As if to compensate for the rocks, the trail began to taper the incline and the rocks became more manageable, then fewer, and the sun came out and turned the afternoon into a beautiful panorama of puffy white clouds and intense blue sky. I reached Zealand Hut midafternoon, grateful for the early finish of the day. The hut was situated in a col, or deep valley, and nearby was a lovely broad stream of clear cold water pouring down over smooth boulders, the rush of the current audible from hundreds of yards away. Quicktime was soaking his swollen knee in a pool of the cold water. Nick, Al, and I soaked our aching feet in the pool, enjoying the warm sun and the massage of the current. The cold water helped my bruised ankle. We relaxed on the rocks for hours, letting our sweaty shirts and damp socks dry out and our feet get numb from the cold stream. Later in the afternoon Eco hiked in and we had another joyous reunion and stories to tell each other.

Dinner was fabulous. This hut had a croo of older folks, and they put on a show for the guests who had come up on a side trail, with funny skits and games for the few children who were there with their parents. I enjoyed the evening talking to thru-hikers and learning from them about their experiences after 1,838 miles from Springer Mountain. A few southbound thru-hikers were among our group, too. They had started at Katahdin in Maine, now a scant 353 miles away for the northbounders. But what they had to say was alarming. Southern Maine, they agreed unanimously, was harder than these mountains in New Hampshire. I went to sleep wondering how that could be.

✑

A birthday present was in order, and the Appalachian Trail delivered right on cue. I left Zealand Falls Hut after a colossal breakfast and turned seventy on a gorgeous day tromping along the nicest, easiest-to-walk piece of Appalachian Trail in all the White Mountains. Hardly a rock or root littered the path, which stretched high above and paralleled a deep valley floor smothered in boulders the size of locomotives and box cars. The trail was straight and gently inclined, the sunlight reflected off the high mountain ridge on the west side of the valley, and the miles rolled away with the morning in an arm-swinging, leg-stretching rhythm that felt magnificent. I had not hiked with such freedom and pace all month.

Our original plan called for ending the day at Ethan Pond Campsite. We passed it after two hours of hiking and barely gave it a glance. New Hampshire Highway 302 and Crawford Notch beckoned ahead, and I arrived there well before noon, not long after Quicktime. In keeping with the spirit of the day, a couple of people manned a grill and ice chest beside the trailhead in a parking lot and were offering food and drinks for hikers—trail magic. I helped myself to a delicious hot dog.

But I also braced myself for what was coming. I had seen my hiking buddy out in front of me limping slightly. Quicktime's knee was still swollen, and improvement was not going to happen, even if the trail was kind to us over the next few days, which we both knew was exactly the opposite of what lay ahead on our path to the north. The hard truth was, we had arrived at Crawford Notch, which was the southern edge of the highest stretch of the White Mountains. The next few days were going to be extremely difficult. So there was no question of my friend pushing on with a badly swollen knee, just as there was no question of me quitting. We both knew it. He would go home; I would continue to hike. The only question was how to arrange things. The Appalachian Mountain Club's Highland Center was a few miles away. If we could get there, we could get cell phone service, Quicktime could get a room for the night and make airline and shuttle reservations, and I could place a long overdue call home to talk to my wife.

The solution to this dilemma knocked us over. Learning of our need, a young woman helping out with the trail magic handed us the key to her Honda. This amount of trust of and generosity toward two strangers defied belief, but she insisted with a wave of her hand, like it was no big deal, and within ten minutes we were walking into the Highland Center.

Al and Nick were there, having taken a different trail down from Zealand Hut. Our friend Eco would be there later in the day; she planned to skip ahead and meet me farther north. But Quicktime was done. He had been my hiking partner off and on since the beginning back in Georgia, and I had long admired his trail knowledge, his powerful pace, and his stamina. His enthusiasm for hiking the Appalachian Trail had rubbed off on me, and we had shared many hours together on the trail and at the shelters and numerous hostels. I was this deep into New Hampshire because of him. But now it was time to say goodbye.

I returned the Honda to the generous woman at the trailhead with a twenty-dollar bill in the cup holder and then hitched a ride to Dry River Campground, where I was able to get a shower and wash my clothes in the campground's laundry machines and charge my telephone. Then I reloaded my pack, feeling clean for the first time in days but very hollow inside. I road-walked back to the trailhead, entered the forest, and soon began an easy climb through spruce and hemlock. I hiked until I could see the trail becoming steep and the first hints of big rock outcrops. I found a level spot far enough off the trail, pitched my tent, ate a quick dinner of dry granola, crawled into my tent, zipped shut the screen to keep out the mosquitoes, and settled in for the night as the sun was going down. I was completely alone now with New Hampshire's biggest mountains in front of me. I said happy birthday to myself and immediately fell into a deep, hard sleep.

Superstars

"Stealth camping" is the hiker term for pitching your tent somewhere reasonably level and off the trail wherever you end your day rather than at a designated or well-used camping area. The idea is that you hike until you are ready to stop rather than hike to a predetermined destination. Trail clubs discourage this because it harms the vegetation and, if repeated in the same place several times over a short period, can result in broad areas that are beaten down and ruined, but if hikers select a stealth camp site carefully, the damage can be minimized. Thruhikers who hike big miles from sunrise to sunset do this often, section hikers less so. This was my first stealth camp on this trip, and I was glad of it in the morning because I was able to get an early run at the big climb to Webster Cliffs. I had my tent stowed, my breakfast eaten, and my backpack ready to go as the glow of the sunrise was brightening the forest.

The fine weather was holding and, if anything, becoming gorgeous. The morning was cool and the air dry. No threat of rain today. The climb was the usual hard, steep work, but I managed most of it without the trouble of stowing my trekking poles. After an hour, when I came to a rock outcrop gap in the trees, I had gained enough altitude to gaze down on Crawford Notch. The view in the clear morning air was incredible, and I had it all to myself. But I was not done climbing. Webster Cliffs is a series of rocky summits gained as the Appalachian Trail parallels the Notch. One after the other, climb then descend a few hundred feet, then climb again. The reward each time was a new, even more magnificent view of the long narrow valley and the mountains beyond. For another hour I bobbed up and down along this ridge, going in and out of the spruce and balsams, alone on this glorious sunny morning.

The next landmark was the summit of Mount Webster, where the trail would make a hard turn to the northeast and veer away from overlooking Crawford Notch. Beyond Webster was Mount Jackson. But these knobs along the ridgeline were confusing. Every time I thought surely I must be at the top of Webster another knob popped up ahead and views of Crawford Notch kept appearing off to the west. From one exposed outcrop I had a bird's-eye view of the Highland Center where Quicktime, Nick and Al, and Eco had spent the night in comfortable rooms. The lodge seemed only an arrow shot away down in the valley, though it was actually the better part of a mile and a half in a straight line.

The first hiker I met sorted out my confusion; he was a local fellow who confirmed that I was indeed standing at the summit of Webster. The trail dutifully turned right and dipped back into the trees. Jackson's rounded summit loomed high beyond me in a perfect blue sky. Hiking to it involved crossing a large bog on boards, then some steep hand-over-hand climbing that sapped my energy level and had me gulping down water and eating the last of my candy bars. A couple of thru-hikers I recognized passed me and surged up toward Jackson. I was finally there midmorning, tired and sweaty.

What awaited me on top of Mount Jackson was a sight I had been striving for since day one of this section hike back in Hanover—the clear-as-day, unmistakable, dark 6,288-foot-high mass of Mount Washington off to the northeast. I could see the weather towers and buildings and even puffs of black smoke on the western flank of the mountain where the cog railroad was making a run down toward Ammonoosuc Ravine, delivering the morning's first batch of tourists back to their buses and cars. Washington was the climax of every Appalachian Trail hike through New Hampshire, as famous to hikers as Clingman's Dome in the Smokies and Katahdin in Maine, dangerous and unpredictable when the weather was bad, difficult under the best of circumstances. The great mountain was only about six miles from me in a straight line, and only a little less than eight trail miles. I would need a full day of hiking spread over the next two days to get there, and I would be above the tree line nearly the entire way.

Mizpah Spring Hut was a welcome sight. My early start this day had earned me an afternoon of leisure at the hut and a big bowl of potato soup and three thick slices of day-old bread for lunch. My energy level had been low over the six miles to Mizpah because I had not eaten enough dinner or breakfast at my stealth camp. I made up the deficit with a long, luxurious nap and then another of the hut's hearty dinners, joined by Eco, Nick and Al, and other friends I had made in recent days. They had hiked up to the hut on a side trail. Someone spilled the beans about my seventieth birthday and the croo brought me a slice of chocolate cake with a candle on it and forty or so people wished me a belated happy birthday.

A fine way to end a fine day, a day so characteristic of hiking the Appalachian Trail in the White Mountains, hours of solitude, a lingering sadness for the loss of Quicktime, lovely long-distance views, hard work climbing, improbable muddy bogs, warm fellowship with new friends, and even a surprise of hut trail magic. I ended the day with the thought that I was one lucky man.

❧

From Mizpah Springs Hut on north, weather was now the number one concern. The trail is exposed above the tree line and the altitude is high enough that strong wind is always possible, as are sleet, hail, or snow and cold temperatures, even in August. Hypothermia is a real threat for anyone in the Whites who is both unlucky and unprepared. The day before had been beautiful, with mild temperatures, little wind, and clear skies. But during the night clouds had gathered, and in the morning we awoke to rain and cool fog. However, the barometer was steady, and the forecast was for clearing skies later in the day. Our destination was Lakes of the Clouds Hut in a col between Mount Monroe and the southern slope of Washington. Eco and I decided to hike together most of the day.

First was the climb up Mount Pierce, a relatively modest 4,312-foot mountain. The climb of just less than a mile took us a little less than an hour, and we were then standing at a historic junction. From here we would be hiking for the rest of the day on the Crawford Path, which was celebrating its two hundredth anniversary. The words "path" and "trail" can only be generously applied when speaking of this old route roughed out by Abel Crawford and his son Ethan to the summit of Mount Washington. Your shoes rarely touch soil on the Crawford Path because there is not much of it on these wild mountains and connecting ridges. Fractured rock mantles the slopes; much of the rock is loose, and all of it is jagged and rough, and scattered in such a way that rock is piled on top of bigger rock that lies haphazardly on the bare rock bones of the mountains themselves. No white blazes here, apparently in deference to Crawford Path's status as the oldest maintained hiking trail in the U.S.A.; rock cairns every few hundred yards marked the path. Those tough New Englanders employed by Abel Crawford who first wrestled this path out of the rock scree in 1819 had plenty of material to work with. Some of the cairns they built looked as ancient as the mountain itself.

In this alpine zone plants seem to cower and cling to whatever cover they can find. But the amazing thing is that flowers and delicate plants are everywhere in wild profusion among the rocks above the tree line, and fragile though they are, these plants are incredibly hardy. They survive winters more in keeping with the climate of the Arctic than New England. And, not surprisingly, many of them are found nowhere else.

It was my good fortune to be hiking Crawford Path in the company of someone who knew a lot about plants. As we hiked through the mist, picking our way among the rocks, and seeking out the cairns that marked the trail, Eco often stopped to take pictures, rapturous over spotting yet another species she had never seen before.

"Three-tooth cinquefoil!" she exclaimed, bending over a cluster of tiny white flowers nestled amid the rocks. "Alpine goldenrod!" she shouted a few minutes later. "And I think that's sandwort!" she said, pointing to a bunch of tiny white blooms wedged like a bouquet in between two rocks. Her excitement was contagious, and I began to sporadically pay attention to the plants I saw almost as much as to the rocks my feet had to negotiate. This was not wise. Whereas Eco knew to stop and observe a new flower or interesting plant, I merely noted them in passing. The rocks were wet, and some were slippery. I slipped and caught myself with my trekking poles and avoided a spill that could have broken something. After surviving this near miss, I resolved to pay more attention to what I was doing and leave the botany to my friend.

Indeed, as we made progress over Crawford Path's torturous rocks and began to steadily climb higher on the ridge, the weather became more of a concern. Despite the forecast of clearing skies, the clouds were blowing over us in darker, lower bands that showed no sign of breaking up. As we approached Mount Eisenhower, I felt an urgency to accelerate the pace. A cutoff trail led to the summit, and Eco wanted to try it. I was not interested in bagging summits, however, and pushed on while she took the cutoff trail. Soon I had to pull on my jacket against a slow rain. Fog descended over the mountain, and for the next two miles I hiked over tumbled, wet rock, occasionally casting an eye westward to gauge the weather.

Two big mountains stood between me and the safety of the next hut, Lakes of the Clouds. First 5,004-foot Franklin and then 5,372-foot Monroe. The trail skirted just west of Franklin's summit and then bent east of Monroe's before descending to Lakes of the Clouds, the biggest hut of the nine in the White Mountains. I pressed on, head bent down against the rain and wondering if my luck with the weather had finally run out. Maybe I was overdue for getting caught in a storm. If so, this was one heck of an exposed place for it to happen.

But when I reached the sign for the trail to the summit of Franklin, the rain stopped. While I paused to switch out water bottles from my backpack and eat a snack, I glimpsed a blue-sky hole in the cloud deck racing overhead that seemed close enough for me to poke at with my trekking pole. I cautiously pulled off my rain jacket, shook off the water beads, and stowed it away in the pocket of my backpack. For the next few hours, the weather was unsettled, one minute ragged pockets of blue above or scattered along a far horizon, and then the next the ceiling was swallowed by gray clouds that threatened to drop down over the mountain and engulf me. White cloud tops formed in the valleys below the ridge and swirled higher on the flanks of the mountain, sometimes reaching the trail but just as often dissipating into a thin mist. This just reinforced the truth of the claim that the Presidential Range of the White Mountains makes its own weather.

As I hiked the flank of Monroe, I was in the lee of the wind and was warmed when the sun finally chased off the last ranks of clouds to make a lovely afternoon. I took note of several signs warning hikers to stay on the path to avoid trampling endangered plants. In places the path was lined with rock on both sides to emphasize the point. I spotted lots of tiny yellow flowers in clumps alongside the trail and wished I had Eco with me to identify them.

I reached Lakes of the Clouds Hut a little after noon, checked in, and arranged with the kitchen staff for a bowl of hot soup and some leftover bread. From the windows of the big dining hall the summit of Washington loomed in bright sunshine, as though tempting hikers to try it in the hours of daylight remaining. But the sun rarely shines on Washington for very long. I enjoyed a leisurely afternoon at Lakes of the Clouds talking to thru-hikers who straggled in one by one, including Saint Pete late in the day. At some point before the call for dinner I realized the sunshine was gone, Washington was obscured in mist, and rain looked likely for the evening. The barometer on the wall in the dining room was holding steady. The next day I would climb Washington and hope my luck with the weather held.

✐

A peculiar apparatus erected over the trail just in front of Lakes of the Clouds Hut needed explanation. It was a cable maybe eighty yards long and twenty feet off the ground suspended from tripods of metal poles and securely anchored with guy wires. One end of the cable was anchored uphill from the trail near a pile of rocks, and the other was down near the hut. The purpose of this device was impossible to guess but the lazy afternoon I spent at Lakes of the Clouds allowed me to ferret out the answer from an Appalachian Mountain Club naturalist, Doug Weilhrauch. The cable, I learned from Doug during a long conversation with Eco around one of the dining tables, was a final instrument in a great and largely unknown success story that had taken place just outside the hut.

Doug had hiked to Lakes of the Clouds to put in a morning of pulling up invasive plant species near the hut, and he was happy to take a break after lunch and talk with two Georgians and answer our many questions. Trail maintainers had erected the cable, he explained, to move rocks from the big pile near one of the anchors down to the trail, where they could position them to help define the path and keep hikers from straying off of it. By ferrying the rocks with the mini zip-line cable, trail workers avoided trampling the delicate and endangered plants that thrived among the rocks.

One of those plants is a superstar in the rare plant world. Dwarf cinquefoil (Potentilla robbinsiana) is a tiny plant that lives only in the rugged high-altitude Felsenmeer above the tree line in the White Mountains between Mount Monroe and the slope of Mount Washington. In 1980, the plant was headed toward extinction and placed on the List of Endangered Species. The venerable Crawford Path, which, of course, is also the Appalachian Trail in the Whites, was relocated in an ambitious attempt to save the little plant. The efforts of naturalists and trail builders paid off over time, the species reestablished itself, and Doug said some fourteen thousand dwarf cinquefoil plants now thrived in a patch of rocky ground that borders Crawford Path just above the hut. These little plants survive winter temperatures of minus forty degrees, require eight to thirteen years to flower, and can live more than sixty years. A few of them had more recently been found on Franconia Ridge, well south of the hut. The hardy little plant was the first ever to be removed from the List of Endangered Species.[1]

This success story illustrates two characteristics of the modern Appalachian Trail that trail clubs and federal agencies constantly wrestle with, trying to strike the right balance. First, the popularity of the A.T. has grown enormously in recent decades, both in the number of serious thru-hikers and section hikers, and also in the number of day-hikers who use the trail for recreation. All those hikers, thousands of them ev-

ery year, even here in these wild and remote White Mountains, can inad-
vertently do a lot of damage to the environment. That was exactly what
was sending the dwarf cinquefoil to extinction in 1980. But serious hikers and the clubs that have the responsibility of managing and protecting
the trail corridor care passionately about the many environments the A.T.
traverses. All along the entire 2,194-mile length of the A.T. these clubs
have heroic people like Doug Weilhrauch, men and women who have
skillfully crafted solutions to environmental problems, fought to protect the trail from encroachment and other threats, and worked hard to
keep the trail passable. I thought of those mostly anonymous volunteers
in New Hampshire every time I crossed a bog on a footbridge of boards
or passed a tree trunk where a blowdown had been cleared by someone
wielding an axe. The success of the tiny dwarf cinquefoil in the harsh
environment below Mount Washington was proof that the Appalachian
Trail, for all the challenges its popularity has generated, can coexist with
the most delicate of environments.

And my destination the morning after my wonderful conversation
with Doug constitutes one of the most popular and incongruous places
on the entire Appalachian Trail. Eco and I set out from Lakes of the
Clouds Hut to climb to the summit of Mount Washington wearing all the
clothes we carried to protect us from the mist and the cold wind. On any
given summer day hundreds of people visit the summit, delivered there
by car or the cog railroad. Today was a Saturday, and a crowd would be a
certainty despite the heavy overcast skies and high winds.

From the hut we climbed a rough rock staircase that had been built
150 years earlier. Rocks the size of sofas and coffee tables had been le-
vered into positions so that a reasonably flat surface offered a stable step,
one on top of the other, a "stairway to heaven" if ever there was one. Not
for the first time I marveled at the toughness and tenacity of those New
Englanders who years ago muscled the scree here into something that
anyone could call a trail.

As the mountain became steeper, of course, the stairs ended, and the
real climbing began. By now this was no longer new to us, and we attacked each ledge and rock face methodically and slowly, not bothered

by other hikers who passed us going up. Often there was no discernible trail at all, just rocks to climb to reach the next cairn, and then the next, the route between them demarcated by what looked the least impossible. This kind of climbing has a one-two-three-four rhythm of hands and feet to it and requires a sharp eye for the best rock surfaces for foot placement and handholds. The rhythm is easy to break if you do not concentrate or if you stop too long in one place or allow your breathing to get out of control. But I found that I could cover ground safely if I got into that slow but steady rhythm of moving, pushing off and pulling up simultaneously, always keeping my weight low and forward, never twisting or reaching too far.

Near the summit we were in the clouds and the wind speed rose another notch. Visibility dropped to no more than twenty feet and was worse for me because my glasses continually fogged over. We more or less stumbled into the sign indicating the trail to the summit. And this was where the incongruity of Mount Washington kicked in. Buildings appeared out of the fog. A grandstand lined with spectators cheering something and people milling around, a PA system blaring excited words I could not understand, children and dogs and parked cars—none of this made any sense until Eco explained to me that the summit this morning was the finish line of a bicycle race that was just ending. The wind and the tumult were so loud she had to shout to be heard.

We ducked into the visitor center to get out of the wind and mist. I got directions from a man at the counter for the little path to the summit sign and then the Appalachian Trail heading north. But back outside my glasses immediately fogged over again and I could not see where to go. We wandered around a few minutes until the path to the summit emerged right in front of me. Photos were in order, of course, but as soon as we took them, I wanted to get off the summit as fast as possible.

The trail northward from the summit was not a steep descent, but it was entirely scattered rock and hard to navigate, especially in the high wind and fog. I needed Eco to lead the way because I could not see well through my fogged-over glasses. We picked our way from rock cairn to rock cairn and soon were startled by an eerie mechanical sound audi-

ble over the wind, a metallic scraping rumble that did not belong on the
north slope of this wild mountain. From out of the clouds suddenly a
railroad car appeared, followed by another one jangling down the mountain. Passengers waved at us like we were an expected part of the scenery, two Appalachian Trail hikers positioned in the fog for their benefit.
It was bizarre. Thru-hiker tradition suggested we should moon the tourists, but Eco and I declined. One of the perks of being section hikers, perhaps.

After the shock of seeing railroad cars growl out of the dense mist and
then disappear down the mountain, I was ready to flee Mount Washington. The problem was we now were hiking high above the tree line on a
difficult stretch of the Appalachian Trail in the Presidential Range, and
we had three big mountains between us and Madison Spring Hut—Clay,
Jefferson, and Adams, all above 5,500 feet. It was a long way. I began to
appreciate what a southbound thru-hiker had told me several days earlier—that this stretch of trail was among the hardest days of hiking she
had ever experienced, ranking maybe just below the Lafayette-Garfield-
South Twin complex, and what made it so hard was not going over Washington. It was the long distance over an exposed trail of nothing but jumbled rock, a trail where a pace of a mile an hour sometimes felt recklessly
fast.

The strong wind began to abate as we dropped below six thousand
feet. The mist lifted and I could finally see farther up the trail. Plenty of
day-hikers passed us heading toward Washington; not so many were
walking north. After an hour the clouds were above us where they belonged instead of all around us. Despite the rock, we were making progress, and the weather now was looking better. We settled into the hike,
and I began to enjoy the day.

We hiked to the west of the summit of Mount Clay and then came
down into the col between the tops of Clay and Jefferson. Here we got our
first good view to the northeast of the Great Gulf Wilderness, an enormous upside-down, heavily forested U-shaped valley that is open to the
south and enclosed to the north by the 5,799-foot mass of Mount Adams and, farther east, the only slightly lower peak of Mount Madison.

Looking down into this half-bowl of wilderness, we saw the white tops of clouds swirling, rising, and then dissipating into mist on the flanks of the mountains. The Appalachian Trail, now sharing a path with the Gulf-side Trail all the way to Madison Spring Hut, curves around this great horseshoe of mountains, first north, then east, and then south, where it starts a long, straight dive toward Pinkham Notch. An hour later we came to Edmands Col just past the summit of Jefferson and had another grand view to the east of a ridge towering above the clouds below. Edmands Col is one of the most dramatic and picturesque places in all the White Mountains, a dip between two giants with a backdrop looking down into the vast forested horseshoe of the Great Gulf. We lingered there to rest, eat snacks, take pictures, and just absorb the wild beauty of the place.

One final challenge remained late in the day. The trail, which had not troubled me with steep slopes since I had climbed Washington, abruptly plunged to the col where Madison Spring Hut was situated. After the long day of balancing and teetering over rocks, this descent was tricky, exhausting, and all the more frustrating because I could see the hut far below. The trail down was narrow, and the rocks were particularly difficult to navigate safely. I resisted the temptation to hurry. These were exactly the circumstances that could produce a serious accident: fatigue, carelessness, jagged rock, and such a steep slope.

I made it down safely but found that even the space in front of the building's door was a jigsaw of irregular rock. Several tired hikers were sitting on rocks and a bench watching me approach. As I struggled toward the door, grateful to finally be done with this 7.2-mile hike, I put both my trekking poles in my left hand and began to slip off a strap of my backpack. The motion upset my balance, my feet splayed out on two different levels of rock, and I nearly fell on my backside. It would have been a perfect final irony—falling on the doorstep of a hut before a bemused audience after safely walking one of the most difficult stretches the entire Appalachian Trail had to offer. But once again, no damage done. I picked up my backpack and poles and carefully went inside to register and find an empty bunk, happy to be in one unbroken piece after crossing Mount Washington.

After more than two weeks on the Appalachian Trail, I had met and come to know a dozen or more northbound thru-hikers. Nearly all of them were young or middle-aged and, after 1,800 miles on the trail, were much stronger and faster than I would ever be, especially in these rugged White Mountains. I marveled at how some of them could bound from rock to rock, could gobble up a difficult climb almost effortlessly or bounce, hop and skip down impossibly steep descents without breaking their necks.

More than anything, however, it was their stamina that was amazing. The hike plan I was following adhered strictly to a hut-to-hut schedule that necessarily kept the daily trail distances low. That was important because some of my toughest days so far had been relatively short, allowing me part of an afternoon to rest and recover at a hut. Anything more than seven or eight miles, however, was exhausting and could take me nine or ten hours to complete at a pace of less than one mile per hour. But some thru-hikers I met thought nothing of reeling off fifteen or even twenty miles in the Whites, arriving midday at a hut that would take me all day to reach. A few of the younger ones seemed to be pushing themselves toward the finish line at Katahdin, now not much more than three hundred miles to the north.

One exception among the thru-hikers stood out. His trail name was Saint Pete. He was tall and skinny as a pencil, wore rumpled khaki pants and shirt, and a floppy wide-brimmed hat, and had a long grey-white beard and a countenance that reminded me of Father Time. At seventy-two, he was the oldest thru-hiker I had met in New Hampshire and the only hiker of any stripe in the Presidential Range older than me. Saint Pete was slow and made no apology for it. The entire hiking community seemed to know and revere him, and with good reason, for he was a kind, gentle man, friendly and conscientious about his hiking, always willing to lend a helping hand. Since leaving Georgia, Saint Pete had been losing weight at an alarming rate, and so when he reached the series of huts in the White Mountains, he decided to stop for the night at each of the huts and take advantage of the opportunity to eat a good dinner and breakfast and sleep on their floors in exchange for a few hours of work each day. And that is how I came to know him, for his slow daily pace happened to correspond with my reservations at the huts. My first minutes spent conversing with Saint Pete had convinced me that he would eventually reach Katahdin. The key to his success thus far was his persistence—he had taken only four days off the trail since he left Springer Mountain in the spring.

"I hike from sunup to sundown," he told me. "And I'm very careful." His only problem, he added, was food. He just could not ever seem to eat enough.

Each late afternoon for the last few days Saint Pete had turned up at a hut and asked the hut master if he could work for food and stay, and, of course, they always said yes. No one could have denied this thin, haggard, modest man a decent meal. So, each evening Saint Pete sat off to the side or even outside the dining room with a few other lucky thru-hikers while the paying guests devoured heaping plates of hot meals—pasta or beef tips, chicken breasts, mashed potatoes, rice, green beans, fresh bread, wonderful soup, salads—the menu each night varying according to the taste of the hut's cook and the supplies that the croo had backpacked up the mountains. But always delicious. And when the guests finished dinner and the croo had cleared the tables and the guests were filing away to their bunks, patting their stomachs, the leftovers of the meal were served to Saint Pete and the few others. It seemed a little mean to make them wait, smelling the aromas of the evening dinner, but that was the routine, and they did not complain. And when the thru-hikers finished their meal, they went to work cleaning or handling other chores while the rest of us relaxed and prepared for the next day's hike. They repeated this ritual at breakfast. And this meant that here in the Presidentials whenever Saint Pete worked for stay at a hut, he got a late start on the trail. Being a man of conscience, he went at his assigned work with the same diligence and care that he applied to his hiking, even if doing so delayed the start of his hike each morning by several hours.

Most days leaving the hut a few hours behind everybody else who was hiking north was not a problem, at least not for the thru-hikers. They were easily strong enough to hike the distance to the next hut in time to check in with the hut master for a work-for-dinner slot. But the long stretch of Appalachian Trail from Lakes of the Clouds over Mount Washington, along the string of lofty peaks, and then down to Madison Spring Hut had tested even the best of the thru-hikers. Even with my early head start, I arrived in the late afternoon. After I settled in, I watched for Eco and soon saw her silhouette high on the mountain beginning the slow, careful descent down the steep trail. Later another thru-hiker, Moonwalk, appeared as a tiny speck backlit by the evening sun and began picking his way down the mountain. Other hikers arrived. The croo began setting out plates on the long tables for dinner.

But Saint Pete did not appear. Moonwalk said he had last seen him when they were climbing toward the summit of Washington. That was hours ago. Several of us who knew him gathered outside the door, watching a spot high above us that marked where the trail fell off the mountain. Moonwalk admitted to being worried about his friend. We all knew how rough the trail was on this section and how the rocks had tortured our feet and slowed our pace during the long day. Hiking that stretch of high trail in the dark would be madness. But there was literally no place to pitch a tent among the rocks. And there was the possibility that Saint Pete had fallen and was injured.

The sun was below the far mountain range to the west and the trail was in deep blue shadow when we saw a tiny dark moving speck appear at the rim of the mountain. The floppy hat was just visible in the last of the twilight. We raised a cheer of relief. Then ever so slowly the tiny figure began the steep descent and disappeared into the dark shadow. There was no way to help him—every hiker in these mountains is essentially on his or her own when it comes to negotiating the trail. And Saint Pete needed no help. He was just taking his time, being careful, using the last of the light and his months of experience to bring himself safely down off the mountain. It was no big deal to him, although he did admit that it had been a long, hard day. And he was really hungry.

The next morning, we awoke to the news that it had rained during the night. Heavy fog obscured the mountain we all had descended the day before and the summit of Madison to the north. The air was noticeably cooler. The forecast posted after breakfast was for rain later in the day, possibly heavy on the summits. We had another long hike ahead of us, 7.8 miles up and over Madison, then curving to the east and finally to the south for a long descent into Pinkham Notch, where we would stay at Joe Dodge Lodge. I left Madison with a word to Saint Pete, mentioning the prospect of rain and hoping he had a good day. He was untroubled by the forecast or the hint from the croo at the hut that the next stretch of trail was every bit as difficult as what we had hiked the day before. Just another day at the office for him.

But not for me. This was all still strange here above the tree line, exotic even, and the degree of difficulty each day posed seemed to ratchet upward while I wanted it to go in the other direction. Hiking on these rocks was taking a physical toll on my feet and a psychological toll on my mind. I had heard stories about Madison from southbound thru-hikers and I had not enjoyed them. The prospect of heavy rain had me worried. It took more effort than usual for me to settle into a hiking rhythm and concentrate on each footstep.

It took a little more than an hour to climb to the summit. It was the usual stuff, very steep, all rock, some of it hand-over-hand crawling like a spider on a tall pile of gravel. But amazingly, at the summit we got little peeks of sunshine, and the cloud deck was not so dark and threatening as it had been back at the hut. We even got some good views of distant valleys and mountain ranges. This was not so bad.

It was the next two and a half hours that were a nightmare. The northern slope of Madison sheared off at a steep angle and was completely covered in a tangle of big rocks, the worst we had encountered so far, rocks piled loosely on top of each other, rocks with no flat surfaces, only rough, irregular and unpredictable shapes, big ones the size of houseboats, smaller ones the size of vending machines, and jammed into the gaps in between them smaller ones yet turned edge on or precariously balanced so they teetered or slid when you stepped on one. And all we had to help us navigate through this mess was a series of cairns of stacked rock at intervals and an occasional faded white blaze painted on a rock face. Describing this as a trail was a joke that wasn't funny. All I could do was constantly remind myself to concentrate on each footstep.

A wrong one would likely topple me over. The only good thing I could think of was that it was not raining. Everything else I tried to put out of my mind. Just focus, just focus, just focus. . . .

The most welcome sight of this long morning was not the snatches of blue sky, it was a scrawny twisted dwarf of a spruce tree in the distance. And then several more scattered among the scree. We were approaching the edge of the krumholtz, the zone of miniature spruce and balsam trees barely head high, the first trees we had seen in three days. But this good news was tempered by the descent off Madison that we now faced. The trail here lost three thousand feet of altitude over a distance of less than three miles, the majority of it in the first mile down.

The slope was so steep I often had to get off my feet and scoot or slide down bare rock faces or turn around facing the mountain and use limber tree branches like cables to lower myself to a ledge or foothold. This was just as hard as the piles of rocks on the summit of Madison, except now I had to resist gravity and worry about the balance of my backpack. But I had done this before coming down other mountains in the Whites, and I knew how to pace myself and how to find reasonably safe routes over the rock. After an hour and a half of this I was tired and sweaty, but I had come down the worst of the slope. The trail still dropped, but the slope was not as steep, and I could actually walk freely without using handholds.

The freedom of being able to walk on an actual trail again through a beautiful evergreen forest brought a flood of relief, even mild exhilaration. I took a break to let Eco link up with me and together we hiked the remaining miles down toward Pinkham Notch at a brisk pace, crossing a brook and then the auto road that climbs to the summit of Mount Washington. We arrived at Joe Dodge Lodge just before 5:00 p.m. and checked in. Showers, electricity, cell phone and Internet service, a well-appointed visitor center and a real cafeteria, traffic out on the road, tourists milling around, enjoying the evening . . . we were back to civilization after hard days above the tree line of the White Mountains Presidential Range. It felt a bit strange and wonderful.

The Trail Provides

A little more than an hour into the hike the next morning I came to a dead stop. I had climbed Moosilauke and Kinsman, Garfield, Washington and Madison, not to mention Smarts and Cube and half a dozen other steep mountains in New Hampshire—all of them were devilishly hard yet none of them had defeated me. But the ledge I was staring at above me on the side of Wildcat Mountain Peak E, the steepest climb on the entire Appalachian Trail, defied belief. Two great smooth inverted rocks formed a vertical V with smaller rocks wedged in the narrow crease between them. There were no rebar steps or wooden blocks or chiseled handholds—just two slabs of inverted and nearly vertical rock. My first tentative attempt to gain a foothold failed when my foot slid off the surface and I skidded backward several feet down to where I had started. No other solution seemed within reach. I was stumped. Not mad, not scared, just befuddled. How the heck was I going to climb this thing?

There is an expression among thru-hikers that I had often heard and had always dismissed—"the trail will provide." I viewed that saying as one of those metaphysical nostrums unsupported by hard evidence and invented from a mix of coincidence, illusion, and wishful thinking. Well, here the trail was providing me something—another smack in the face, very different from Wolf or Spivey Gap but just as hard. I saw no way to scale the fifteen to twenty feet of smooth rock looming over me. Eco and I stood at the narrow base of the monster and stared at it, and I felt a

sinking feeling of hopelessness and ineptitude. Meeting that ugly buddha . . . again.

Within a few minutes two thru-hikers climbed toward us, a tall,
young, robust, and athletic fellow with a red beard any Viking would
have been proud of and a short, stout older fellow, a salty Australian—
Red and Stump. I stood aside and Red expertly scaled the obstacle in a
couple of quick, precise, and powerful movements. Wonderful, I thought
glumly, expecting him to disappear on to the next series of rocks. But instead, Red turned around, leaned over the ledge where he was kneeling,
and asked me to hand to him my trekking poles. Puzzled, I did what he
asked. Then from his perch high above me, he leaned over the ledge and
began coaching me, using a pole as a pointer—put your right foot there,
your right hand here, now push up and reach this cleft in the rock with
your free hand and swing your left foot high up to here. . . .

To my amazement, it worked, and I was halfway up, clinging to the
narrowest of crease and hugging the rock close. A new handhold was just
within reach on my left, then the indention Red pointed to for my foot,
and another, and I was standing on top of the thing with him. Next it was
Eco's turn, with a little help from Stump below and Red coaching from
above, only Red chose a slightly different route for her, straighter up the
V, whereas I had zigzagged to the left, probably because I am taller and
had a longer reach with my legs. Within minutes of meeting these two
thru-hikers, total strangers, Eco and I were standing on the little platform above what the trail guides deceptively term a "rocky crevasse" at
mile 1,874.6, the steepest single place on the steepest climb on the A.T.
We expressed our gratitude to Red and Stump, but they shrugged it off as
a small thing, all in a day's work for an Appalachian Trail thru-hiker.

"The trail provides," Red said matter-of-factly. And then they continued their climb, Red scampering up the rock in great powerful bursts and
Stump attacking the rock slowly, muttering under his breath and huffing
occasionally like a steam engine, but chugging steadily up, up, up, and
he was gone.

Over the course of the day, I had plenty of time to think about this.
The mountain we were climbing, Wildcat, is not a single peak but rather

a confusing series of peaks and knobs. After the initial long ascent, each required a short, exhausting climb and an equally dangerous descent, with patches of muddy bog in between. Wildcat E plus D claimed the title of the steepest climb on the entire Appalachian Trail, but C and A were tough in their own way, and so the morning stretched out into a long slog and eventually I did not care whether we were on top of Wildcat D or C or whatever it was. We even emerged from the trees at one point to find a clearing with a Jetsons-like spaceship building perched on stilts overlooking the valley below—actually the Wildcat Mountain Ski Gondola and Observation Tower.

"The Appalachian Trail provides." What does that mean? Maybe the thru-hikers who use that phrase intend something mystical, something metaphysical, implying that the trail itself has a power to bend or shape people and events or even offer protection to those who know and adhere to its ways and follow the trail's white blazes like religious pilgrims. Or maybe they have just benefited from enough coincidences and kindness over a thousand plus miles of hiking to believe that it will all work out for the best somehow. Maybe "the trail provides" means that some hikers have been lucky, and their good fortune obscures all the rest.

I do not know the answer, but I can offer this: the Appalachian Trail is nothing more than a very long footpath. But for the people who hike it seriously, day in and day out, week after week and month after month, it becomes a well-honed state of mind as well. And success on the A.T. requires this particular attitude, one that deeply respects the trail's many hazards while it also believes fiercely in the worthiness of the endeavor and confers honor on all who share its travails. The northbound thru-hikers who had made it as far as New Hampshire possessed this state of mind; the southbounders who had hiked only 350 or so miles from Katahdin did not quite grasp the full dimensions of it yet, and I could sometimes tell the difference just by spending a few minutes with each one. The veterans knew they would find a way. The new hikers, those headed south and still in mild shock at the difficulty of it all, hoped for the best.

Would Eco and I have found a way up the crevasse on Wildcat E without the help of Red and Stump? Maybe. The alternative was turning around and scrambling back down that wickedly steep mountain I had just spent a tiring morning climbing. The solution was waiting there in the rock—Red just pointed it out to me. Maybe I would have found it on my own. Instead, I have to admit the trail provided.

⤚⤙

A bubble is a useful metaphor for a lengthy hike of the Appalachian Trail. You live inside a frame of mind physically reinforced by the forests and mountains that isolate you from the everyday world. Within the bubble are the weather conditions, the rocks, the mud, the rain, the crappy trail food, the fellow hikers you meet, the fellowship you enjoy at the shelters, the tent sites, and, here in the White Mountains, the huts. A minimalist mindset prevails. Outside the bubble is everything else going on in the world. Inside the bubble is hard, sweaty work, sometimes suffering, loneliness, and exhaustion. But it is also wonderful because so much stuff, ranging from the mundane to the truly awful, is outside the bubble, and when you attend to nothing but the business of hiking you are not aware of it, you do not worry about it or discuss it. You just hike.

Bubbles are fragile things, of course. They burst easily, and so it is with the hiking bubble. Early in our New Hampshire hike I learned about a mass shooting when I went into a grocery store and saw a day-old newspaper headline. The shooting had happened three days earlier and I had been oblivious to it. On the trail the Internet is all around us all the time, and some hikers cannot resist its pull for very long. But mostly hikers talk of weather forecasts or keep track of other hikers they have met through podcasts or social media. The bubble may screen hikers from the turbulence of the world but that does not mean it is not busy inside. Trail news travels within the bubble at amazing speed, usually the old-fashioned way. Word of mouth spreads quickly both north and south about hikers, weather, friends, trouble, and, most of all, trail conditions. Trail news I had heard from the southbounders had a consistent thread—the last miles of New Hampshire and the first miles of western Maine were very difficult. One young man I talked with expressed it this way: "I was shocked at how hard it was."

What was it that was so tough? I asked.

"Everything," he said mournfully.

The day Eco and I left Pinkham Notch and began climbing Wildcat E Mountain was my unofficial entry into this zone of hiking horror, for the Presidential Range was now behind us, and the A.T. took a northeast compass heading pointed toward Katahdin. The Maine state line was only 37.6 trail miles ahead.

The crevasse we had encountered that morning going up Wildcat was merely a warning sign that the hiking was about to become seriously mean. I had arrived at Carter Hut that afternoon exhausted and sore after the hardest day of hiking I had ever experienced—by far. I had walked, crawled, scooted on my backside, stumbled, and climbed only 5.7 miles in eight hours. I had suffered periods of doubt again and had thought of quitting and going home. The southbounders were right—everything about the trail here was devilishly hard. Even Saint Pete, when he ambled in that evening, admitted that it had been an especially tough day.

But the amazing thing was that I felt, for the most part, pretty good. Tired, yes, and happy to be arrived safely at the hut, but overall, I finished the day in a good state of mind in spite of the occasional dark thoughts that had hovered over me at the worst moments. The good fortune of meeting Red and Stump at exactly the right moment in front of the crevasse had helped, but another chance encounter with a man on the trail a few hours later had sustained my mental momentum for the hard day.

The man Eco and I met was tall and athletic, had a well-shaped full salt-and-pepper beard and shoulder-length dreadlocks, dark brown skin (which, of course, set him apart from the majority of hikers on the trail), and a golden tenor voice that was instantly friendly and cheerful. He was a northbound thru-hiker, and he came up behind us in long, graceful strides. His trail name, he said as we exchanged greetings, was Doc.

"Oh, you're a doctor?" Eco asked.

"No, my friends gave me that name because I played one on TV."

Grey's Anatomy, specifically. Doc had the presence of an actor, that magnetism that is so hard to define and yet shines through so sharply in person. But he in no way carried himself like a Hollywood star out here on the trail. He was happy to meet us, interested in our experiences, encouraging and open about himself in every respect except one—he was not eager to talk about his television work. That phase of his life seemed to be over now, or at least on hold, and his focus was on one thing only—hiking the Appalachian Trail. All that he would say about his time on the show was that most of his scenes had ended up on the cutting room floor. And he laughed when I admitted that I had never seen the program.

Like all thru-hikers, Doc could far outpace us. But he had walked with us a while, and we had bantered about all kinds of things, and then he had pushed on. Then a few hours later we saw him again—he had stopped to rest at a view off the trail and we had passed him, and later he caught us again. Doc liked to take his time, see the sights, engage in good conversation, and enjoy himself no matter the circumstances. He was genuinely interested in the history of the A.T. and fascinated to learn that I maintained a short section of it in Georgia. Our conversation seemed to lap up the miles over this rugged piece of trail, even though we were together for a brief time.

When I arrived at Carter Hut, Doc was sitting outside on a bench with another thru-hiker we had met earlier, a young lady named Atoms, a trail name that befitted her status as a scientist at a research facility. He was going to work for stay at the hut along with Saint Pete, Atoms, and several other thru-hikers. Doc waited his turn to eat the leftovers, and he pitched in to clean up. We chatted briefly after dinner, and I then retired to my bunk, happy inside the hiker's bubble, where the only sounds were the snores and grunts of bunkmates and the distant screech of an owl. Thoughts of quitting were long gone. I went to sleep wondering what would come next.

⌇

I awoke to a clear blue sky and a cool wind at Carter Hut. I felt recovered from the exertion of the day before and ready to go after another great breakfast, the last meal I would have at a New Hampshire hut. Things were about to change yet again. The hike today would take us over a mountain called Carter Dome. At 4,832 feet, Carter is the last of the tall mountains for nearly one hundred trail miles north. Carter, like Wildcat the day before, is not one peak but several, all of them above four thousand feet. Carved out between the peaks is Zeta Pass, where several side trails intersect with the Appalachian Trail. At Zeta Pass, Eco and I would say goodbye. She would take a side trail down the mountain to a road, catch a shuttle to an airport, and fly back to Georgia. I would press on.

We climbed Carter without much trouble. This was now routine, an hour and a half to cover 1.7 miles, all of it steeply inclined to the summit, but something extraordinary was awaiting us there. From the bare rock of the summit, we could look back due west and distinctly see Mount Washington glowing in the morning sunshine. Every feature stood out in the clear air, the towers were tiny filaments poking up into the blue sky, the visitor center a flat smear, the auto road curving down off the mountain, and as we watched, a glint of sunlight off a windshield identified a vehicle driving up. We could trace our route down off Washington, following the ridgeline to the north as it fell toward Clay, then the hump of Jefferson, and there was the deep V of Edmands Col and then the sharp point of Madison and the incredible drop-off, scary to look at even from this distance. To think we had hiked those miles and to see it all laid out in front of us was remarkable—a sight to remember, the last clear view of Washington and the Presidentials and on such a splendid morning.

We reached Zeta Pass midmorning and Eco said goodbye and set off down the side trail. She had a shuttle to meet and a flight to catch, the timetables and deadlines of life outside the bubble. I just had more miles to hike. My destination was Imp Campsite, and I arrived at 3:00 p.m. after scampering up and over and down the series of Carter's secondary summits. Imp Campsite had a caretaker, a young man who had lived there all summer collecting the eight-dollar fees of hikers and living in a half tent, half shelter with a little wooden porch and two chairs outside. I was the first hiker of the day to arrive, and we sat awhile in the chairs and talked about life on this mountainside. He appeared to have enjoyed it, but the summer was coming to an end, and he would soon be leaving for home. He seemed ready for that.

I walked down to the shelter and decided to sleep inside on the platform instead of pitching my tent. The caretaker had a radio and received the daily Mount Washington weather forecasts. He had mentioned the likelihood of rough weather tomorrow, maybe as soon as early afternoon. Possible thunderstorms.

"You don't want to be on a summit if we get storms," he had warned, and his voice had the somber tone of a man who had experienced exposure to lightning on a high place more than once in New Hampshire. I had one more summit to climb, Mount Moriah, and then a very long descent. I wanted as early a start in the morning as possible.

That afternoon I swapped stories with two northbound thru-hikers, a lean, athletic young man, Hollywood, and an attractive young woman, Little More, who were resting and eating dinner. They had about three hundred miles remaining to reach Katahdin. I asked how it felt to be so close to the finish of their great adventures. Both grew wistful and had trouble finding the right words. Little More was from Texas; she had sold everything she owned, quit her unfulfilling but lucrative job, and set out from Springer Mountain months ago. Now the end was tantalizingly close, and she did not know what she was going to do when it was over. She expressed the same conflict of emotions I had heard in New Hampshire from other thru-hikers, the fierce desire to stand on Katahdin's famous summit but also reluctance for the experience to end.

Not long after our conversation I was boiling water for my dinner, and I overheard them discussing something. To my surprise, they hefted their backpacks and gathered their trekking poles. They had two hours of daylight left, and six miles of hiking would bring them to the spot on the trail where Katahdin was exactly three hundred miles north. Hollywood was clearly impatient to get back on the trail, his powerful leg muscles tense and his face set in a hurry-up frown while Little More fiddled with her backpack pockets. I wished them good luck, and off they went, focused on putting miles behind them before dark.

Like magnetism working on a compass needle, the big mountain in Maine exerts an invisible tug on northbound hikers. In Georgia the magnetic force is a remote, weak, and almost mystical thing, hardly worth mentioning. "The mountain that shall not be named," some thru-hikers call it. But this near the end of New Hampshire, we were close, so close the pull was a tangible and strong force, a constant presence in hikers' minds.

"Be careful," I called to them as they turned onto the side trail that led up the mountainside to the Appalachian Trail. Hollywood flicked his hand my way in recognition, his handsome face set forward on the trail, but Little More looked back at me and nodded. I think she knew. There is danger in being so close and yet still far away.

In the early morning hours, long before sunrise, I tossed myself awake in a troubled state of mind. Late that previous evening a number of hikers had arrived and spread out their equipment in the shelter. After I went to bed even more must have arrived because every space inside the shelter was now taken and someone was curled in a ball wrapped in a sleeping bag on the open wooden lip of the structure next to my backpack and trekking poles. During the evening some of the new arrivals had smoked cigars inside the shelter, and I could distinctly smell the rich tobacco smoke in the cool darkness. From inside my sleeping bag before I went to sleep, I had heard laughing voices nearby. An empty beer can sat on the edge of the shelter deck and confirmed my suspicion that considerable drinking must have been on the agenda.

This felt all wrong. A violation of something, although I could not think of any rules they were breaking, and besides, this wilderness was hardly a place where laws and regulations applied, much less could be enforced. The partyers had as much right to be here as I did. What did it matter that they had hiked up a short side trail to get here while I had hiked 136 miles from the New Hampshire-Vermont state line? Still, the noise and the beer and the cigars belonged on the other side of the bubble, not here in this beautiful forest. I wanted to be gone from Imp Campsite, and even though it was pitch-black inside the shelter, I began to silently pack my sleeping bag and equipment by the red light of my headlamp. By 4:00 a.m. I was almost ready. Pale moonlight cut through the gloom of the spruce forest. Previous experience had taught me to begin every morning by eating something, so I walked toward the care-taker's camp until I found the steel bear box provided for hikers to se-curely store their food at night. I retrieved my food bag from the bear box and sat on the cold lid while I ate a breakfast of dry granola and chopped dates. Slowly a plan resolved in my head. I decided to hike in the dark-ness.

On many stretches of the Appalachian Trail in New Hampshire hik-ing in the dark would have been madness. An invitation for disaster, es-pecially for an old man. But the trail here was not too bad. At full illumi-nation strength my headlamp and the moonlight gave enough light for me to see where to put my feet, and the rocks were not so numerous or difficult. I had a little less than a mile of trail to hike before I reached the base of the steep climb up Mount Moriah, a total of eight miles to hike to reach a road and the Rattle River Hostel, where I planned to stay for the night. If I could manage a mile before sunrise, I would then have a good chance of going over the summit of Moriah well before any rough weather closed in on me. I might even make the hostel before noon.

So I began this experiment, slowly and carefully feeling my way along, using the beam of light to guide my footsteps. To my surprise, I found I could hike pretty well this way, even when the trail had me climbing or descending over rock. All my previous experience on the difficult moun-tains behind me kicked in and I managed a decent rhythm. The darkness, the cool air, the solitude, and the silence of the forest all helped. I was ac-tually enjoying this.

The first gray light found me at the junction of the Stony Brook Trail peering up at the steep slope of Moriah. I was able to put my headlamp away, eat a little more, and drink plenty of water while I waited for the light to strengthen. I had hoped for a pretty sunrise at the summit, but clouds were building fast from all directions. Up I went, my last climb in these mountains on this last day of my hike across New Hampshire. It was old hat by now, just another steep, rocky slope, more seeking foot-holds and handholds and carefully pulling myself up to the next one and the one after that. The work required plenty of muscle power, and I was sweaty in spite of the cool morning when I reached the summit after more than an hour of climbing. Moriah's peak was a tiny patch poking above the trees. I crossed the bare rock and paused for a last view of New Hampshire's mountain vistas below the cloud deck. Washington was behind me, plainly visible but not as imposing as it had been the day before in the sunshine from the top of Carter. I took it in for a moment, knowing I would never see the famous mountain from this vantage point again, and then I scrambled down the dark side of Moriah.

The descent of Moriah was another rugged, knee-jarring exercise in defying gravity. The rock here was different from that in the Presidentials, often broad and smooth and steeply tilted so that the only way safely down was sliding on my backside or turning around to hug the rock and feeling for a secure landing for a foot while holding on tight with my hands to a tree or rock edge. I did this for the better part of an hour and then was startled by the sight of a day-hiker climbing toward me.

He was a local man dressed in a red-and-black checked shirt and tan hiking pants with huge pockets, and he carried a heavy walking stick almost as tall as he was. Obviously an experienced and tough hiker. We exchanged the usual greetings, but his craggy face was fixed in a somber expression.

"Bad weather coming," he said with that characteristic New England accent. "Severe thunderstorms predicted on the summits and maybe in the valleys."

"How soon?" I asked.

"Around noon," was the answer.

I knew I had pushed my luck out to the edge in New Hampshire with the weather and now, on my last day, it looked like I was finally going to experience a downpour at the least. We said goodbye and I continued down the mountain and had gone a hundred yards or more before it dawned on me that the fellow was headed up Moriah, not toward the safer terrain of the valley like I was. These New Hampshire hikers are tough.

The descent soon began to transition into a more manageable slope, and I was able to safely increase my pace. I reached the Kenduskeag Trail and then an hour later the Rattle River Trail. I hiked through a section of trail strewn with blown-down trees, some of them cleared but many smaller ones still across the path, requiring an awkward climb over or detour around a tangle of limbs that slowed my progress. It was also a vivid reminder of why I did not want to be out here in a thunderstorm.

Once I was on the Rattle River Trail, however, the hiking became easier down a gentle slope. I crossed the Rattle River on a bridge of stepping stones and then hiked beside it, and the miles began to roll by since I could manage a longer stride. Mosquitoes, which had not troubled me for days, suddenly discovered me and began coordinated attacks on my arms and face. At first, I swatted at them but finally I surrendered to the reality of it and took off my backpack so I could pull out a long-sleeve shirt and put it on.

The overcast was still building, and the air was growing humid. But the trail was arrow-straight now, wide and easy to walk, and I was thumping along faster than at any other time since I had set out nineteen days earlier. And soon, remarkably, I saw ahead of me a hiker I was overtaking. This had not happened on the entire trek. I hardly knew what to do as I approached the lady from behind. When I was close, I called out "Good morning!"

My voice startled her. She turned around and quickly regained her composure when she saw me coming down the trail. We exchanged the usual greetings, and I learned she was a local, a native of New Hampshire and just out for a day hike in the woods. I remarked on the beauty of her state and pressed on. And then, from behind, I heard her ask a curious question.

"Are you a southerner?"

I turned around and smiled at her as the first rumble of distant thunder drifted our way. Her weathered face, wrinkled hands, and frayed old-style canvas day pack suggested that her age was somewhat more than mine, but there was a strength there also, a toughness unperturbed by thunder or snow, rough trails, or steep mountains.

"Yes, ma'am," I said. "Georgia."

In the pause while she reflected on that I heard the sound of a truck grinding away on the road that was my destination.

"And are you by yourself?"

Aren't we all out here? I thought. But then no, that wasn't entirely true, was it? At least not at moments like this.

"Yes, ma'am. My friends had to go home a while back."

"Well," she said. "Welcome to New Hampshire."

I smiled, thanked her, and pushed on, the tire noise of cars plainly audible in the distance and more thunder, closer now. Welcome indeed.

At Rattle River Hostel I spent a pleasant afternoon watching the thunderstorms roll overhead and listening to loud booms of thunder and the downpour of rain hammering the metal roof of the old clapboard house where I was staying, warm and dry in clean clothes after a hot shower. I watched hikers come scurrying in seeking shelter, dripping wet and still shaking from the lightning bolts on the flank of Moriah. That evening some twenty of us shared an enormous spaghetti dinner family-style around a huge dining table. Trail stories abounded over great heaping plates of pasta. I had a fascinating conversation with a wiry thru-hiker named Popeye, not quite as old as me, with a big scraggly beard, muscled arms, dragon tattoos, and a steady glint in his eyes.

Popeye was a martial arts master, a former prison guard, and a fast talker. He claimed that hiking in the Whites was like the forms of karate, a series of rhythmic movements, and that successful hiking up there required the same focus and intense concentration of the martial arts discipline.

"It's all in the mind," Popeye said, tapping the side of his shaved head. "Once you master the movements, it's all about concentration; you attack the rocks the same way, you don't think, you just move, move, move! You move where the trail lets you move with your hands and your feet. When your mind is focused like that, the trail almost tells you what to do. Once you learn how to read it, you aren't fighting it anymore and the trail will just unfold itself for you."

There it was again, in a slightly different form, but there nonetheless—the trail provides. At least it does for the hiker who can empty his mind and focus on each moment, each footstep, and each breath. Popeye polished the last of his spaghetti sauce off his plate with a crust of bread and the glint in his eyes turned a little mischievous. He had a surprise for us—cheesecake for dessert. He had bought a sackful of cheesecakes in Gorham and hidden them in a cupboard. He made a big deal out of giving me the first slice. No words can describe the taste of cheesecake to a man who had lost eight pounds in nineteen days of hard hiking. My slice vanished in a twinkling.

But then I thought of Saint Pete and Moonwalk, Red and Stump, and Doc and Atoms, Hollywood and Little More. They were all out there on the trail, hunkered down somewhere against the storm that was just then playing out over the mountains. And the next morning while I waited for my rental car to pick me up to begin the long drive home, I stood outside the hostel and stared across the wet two-lane highway at a little side road that pointed north. The Appalachian Trail white blaze was painted on its guardrail. The trail followed the little lane, crossed the Androscoggin River, and disappeared into the woods. While I watched, Doc waved at me as he set out, his backpack riding easily on his back and his long, graceful strides eating up the asphalt. He had come in early that morning after a wild night high on the mountain. He was untroubled by it.

Maine was only 16.5 trail miles to the north. Katahdin was 281.8 miles from the state line. Up there was the fearsome Mahoosuc Range I had heard so much about, the Mahoosuc Notch, the lakes and bogs, the Kennebec River where A.T. hikers ferry across in a canoe, and the famous One Hundred Mile Wilderness. And then, of course, Katahdin itself, the holy grail of every northbounder who sets out from Springer in Georgia.

And so, the question: Would I ever go back to New Hampshire? Would I cross the Androscoggin River over that bridge I was staring at and continue toward Maine, following in the footsteps of Saint Pete and Doc, Popeye and Red and Stump and all the others I had met who were hiking north?

At that moment I could not say. Not that year, but maybe in time, I thought, the trail would unfold itself and provide an answer.

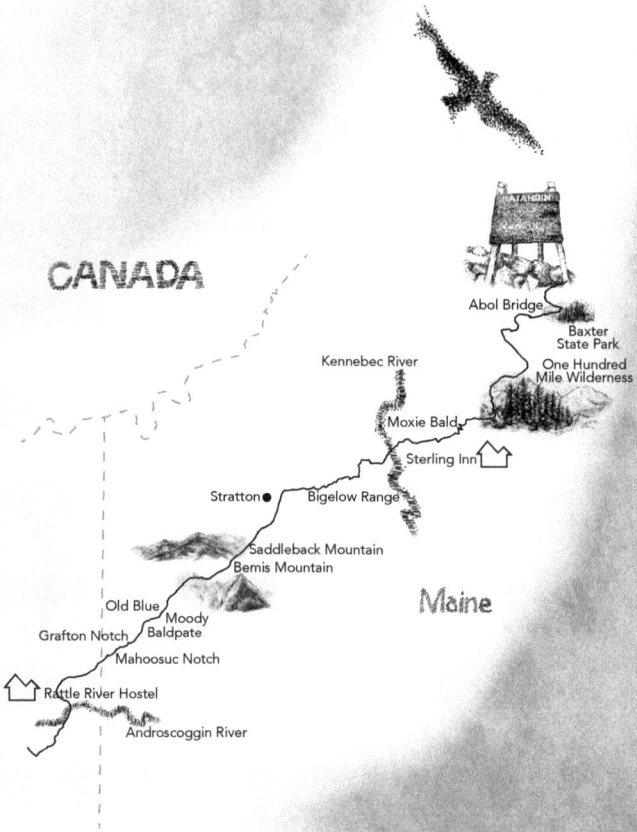

Sum over Paths

Two years passed. Months in which the idea of hiking the entire Appalachian Trail swelled and ebbed, zoomed into and then out of focus, seemed possible, then less so and wavered just out of my reach. Two years of more hikes, little gaps filled in, more states checked off, all of Virginia and then all of Pennsylvania, the miles adding up and the long, completed line on the map from Springer Mountain inching north in fits and starts. Over those months the ambition of ever completing the entire Appalachian Trail reduced itself down to a single word—Maine. Either travel north and start hiking where I had watched Doc disappear up the trail or quit dreaming about it. The decision had a bracing simplicity—face the challenge or be done with the quest. The COVID-19 pandemic intervened and made everything about life harder and anything related to hiking seem trivial, but another year elapsed, and the situation clarified. I was not getting any younger. It was either 2021 or forget it. I bought the airline ticket, made the arrangements, sweated the countdown. And then it was time to go.

Twenty-three months from that moment of wistfulness watching Doc cross the road, the answer was yes, and the day arrived that I had been hoping for and I was standing almost exactly where I had stood to watch him walk across the road from Rattle River Hostel and cross the bridge. Now it was my turn. I found it a little surreal, a little hard to believe. I was actually going to hike the last miles of New Hampshire and north into Maine toward Katahdin. I had set aside the month of August—not enough time for me to hike the entire 298-mile distance to the northern terminus, but enough days to put me deep into Maine and possibly, by skipping a section, to attempt to climb the great mountain.

After crossing the Androscoggin River near Gorham, New Hampshire, the Appalachian Trail alters in ways that are neither subtle nor mysterious, and I had spent months pondering those changes. Hikers climbing out of the river basin enter the Mahoosuc Range, and the very name Mahoosuc puts a stamp on what is different. The day-hikers and tourists and spectacular wide-open five-thousand-foot peaks of the Presidential Range are left behind and the Appalachian Trail becomes a rugged, lonely, and largely inaccessible ribbon of rocks and roots and mud pointed northeast toward the great mountain—Katahdin. The A.T. was hard through most of New Hampshire. Now the trail would become even harder, although in different ways. The mountain peaks are jammed close to each other, separated by deep defiles and gaps, one after another after another. Northbound hikers who cannot bring themselves to fully believe that Maine could be harder than what they have already hiked in New Hampshire are soon rudely disabused of their skepticism.

I walked across the bridge over the Androscoggin on a balmy August morning, tracing the same steps that Doc and Saint Pete and the other thru-hikers I had met that season two years earlier had walked, thinking that I knew approximately what was coming. I also knew that once again I was not prepared for it, certainly not in a physical sense, and probably not in my head either. No sometime section hiker can step off an airplane, load his or her backpack with four or five days of food, and set out on the Appalachian Trail fully prepared for the rigors of the Mahoosuc Range and the mountains beyond in western Maine. As I knew so well from previous experiences on lesser Appalachian Trail challenges, only by hiking for months in the cold and rain and heat, by enduring the mosquitoes and the bumps and bruises and outlasting the interminable climbs and descents, day after day, can a hiker develop the leg strength, stamina, and mental toughness to tackle Maine with any degree of preparedness. My efforts to prepare for the challenge of Maine were pitiful in comparison—hiking the trail in Georgia a few days each month, spending hours on a treadmill, and more hours poring over maps and making plans. My only option for a successful strategy to hike Maine, especially at my age, was the same as it had been for New Hampshire two years earlier: begin very slowly, just a few miles each day, and adjust my daily average to the conditions as I encountered them.

I crossed the river alone, excited to be back on the A.T., a bit nervous, anxious even. And within a couple of hours of climbing a steep, tough trail, I had gained enough altitude going up Mount Hayes to turn around and look behind me through a gap in the young spruce trees. Laid out along the horizon to the southwest in forest greens and then muted blues were Moriah, then the Wildcats, and beyond them the Whites, mountains I had hiked two years earlier, enormous mountains that filled the screen of my camera, Mount Washington, the highest of them, clearly poking its clouded peak into the sky. Ahead, in the opposite direction, the mountain peaks were modest by comparison—Cascade only 2,631 feet, and Mount Success a day's hike farther north just 3,565 feet. But the lower altitudes of the mountains in the Mahoosuc Range and the bigger mountains beyond Grafton Notch are deceptive—dangerously so. The peaks come at you like the teeth of a saw blade. What counts is the difficulty of climbing and descending them, as I was about to learn firsthand.

My first night on the trail I lay in my tent at Trident Col listening to a group of ravens roosting in tall white pines nearby. Toward evening they began to congregate and carry on like a bunch of juveniles turned loose in an empty mall parking lot. Back and forth they flew at treetop level above the spruce and pines, squawking, chattering, clicking, and jiving at each other with a ruckus of sounds that echoed in the forest. *Rrrr* and *kak kak kak* sounds mashed together, rapid-fire taps like rapping a drumstick on a hollow tree, eerie mixtures of squawks and almost shrieks and purrs that must have meanings in the raven world. I stretched out on my back on my sleep pad listening, mesmerized by their performance. Then, just before the twilight faded, the racket suddenly stopped, as if one of them had barked a command, and the forest became silent. I went to sleep wondering if I would ever again hear such a wild avian jabbering or whether this was a common phenomenon in these remote woods. Weeks later the answer was clear—I had been privileged to hear ravens calling to each other in such numbers and with such a variety of sounds.

Two days after camping at Trident Col, following a long, hard slog up Mount Success, I faced an equally long and difficult descent down into a deep gap toward the New Hampshire-Maine state line, another of those Appalachian Trail milestones that thru- and section hikers treasure, this one more meaningful than most since I would be completing New Hampshire and entering the trail's final state, a state that at one point a year prior I thought I might never see.

Near the bottom of the descent, just before the trail climbed again and less than half a mile after I celebrated crossing into Maine, I arrived at a spot that was all wrong. Staring over a forty- or fifty-foot plunge nearly straight down, I thought surely this must be a mistake—it could not be the route of the Appalachian Trail. Here the boulders squeezed a sloped passage to barely two feet of width between two giant slabs of rock. I scooted sideways through the gap, dropped down between more boulders, carefully eased over one ledge and onto another, and came to an abrupt halt. The trail literally disappeared before me, straight down into a pit of broken stone.

In front of me were a middle-aged husband and wife, both thruhikers, the husband leading the way and coaching his wife on what to do. Pausing to let them negotiate the tricky drop into the rock pit, I made a serious mistake, something I knew better than to do but was fooled into doing by the apparent impossibility of getting down safely any other way. I followed them, choosing the exact spot and method they had used to drop off a twelve- or fifteen-foot smooth rock. What I should have known was that the husband had helped his wife down—he was tall and athletic and had managed the big drop okay and, unseen by me, he had given his wife a foothold with his hands to bring her down safely. But now they were gone and I was stuck—there was no going back up through the narrow split in the boulders above me to find another way. I had no choice but try the same method.

It did not work. With one hand grasping a tree branch, I eased my body over the edge of the rock I was sitting on, and my left foot found a tiny crevice for support—and then slipped out of it. Immediately I slid down about three feet and was dangling above the pit, holding desperately on to the tree limb with one hand. It felt like falling into an elevator shaft. With nothing underneath me, for several seconds I flailed away for something to grab with my free hand. I found something and the rest of it was a blur—I am not sure how I was able to shimmy sideways and find a support for my foot and lower myself down, landing with a hard thump.

From down in the pit, I heard someone above me ask, "Are you okay?"

Yes, I insisted as I looked up in disbelief at the rock I had just dropped off of and waved at a thru-hiker preparing to come down. My right arm was bleeding from scraping the rock, but I was otherwise okay.

Except I was not okay. The near-fall had badly shaken my confidence in my ability to hike these tough mountains. All the old familiar negative thoughts tumbled through my head in the next thirty minutes as I headed for Carlo Col Shelter to patch myself up. Here was the buddha again, sneering at me this time. What in the world was I doing out here in this wilderness alone and so physically unprepared? Who was I fooling? And the only way out now was to walk myself out, and what lay ahead was going to be much harder than what I had just faced. The tough miles were just beginning. This was just the warmup for the big one—the Mahoosuc Notch.

In the shelter that night I shared the space with a quiet, tall, young thru-hiker who exuded confidence and intelligence. Talking with him, listening to his stories of awful weather in the Whites, of weeks of rain and mud in Vermont, and sore feet, worn out shoes, and losing weight he could not afford to lose brought me some needed perspective on my own condition. I *was* okay. I had survived, had hung on to that tree branch and in fact squirmed my way out of a dangerous spot. How, I was not exactly sure, but I had done it, maybe with considerable skill, maybe because of the experience I had gained when I had survived something very similar in New York on the same day earlier in this year when Wanderer broke his arm and I nearly fell fifteen feet. Like then, I did not panic in a terrible situation, one in which I could have been seriously injured. That should count for something.

My young new friend in the shelter listened to the story of my fall and nodded his head sympathetically. "Yeah," he said, as though he was remembering something, maybe a near-miss accident of his own. "This trail can bite you."

Almost the same words Cogs had spoken back in Virginia. It seemed so long ago, so many miles, but what Cogs said then applied now more than ever. The big difference now was the strength of the bite. And this time I had no easy way out. The only choice was to keep going.

⨎

The English poet John Keats said, "Nothing ever becomes real till experienced." For hikers of the Appalachian Trail who have walked from Georgia to mile 1,917 in Maine, this bit of wisdom does not quite ring true when the topic of Mahoosuc Notch comes up. As Maine gets closer and closer, the Notch looms so large in Appalachian Trail lore that it begins to insinuate itself into thru-hiker conversations hundreds of miles to the south, long before it is experienced, a bit like what happens with the Whites. The Notch becomes a real thing, it gets in the hikers' heads and lives there, rattles around with stories passed along about how hard it is, or fun, or dangerous, or all the above. People do get hurt in there. I had already heard some of the stories at Rattle River Hostel when I was preparing to set out. Around a dinner table one southbound fellow spoke of watching his friend lose his balance on a rock and "disappear," miraculously surviving a big fall with no broken bones but with multiple serious cuts and contusions that ended his hike. And on my evening at Full Goose Shelter, the last one before entering the Mahoosuc Notch, I heard talk from hikers that a young woman had been rescued in there just the day before with a broken arm, her northbound thru-hike attempt ended so tantalizingly close to Katahdin.

The Mahoosuc Notch is a mile-long narrow canyon filled with piles of boulders. There is one way in and one way out. To look at it from the air, from the point of view of, say, a raven, there is certainly no "trail" through the gulch in any common meaning of the word, and it probably appears impossible to navigate on foot. And indeed "walking" in the Notch from end to end is impossible. Hikers put away their trekking poles at the entrance and for the next few hours crawl, scoot, shimmy, squirm, hop, lift, stretch, straddle, and tiptoe over, under, around, up and down, and sideways through a bizarre three-dimensional crazy land of rock. To be in there feels as though a cubist painting by Picasso has jumped off the canvas and become hard, rough stone gleefully defying all the geological rules. Add to that the fourth dimension of distorted time—a Salvador Dalí painting dripping minutes into infinity and back out through a black hole of space into hours—and the experience is a unique and salient feature of an Appalachian Trail hike, or any hike anywhere.[1]

Indeed, so truly outlandish are both the physical and mental characteristics of the Mahoosuc Notch that traversing it becomes something like an exercise in quantum mechanics. The brilliant physicist Richard Feynman surely was not thinking of hiking or Maine or the Appalachian Trail when he came up with one of the craziest-sounding ideas in quantum mechanics, his theory of the "sum over paths." Utterly bizarre though it sounds, Feynman's theory has held up well as a deep insight into the reality of the universe. I don't pretend to understand it, but the basic description of his theory seems to jibe nicely with what I found in the Mahoosuc Notch. In elemental textbook physics, subatomic particles riding along with a hiker traveling from one place to another, say from one white blaze to the next one, simply take the shortest path, Issac Newton's classical path. But Feynman said no, reality is not exactly like that. To comprehensively trace the route from one blaze to another, he said, you first must consider all the possible paths connecting those two white spots. An infinity of imaginable paths. That means paths that go to London. Or around Pluto. Or even backward in time to stars that blew up eons ago. Or even farther. . . . And our reality—what we actually see in the physical world—Feynman says is a blending, through complicated mathematics I will never comprehend, of all those infinite possibilities, resulting in a "sum."[2]

When I entered the Mahoosuc Notch, alone and more than a little nervous, I unknowingly began doing something that imitated what Feynman postulated. For there was no classical Newtonian path. The few faded white blazes painted on the rocks here and there were little more than suggestions. Boulders the size of wooly mammoths and blue whales, angles, corners, ledges, cracks, deep crevices, blind alleys, jagged edges, holes, creases, and smooth sloping faces—every shape and size and facet that stone can be hewn into by the forces of nature choked the Notch for every foot of its one-mile length. Therefore, to navigate from the south end to the north end required something like Feynman's crazy idea for the quantum world of subatomic particles; consider all the possible paths, or at least the most feasible ones. Pick one, try it, abandon it if it ended in a twenty-foot sheer drop or impossible-to-scale wall. Try another and another until you gain ten or twelve yards, then do it again. And again. And again. Maybe a trip to Pluto was not a consideration, but at one point, after laboring for longer than I thought was possible to make progress, I might have wished for any path, even one straight toward Pluto, if it would get me out of there.[3]

For an hour I scrambled alone in this stone madhouse. The concentration required was more exhausting than the physical effort, which was itself considerable. Then a young man passed me, bounding from one surface to the next with the freedom and agility of a leopard. He disappeared in two minutes, having the time of his life, quickly and expertly calculating the fastest path over the jumble of rocks, a veritable Michael Jordanesque physical performance of defying gravity combined with rapid-fire Feynman's sum-over-paths mental gymnastics.

I toiled on, not pausing, not hurrying, the mental calculations clicking off in my head—this way to the left, this rock, this surface, not that one, scoot on my butt here, turn around and go down hugging the rock there, belly crawl here, turn around and find another way out of this dead end, don't look too far ahead because it is just more of the same, always keeping my center of gravity as low as possible. Finally, I heard voices behind me. Three middle-age thru-hikers—two men and a woman—tackling the Notch as a team, working together to find the best path. I followed them for a while but soon fell behind. They were too fast for me, and we were now in the teeth of the Notch, the most difficult part, where boulders the size of a New York studio apartment were jammed one on top of another so that going over them was impossible. Holes and tunnels and dark, narrow alleys between the rocks were the only way forward.

And about this time, I met Popsicle. A petite young lady, soft-spoken and unassuming, Popsicle was a military brat "from everywhere" who was hiking the Appalachian Trail as a flip-flop—walking north from Harpers Ferry near the midpoint and then, after reaching Katahdin, turning around and walking from Georgia north back to Harpers Ferry. In the Notch we had time only for cursory introductions, but we began to work together almost without realizing it. In several places we had to remove our backpacks and pass them through to each other in the tunnels and holes too tight to crawl through with them on our backs.

At some point, somewhere toward the last third of this weird mile between two high cliffs, where the air was often cold and water gurgled invisibly somewhere down in the crevices where patches of snow remained, something totally unexpected happened to me. The doubts and worries about my hiking ability provoked by my near-miss fall two days earlier evaporated. I knew what I was doing down here in the Mahoosuc Notch on those crazy rocks. Slowly and methodically and carefully I wormed my way out to the southern end, calculating Feynman's sum over paths and finding a solution each time. Just before noon, after three and a half hours of work, I reached something that resembled a real trail where I was able to finally walk erect alongside trees on real soil instead of scrambling over bare rock. The relief and exhilaration made me want to shout for joy but instead Popsicle and I did a fist bump to congratulate each other and hiked on. Like it was no big deal. Like it was just another day and another mile on the Appalachian Trail. Just a tidy little application of quantum mechanics.

⚘

Luck plays an outsized role in any long-distance hike of the Appalachian Trail. The evening before I set out to cross the Androscoggin River, I was eating a sandwich at the dinner table of the Rattle River Hostel and raptly listening to a tall, amiable Texan named, appropriately enough, Rodeo, as he told of the horrible weather in the Whites over the previous week. Rodeo had laid up for two days before attempting the big peaks, Washington and Madison, to let the weather improve. He had hurried over those big, exposed summits in a skinny window of barely acceptable but nonetheless miserable conditions and narrowly escaped disastrous weather behind him that had brought all hiking on the mountain to a halt. The day before our conversation, the observatory had reported screaming one-hundred-mile-an-hour winds on Mount Washington. In contrast, my own trek across the Whites two years earlier had been mostly through fine or at least tolerable weather, and hearing Rodeo's stories of slamming wind and rain up there made me appreciate how lucky I had been.

But good fortune on the trail often comes in other, unexpected forms. What can seem to be a logistical calamity at the time can turn into a benevolent twist of fate farther up the trail, and so it was for me when I finished the long descent out of the Mahoosuc Range to the trailhead at Grafton Notch. When I was on a summit several days before I had called to arrange a shuttle to meet me at the parking area at Grafton Notch, where cell service would be unavailable. To preserve the battery on my cell phone, I kept it powered off. What I did not realize was that the shuttle service had later sent me a text message telling me to confirm the shuttle time of 1:00 p.m. when I was near the summit of Old Speck Mountain and headed down. This error on my part would leave me stranded at a remote trailhead without any good options—and I was almost out of food.

But when I arrived at the trailhead before noon, a welcome sight greeted me. The Appalachian Long Distance Hikers Association had erected a canopy and was feeding hikers scrambled eggs, sausage, cold drinks, and fresh fruit. Even better, I recognized one of their members, and he remembered meeting me from a chance encounter on the Appalachian Trail in Georgia back in the spring. I eagerly gobbled down the hot food and chatted with the other ALDHA members about my hike so far and my plans for the next section. I knew that I would not have enough time to complete all 281 of the remaining miles of the A.T. in Maine before I had to fly home, but I was not sure what sections would be best to skip. Learning of my dilemma, one of the ALDHA members, an elderly, very experienced Maine native and trail maintainer, patiently guided me through a new plan to leapfrog some of the miles in southern Maine and put me on track to reach Katahdin by my deadline. With my new plan firmly sketched out, I waited in a soft rain for my shuttle to pick me up.

Which, of course, did not come because I had not called with the confirmation. An hour passed, then two, and I knew I was in trouble, with no food, no ride into a town, and no prospect of getting one either.

"Hop in the car," one of the ALDHA members said, pointing to his SUV in the parking area. "I'll drive you wherever you want."

He was Dennis "Trail Pilgrim" Newton, a retired army chaplain, and by late afternoon he had delivered me to the little town of Rangeley, where I secured a motel and was able to take a shower, resupply, and regroup for the next leg of my hike with my new plan. Which turned out to be exactly what I needed. There it was again—the trail provides. And not for the first time, transportation when I most needed it. Missing the shuttle—a blunder on my part—turned out to be the best fortune I could have asked for. A better path from point A to point B, in a quantum sense.

Trail Buddhas

A central tenet of Buddhism, as I understand it from decades of casual study, is that anyone you meet might be an authentic buddha, an enlightened one. And being a buddha is therefore nothing really special. It is a state anyone can attain because everyone already exists in that state. A lot of people just do not know it. They think and act like they are not a buddha, and they suffer to various degrees for that illusion. The way to realize you are a buddha, Buddhist teachers advise, is to stop trying to be a buddha, to calm down, put away all the worrying and self-help exercises and psychological fads, stop thinking about the Buddha, put aside the dualism that saturates our Western culture, and stick to the discipline of living in the moment. It sounds ridiculously simple, but the basic idea has thrived for about 2,400 years and is practiced in one form or another by people all around the world, across many religions and cultures and ethnicities.

Aside from the misapprehension that what we fiercely regard as our individual and separate selves are independent of others—what Buddhism calls ignorance of our true selves—it is the sticking to the discipline that is the tough part. Discipline does not seem to be a plentiful commodity in our modern world. Maybe it has never been, but twenty-first-century life, with its myriad distractions and troubles, seems particularly at odds with the idea of regulating and controlling oneself in such a way that every moment is lived with full attention to that moment only. Achieving this focused state of mind is one thing; sustaining it over

any length of time is entirely another. A teacher or master and a rigor-
ous system of meditation or other form of study and years of practice are
usually necessary for a layman to get anywhere, and great effort is demanded. Which is a contradiction right at the start because Buddhism
also teaches that every person must look solely to themselves for enlightenment. There are no shortcuts on the Middle Way. Worse, for the beginner especially, is learning there is nowhere to get to. You finish where you
started, which, in one sense, means you never really finish. And yet when
you do finish, everything about you is different.[1]

At the risk of trivializing one of the world's great religions, this is
pretty much the state of play for anyone who sets out to hike the Appalachian Trail for any substantial distance. You are going somewhere, of
course, in a physical, geographical sense, but in a practical sense of going somewhere you *need to go*, you could just as easily be tracing spirals
and loops in a vast maze. From this utilitarian perspective, Bill Bryson
had a valid point: south to north or north to south or midpoint to another
point—the direction does not matter at all as long as you arrive. Feynman's sum over paths again.

No matter who may be traveling with you, you must rely entirely on
yourself, and no one can walk the miles for you. There are shortcuts to
take and a hundred ways to cheat the miles, but those actions always
eventually reveal themselves for what they are—less than the whole. You
are your own master, your own guru out there on the trail, and yet others on the same journey will be your companions and even help or en-
courage you, often when you need it most, as I had discovered several
times already on my trek north. The work is hard; it requires discipline,
determination, and courage. Yet it is ridiculously simple. You just get up
and walk every day. You finish wherever you finish, on Katahdin's summit or Springer Mountain or Harpers Ferry or anywhere else along those
2,193 miles that you choose. You are fundamentally the same person as
you were when you started. If you were a jerk when you began your hike,
you will likely still be a jerk when you finish, if you finish, for in my experience jerks do not last very long out there on the trail. And to deepen
the paradox even further, the ancient Zen masters command that if you

meet the Buddha on the trail, you must kill him straight away, because grandly proclaiming that you are a buddha, or enlightened or awakened, a guru or a master of the trail, or whatever superlative you want to apply to yourself, is a surefire indication that you have missed the mark and are headed for trouble. A jerk, if you will.

The obverse is equally true. Bemoaning your worthlessness, surrendering to self-pity, doubting your ability, quaking in fear of the unknown, and the long list of other misgivings and mental infirmities that can plague us from day to day are foibles that can hobble even the strongest hiker. The master admonishes you to kill all of that.

And in time, if you keep at it with the proper attitude, neither smug nor despairing, the miles will pile up, there will be something about you that is different, something discernible, something perhaps difficult to articulate or explain, but something very real and consequential. And it is not just the strong muscles and the bug bites and the skinny waistline and body odor that will set you apart. It will be both a physical and a mental metamorphosis. Thru-hikers begin to realize this toward the end of their journey, but the overwhelming majority of them resist the temptation to discuss or even think about it. After two thousand miles of walking, they are too focused on their immediate tasks and their daily routines to delve into such weighty matters. And it sounds premature to them. Stuff can still happen. You have not climbed a mountain until you stand on its summit, and even then, you have to get down off the thing and figure out what comes next. In that sense, you are not ever finished.

Being a former journalist and possessing a curiosity about what the trail does or does not do to a person who hikes it, I developed the habit of asking pesky questions whenever I encountered a thru-hiker who had either completed the Appalachian Trail, or nearly had, and was willing to consider my queries seriously. Over the several years I was on the trail, I informally collected the answers. There were a few common denominators among them. "I know I can do anything now," was the answer a young woman gave me with a serious look on her face that said she was not going to elaborate. "I learned a lot about myself," was a frequent answer, followed by awkward silence. "It restored my faith in humanity," was another, sometimes highlighted by a story of kindness or compassion encountered on the trail. Not one thru-hiker I ever questioned bragged about their achievement. Successful thru-hikers were instead mostly humbled and amazed by what they had done. Proud, yes, but also aware that they had received a rare and valuable gift. Speaking too much about this gift apparently was unseemly, even wrong. Many thru-hikers I buttonholed to ask about their experiences and how it had affected them soon found a way to change the subject entirely or divert the discussion away from themselves.

Hiking in Maine, I began to ask the question with a sharper purpose. The northbound thru-hikers were close now, just a few hundred miles from Katahdin. They had to be thinking about the end, if for no other reason than to arrange the logistics of where they would go afterward and how they would travel. And as I hiked up and down the peaks of the Bigelow Range of mountains, headed north, I realized that meeting these hardened, tough, trail-wise thru-hikers was a bit like meeting an authentic buddha, a bodhisattva, not the pretend kind reflected in a mirror. They just knew. I could spot it in their manner, the way they walked, the way they went about their camp chores, the look in their eyes, the massive sinews in their legs, the raggedness of their clothes, and even the way they carried their backpacks. Among the cadre of young men nearing the completion of their thru-hikes the wild scraggly beards and long uncombed hair and mud stains no detergent could remove were the first giveaways. Among the young women it was often the deep tans of their bare arms and legs, the lean, muscular gracefulness of their bodies, and an all-grown-up-now warrior fierceness in their eyes. Older hikers, middle-aged or so, possessed these qualities but also radiated a calmness and a less energetic demeanor that bespoke their age and the wear and tear the trail had inflicted on their bodies. A limp in their gait, or a stooped shoulder, or multiple bruises and healed cuts, plus a world-weary, beat-up-but-still-plugging away look were the tells. Wanderer, the hiker I met in New York who broke his arm and kept hiking, was the best example I knew of this iron-hard, printing-peace-and-serenity-with-every-step tranquility. As was Saint Pete two years earlier, a man who kissed the earth with his feet if ever any hiker has. The image of a wandering monk, sage, or modern-day hermit is not too far afield from the look of an Appalachian Trail thru-hiker, young or old, after two thousand miles of walking every day.

I knew that I had not earned entry into their class. A photograph I took of myself on a mountaintop in southern Maine with the mist-shrouded peak of Avery Mountain in the background that shows my backpack askew and a bewilderment at the wildness of it all on my face is evidence of what I must have looked like to the hardened thru-hikers who encountered me on the trail. But the amazing thing is that the northbound thru-hikers I met in Maine without a single exception accepted me as one of their own and without any reservation or smugness that I could detect.

"You're out here, man. That's what matters," was the way a young army veteran put it when I brought the subject up at Gentian Shelter on a rainy evening. There it was again, what Cogs told me back in Virginia, very nearly the same words. Again, the words of someone who knows. A buddha, of sorts, but a buddha too humbled by the miles to claim any labels or status.

On the morning of my seventy-second birthday, I was thinking about these things when I lay in my sleeping bag inside Bald Mountain Lean-to waiting for first light. I had hiked fifteen miles the day before—the longest one-day stretch so far on this hike—and I had made a good decision not to stay at a shelter along the way that had a poor water source and was probably infested with mice because it was close to a public road and obviously used by day-hikers and overnight campers since scraps of food wrappers were scattered on the ground. After paddling across the Kennebec River in a canoe with the white blaze painted on the bottom below the seat I was sitting on, I had spent a day at Sterling Inn near Caratunk recovering from hard miles and had again enjoyed the company of Rodeo, the thru-hiker from Texas I had met way back at Rattle River. I was eating better and hiking better, and the climbs were not as agonizing. I could feel a new strength in my legs. But these things were superficial, and I knew better than to think the hiking would no longer be so hard.

And as I set out on the trail from Bald Mountain Lean-to a rumble of distant thunder announced an approaching storm. About time, I thought. No hiker goes any substantial distance on the Appalachian Trail without dealing with thunderstorms, and today was evidently going to be my initiation into what a Maine thunderstorm could be. I slid the rain cover over my backpack, put on my rain jacket, and got on with it. Facing me was a climb up and over Moxie Bald, a mountain not particularly tall but peculiar in that it stands alone, protruding off a low plain. The broad summit is exposed rock. As I began the climb the rain caught me and came down hard. Within five minutes everything I was wearing was wet to my skin. Rainwater poured down the trail, filled every depression, and overtopped my shoes with each step. In places the trail immediately became a rushing stream. I climbed steadily, resisting the temptation to either hurry or slow down, the roar of the rain and the thunder echoing loud under my rain hood. I had to endure this, to tough it out. Actually, the storm was no big deal. Lightning lit the dark sky occasionally but was not directly on top of me.

The climb was no more difficult than any of the others I had already made, and after thirty minutes in the downpour I was close to the summit. The hard rain weakened to a steady drizzle and the rumbles of thunder were more distant, now rolling off to the east as the storm passed Moxie Bald. I was relieved not to have lightning bouncing around as I leveled off on the mountain in swirls of fog and a thick mist, for the summit was in fact shaped like the top of a loaf of bread, a long, rounded ridge of exposed, smooth rock and widely scattered young spruce trees and low alpine shrubs—not a good place to be if lightning was striking in the vicinity. The rain tapered off more as I began to descend, and I gave some thought to what I might do next. I decided to pull into Moxie Bald Lean-to at the base of the mountain to see if I could dry off and eat lunch out of the rain. When I arrived well before noon, I was pleased to find that the shelter was situated in a handsome grove of tall spruce trees on the shore of a beautiful Maine lake. The rain had finally stopped but under the tree canopy raindrops were still dripping off the spruce needles. I dropped my backpack and walked down to some rocks at the water's edge. A rocky island populated with a few spruce trees, a tree-lined distant shore, clear blue water, the clouds breaking up and patches of blue sky appearing—it was postcard lovely. Even though I had put in only a few miles, this was where I would spend the rest of the day, I decided on the spot. I stripped off my wet clothes, wrung them out, and spread them on the rocks to dry in the sun; pitched my tent; ate a leisurely lunch down by the pond; and basked in the freedom to do nothing at this serene place for the rest of the day.

Around mid- to late afternoon a young northbound thru-hiker arrived. Lean, of course, but also neat and tidy and clean-shaven, unlike most male thru-hikers his age. His trail name was Ice Cube and there was something else unusual about him that at first I could not define. Soft-spoken, almost shy, but also exuding the confidence and toughness of a thru-hiker, he decided to camp by the shore, and he quietly put up his tent and arranged his gear in a methodical manner. After a while, he joined me at the rocks where I was sitting in the sun in my underwear.

Something about the sunshine, the wavelets lapping at the rocks, the clear water of the pond, the blue sky after the thunderstorms of the morning, the distant line of trees and the craggy island that made a pretty picture—something induced this reserved young man to begin a conversation with me. He was from Indiana. He had left Amicalola Falls State Park and hiked the Approach Trail up to Springer Mountain to begin his thru-hike on May 17. Upon hearing this my mouth must have fallen open. That meant he had covered 2,060 miles in ninety days—an average of almost twenty-three miles per day, *every one of those ninety days!* And with only 133 miles to go, Ice Cube expected to climb Katahdin within a week and be back home in time for university classes to begin. During his hike he had seen twelve bears, three moose, and one bobcat. He had not hooked up with other thru-hikers or joined a trail "tramily," as these informal groups are called. He had sworn off all social media and unplugged himself from phone calls, music, and other distractions. He had not taken time off. He had slowed down to "only" fifteen miles per day in the Whites because of the horrible weather, but now he had resumed his accustomed twenty-four-to-twenty-six-miles-per-day pace here in Maine. And yet he was not in a hurry. He had decided to quit early this day because he liked this beautiful spot and he wanted to enjoy the evening in the sunshine. And possibly a little companionship with an inquisitive old man.

So I asked Ice Cube the question I had posed to other northbound thru-hikers: "Has your experience on the trail changed you in any way?"

He did not answer immediately, just gazed across the pond at the distant tree-lined shore, squinting against the sun. "No, not really," he finally said. But then he shifted his weight on the rock and his face took on a new, serious expression, as though something inherent in the contradiction of what he had just said had made him want to amend his answer.

"But it has made me realize what can be done in ninety days," he said. "Ninety days to get here . . . to a place like this . . . it's amazing. I will never again waste time. If I can do this in ninety days, just think. . . ."

His voice trailed off, as though he were making a mental list of all the things he could do in ninety days. Incredible things. Important things to do and to know from having done them. And he had made this statement in all sincerity while sitting on a warm rock in the evening sunshine beside a Maine pond conversing with an old man celebrating his seventy-second birthday by eating a honey bun that he had carefully stashed away in his food bag just for this occasion.

We did not talk much after that. Instead, we watched the sun drop toward the far tree line and the light on the pond go golden orange, then soft pink. We watched frogs paddling in the shallow water amid the rocks. One frog waddled onto a rock beside my shoes drying in the sun, attracted by the honeybees that were crawling over it. With a deadly aim, the frog zapped a bee, swallowed it, and plopped back into the pond. We looked at each other in amazement. Ice Cube nodded, as though this discovery that a frog could eat a honeybee belonged on his list of incredible things to know, incredible things he had seen since Springer Mountain.

I was in the presence of a young trail buddha. The genuine article. What a wonderful birthday gift for an old man.

❧

The next day brought a change. The Appalachian Trail north of Moxie Bald begins a long and gradual, almost imperceptible twelve-mile slope down to the West Branch of the Piscataquis River and on to the East Branch. From the river crossing of the East Branch, it is just a few bumpy miles to Maine Highway 15 and the nearby village of Monson. When

northbound hikers cross that highway and reenter the woods, almost the
first thing they see along the trail is a sign proclaiming the beginning of
the famed One Hundred Mile Wilderness. A trip into Monson for rest
and resupply is therefore usually in order because no more opportunities arise until the end of the Wilderness at a little store and campground
at Abol Bridge. And at Abol Bridge, hikers are standing in the shadow of
Katahdin itself.

I had long before planned to take a break from the trail in Monson
at the famous Shaw's Hiker Hostel run by Poet and Hippy Chick, a well-
known and very respected couple who thru-hiked a few years before and
then bought and renovated the hostel. But before I could enjoy the luxu-
ries of a shower and a real bed, clean clothes, and good food, I had those
long, mostly flat miles to hike. I naïvely thought the distance to Monson
would be a breeze compared to the mountain climbing and rough terrain
I had already traveled, but I was dead wrong about that. I should have
known better. After all, I was still in Maine, and the state is notorious
for its difficulty over the entire length of the A.T. all the way from New
Hampshire to Katahdin. No more big, rugged climbs for a while, it was
true. Instead, the trail introduced me to river crossings and Maine's infamous miles of rocks and roots.

The rivers and streams in central Maine were at record low levels
due to a drought earlier in the summer. I was able to rock-hop over Bald
Mountain Stream, Marble Brook, and even the broad West Branch of the
Piscataquis, which the trail guides had said would require a ford because
it was normally knee-deep. Even though the weather was beautiful, the
evergreen forest was lovely, and the trail was not burdensome, I found
myself struggling through the morning. What was wrong with me? I
wondered. My energy was low, my back and neck hurt, my backpack was
not riding correctly on my hips, and I kept stopping to adjust the straps,
to no avail. My attitude turned rotten. How was it that this many miles
and days into a hike I was having such trouble? Why had I not figured this
out by now?

I was supposed to be getting better at hiking, not worse. Stronger,
not a walking box of pains. My shoes were still wet from the rainstorm
the morning before, and my feet hurt. The trail, after crossing the river,

paralleled the stream for a while but deteriorated into a never-ending series of little ups and downs chopped and webbed and cluttered by rocks
and roots so thick the walking was like frog marching across a bed of hot
coals and broken glass. What should have been a fine day instead slid me
ever deeper into a funk of my own making, and I took it out on the Appalachian Trail, on Maine, on those damn rocks and roots, and finally,
when I had exhausted all other targets to vent my frustration, on myself.
Here we go again, I thought.

The Zen Buddhist master Shunryū Suzuki calls this type of negativity "mind weeds." And he reminds us that just as we must weed our gar-
dens each day, we must do the same for our minds, for it is inevitable
that some weeds will sprout alongside the desirable plants. And that
rather than being frustrated by the weeds, we should understand that
mind weeds are just waves in our mind. Suzuki said we should actually be
grateful for these weeds because if we recognize them for what they are
and learn how to convert them into "mental nourishment" the weeds will
help us maintain a balanced state of mind. Food for better thoughts, so
to speak.[2]

Weeds left unchecked can, of course, choke the life out of a garden.
And on this day, I was getting perilously close to full-bore hiker rebellion
from all those weeds. At about the moment in the early afternoon when
I was ready to throw my trekking poles into the nearby river and my legs
were on the verge of going on strike, I crested a hill and looked down on
a remarkable sight. Coming toward me was Nimblewill Nomad. I recognized him immediately, though we had never met. Nimblewill Nomad
is a celebrity among Appalachian Trail hikers—one of the great sages,
a master of the practice of simply walking. Nearing the age of eighty-
three, he was attempting to become the oldest man to thru-hike the Appalachian Trail, a feat he accomplished a few months after I met him. He
was heading south on this day, but his hike had started at his home in
south Alabama, where he took the Pinhoti Trail 348 miles northeast into
Georgia, then the Benton MacKaye Trail seventy-two miles south out of
the Cohutta Mountains and up to Springer Mountain, and then the Appalachian Trail on toward Katahdin—fifteen states and 2,620 miles. He
had already thru-hiked the A.T. several times, plus tens of thousands of

miles along roads and byways on more than twenty long-distance treks, including a famous one from Key West to Nova Scotia. This one, "Bama to Baxter," he claimed, was his "last, last time."

Nimblewill had fallen on the trail not long before we met. His left arm sleeve was bloody, and his legs were scraped and bleeding from several cuts. Yet he smiled broadly at me from behind his enormous gray beard and gladly stopped to talk.

"Can I help you?" I asked after I introduced myself.

"No, I'll clean myself up when I get to the river crossing. The old A.T. is just beating me up a little today, that's all."

He was a small man and a bit frail, but his eyes retained the sparkle of a fellow enjoying life, doing what he loved to do. Even if blood was running down his arm. He understood the Appalachian Trail probably better than any hiker who has walked it since Earl Shaffer or Dan Bruce. He expected tough days. Even when the sun was shining. Nimblewill said that he fell at least once every day he was on the trail now. But each time he just got up and kept walking. Complaining does no good, he said. The trail was different now from when he first thru-hiked it years ago, he said. More worn and ragged and rough. Like him. But still wonderful, and there was nowhere else he wanted to be than out here.

I told him I had been having a wobbly day of my own and I was grateful for having met him and hoped I could make it all the way to Katahdin on this trip, but I wasn't sure.

"Oh, you'll make it all right. Don't worry about that," he said, and his Southern drawl was so sincere that I believed him.

I left Nimblewill and continued on toward Horseshoe Canyon Lean-to bouncing over the rocks and roots and humming a tune, my pains and aches absorbed into a new feeling of gratitude. Gratitude for the mind weeds, for the incredible beauty of the forest and rapids and waterfalls of the river, for the chance meeting with Nimblewill Nomad, for just the simple fact that I was on the Appalachian Trail in Maine walking upright in one piece with the scrapes on my arm from my fall two weeks earlier healing nicely. Another day, another authentic trail buddha. How lucky was that?

Dangerously Close

The scene at Shaw's Hiker Hostel during the thru-hiker season is like something out of a late sixties rock festival except that most of the people there, the hikers and the small crew who run the place, were not born then, and Jimi Hendrix and Janis Joplin are no longer around to supply the live rock music. Shaw's consists of a cluster of adapted buildings, a home-hostel with a few private rooms and a kitchen, a bunk house, a converted barn-bathhouse, a laundry, and another house on a quiet back street in the village of Monson, a municipality that does just fine without a stoplight. Hikers headed both north and south flock to Shaw's for several reasons. The proprietors, Poet and Hippy Chick, are well known among the hiking community for their hospitality, infinite patience, enthusiasm and love of the Appalachian Trail, respect for thru-hikers and section hikers, and, mostly importantly, deep knowledge of the ins and outs of the One Hundred Mile Wilderness that begins on their doorstep. Monson is the closest supply point for northbound hikers entering the Wilderness, and it is the first refuge for the southbounders exiting the Wilderness. And Shaw's is a fun place.

On a typical August evening, between twenty and thirty-five longhaired, bearded men and lean and tan women in tank tops and shorts were milling around the small yard between the buildings, swapping trail gossip, meeting trail buddies they had not seen in weeks, eating pints of ice cream from the corner general store up the street, playing guitars, drinking beer around a fire ring, and openly lighting up a few marijuana joints to pass around. The beer flowed, the joints circulated, the laughter and songs reverberated in the soft Maine evening air. When the bunk house and private rooms are full, Poet and Hippy Chick allow late-arriving hikers to put up their tents on the grass between the buildings. On the August evening I arrived and did just that, I counted seventeen tents on the grounds. Every morning Poet fires up a big restaurant-capacity range in the kitchen and turns out a huge breakfast of eggs, bacon, hashbrowns, and blueberry pancakes delivered to the tables by a couple of hard-working staff. Then around 9:00 a.m. Poet opens his gear shop and hikers crowd inside to buy supplies for the next leg of their hike or to arrange food drops in the One Hundred Mile Wilderness so they do not have to lug seven or eight days of food with them when they set out at the trailhead.

I arrived at Shaw's badly in need of some rest and decent food. I had lost enough weight that my pants were loose around my waist, and my feet now had that familiar odd tingling sensitivity that would not go away, even when I propped them up at night. Shaw's was the perfect spot to recuperate, clean myself up, do some laundry, visit with hikers, and eat a few of Poet's enormous breakfasts. Soon after I arrived, Rodeo and his two trail buddies, Brass, a retired marine colonel, and Bongo, a Philadelphia emergency responder, pulled in, hauled off their backpacks, and went looking for food. We sat around a picnic table outside in the twilight telling trail stories, each of us devouring a pint of Ben and Jerry's ice cream.

And the next day I had a wonderful surprise—Wanderer and Merlot arrived on a shuttle from the trailhead. I had not seen either of them since the day in New York when I met them at a trail junction three days after Wanderer broke his arm. Now his arm was no longer in a sling tightly strapped to his chest, but it still was in a cast and he still could not use his hand.

"The doctor said I should have surgery to fix it," he said after we exchanged greetings and I asked about how he was managing. "But I told him not until I finish."

How in the world, I wondered aloud, could Wanderer have climbed the mountains in the Whites, then the Wildcats, and then managed Mahoosuc Notch and everything else Maine fires at a hiker with a broken arm in a cast?

"I've adapted," he said quietly. "I've learned to use my elbow to push on the rocks." His biggest problem was still hauling on and off his backpack but even that was getting better.

And Merlot, was she still enjoying a plastic cup of red wine every evening on the trail? She gave me a sheepish look and said no, she had to quit doing that. From the barest hint of a grin on Wanderer's face as she said this, I guessed a story lay behind this decision. He provided few details but evidently Merlot had learned a hard lesson somewhere in New England about drinking wine and hiking in tough conditions.

And what about Hammer, where was he?

"A week or so behind us, but he's catching up pretty fast," Wanderer said. Hammer had gotten off the trail to attend a wedding and handle some personal business. Horizontal intersecting with vertical again.

Every hiker at Shaw's was making plans. The northbounders did not really care to know much about the One Hundred Mile Wilderness that the southbounders had just completed. They had already walked the meanest miles Maine had to trouble them and they were not worried about any stretch of the trail anymore. The topic dominating the northbounders' minds was Katahdin and the intricacies of negotiating Baxter State Park's strict rules for hikers. The southbounders, and there were a surprising number of them at Shaw's, wanted to know what was coming at them next, how hard was southern Maine, the Mahoosuc Notch and the Whites. Neither group could really fully satisfy the curiosity of the other. As Keats observed, it would not be real until the hikers experienced it firsthand.

For me, the next challenge was the One Hundred Mile Wilderness. After two days enjoying the comforts and companionship of hikers at Shaw's, I was eager to get back on the trail. And I had decided to take advantage of a not-so-secret weapon to get through the first half of it—slackpacking.

How do you define success when you are attempting a hard thing? Completing the thing, of course, but is success always that simple? If you set your mind on running a marathon, and on your first attempt make it only twenty-five miles instead of the requisite twenty-six, is that total failure? Or a partial success? Or is partial success an oxymoron, a cop-out, a chiseler's way of making excuses? And what about hiking the Appalachian Trail? The Appalachian Trail Conservancy defines a thru-hike as hiking the entire trail in a one-year period, but does that mean you have to string the miles together in some sort of geographical continuity or can you skip around—say hike the New England portion in the summer and drop down south to hike Georgia to Virginia in the late fall and early winter? And slackpacking . . . is that in some perverse way the same as taking a shortcut? And what about the fact that the route, and therefore the length, of the Appalachian Trail is not a fixed or permanent entity?

Relocations and closures due to bridges out or other issues are constantly altering in small ways the experience of hiking the A.T. Over a few years, those small changes add up to new distances and new places. In 2021 the trail gained 1.2 miles of official length due to relocations in West Virginia, Pennsylvania, and the New York-Connecticut state line. And the relocation in Pennsylvania abandoned the tortuous climb up the Palmerton Zinc Rock Pile where I had fallen while sitting down and bloodied my hands. The trail now goes *around* the Pile instead of over it. The COVID-19 outbreak completely upended the ability to hike the Appalachian Trail safely in 2020 and had spillover effects the next two years. So hiking the trail in one year is not the same as hiking it in another. My section hike, if I completed it, would be 2,193 miles. For hikers setting out in 2022, the distance would be 2,194 miles, and the year after that the trail would no doubt grow or shrink by a small fraction again.[1] Does that mean some thru-hikes or section hikes are marginally better than others? Or is this all just trail trivia and meaningless confabulation?

And for a section hiker like me, these questions only multiplied over the time I spent on the trail, planning to get back on the trail, and wishing I could be out there but knowing that I could not. Time . . . that was my most precious commodity, time to be out there, away from home and responsibilities, time that could be cut short unexpectedly at any juncture. I had been thinking about these questions at Shaw's as I frittered away the hours talking to hikers, eating ice cream or hot sandwiches, and studying trail maps. My time was running out. Not just for this hike in Maine but for the whole thing. When I began, way back in Georgia with my day hikes, my idea was just to explore the Appalachian Trail sections that were an hour's drive from my home. That evolved into sampling the trail as a backpacker in the Smokies, which despite all my mistakes up there morphed into the idea of seeing how far north I could go toward Virginia, which serendipitously took me to New Hampshire, which then somehow became the crazy notion that I could hike the whole thing. Behind all this was the specter of failure that had stretched all the way back to Africa and had followed me like a dark shadow for all those years. Would hiking the A.T. be yet another failure? And now I was tantalizingly but dangerously close. If . . . and it was a very big if . . . if I could make it all the way to the summit of Katahdin on this trip, I would have exactly 309 miles of Appalachian Trail remaining. Maybe that was not success, but it was darn close to it, much closer than I had expected to get when I started in the Smokies years earlier.

But there was a problem with this line of thinking about success. The seventy-nine miles I had already skipped here in Maine covered some of the Appalachian Trail's most intimidating stretches, with Baldpate, West and East Peaks, Wyman, Moody, Old Blue, Bemis, Saddleback, The Horn, Saddleback Junior, Lone Mountain, Spaulding Mountain, South Crocker and North Crocker, in that order, fourteen major peaks, one right after the other, just daring an old section hiker like me to try them. The northbound thru-hikers at Shaw's spoke of this stretch of the Appalachian Trail with awe, reverence, and tremendous respect. No hiker of any definition who presumed to claim full A.T. success could do so without hiking those giants.

So, was skipping them a mistake? Should I have kept going north from Grafton Notch? No . . . my decision had been the right one, and I would live with the consequences of it. Whether I could ever come back to Maine and dare face those monsters would have to be a question without an answer for at least another year, just as it had been when I completed the Whites and watched Doc set out to cross the Androscoggin

River and head up into Maine. Next for me was the One Hundred Mile Wilderness. I had just enough time to complete it in a reasonable fashion, and I knew better than to believe anyone who told me it would be easy. Nothing about the Appalachian Trail in Maine is easy.

But the slackpacking would help, and I rejected any notion that I should feel guilty about hiking it that way. The One Hundred Mile Wilderness has the reputation of being a vast chunk of inaccessible forest between Monson and Baxter State Park, but a number of dirt roads cross this immense tract of land. The difference is that timber companies own and maintain these roads, and they restrict access to them. Find someone who has access, and you have the key to cutting the One Hundred Mile Wilderness into manageable sections. And at Shaw's, Poet had the access and the knowledge to do just that. He routinely shuttled hikers into the first half of the One Hundred Mile Wilderness at various spots, picked them up at the end of the day, and even met them with food drops.

My first day tackling the One Hundred Mile Wilderness was fabulous. With my backpack weight reduced to just a few pounds of snacks, water, and survival essentials, I attacked the trail at a pace that I had never experienced before. The climbs were modest, and I got up and down them well. I enjoyed the variety of ponds, forest, and exposed bare rock. The feeling of walking along with a freedom of movement and the absence of aches and pains was unique and wonderful. The miles rolled by, and at the end of them I had a shuttle back to Shaw's, a good dinner, a shower, and a bed to sleep in. What could be better?

The next few days were progressively harder as I climbed Barren Mountain, Fourth Mountain, and Third Mountain, and then hiked through the Chairback Range. Though not as tall as the Bigelows, the terrain over these mountains was very rugged and my pace slowed considerably. Some of the forests through this area were beautiful, with larger spruce and big white pines, but the land was a tumult of ridges, small peaks, deep gaps, and mountainsides with the ever-present rocks, roots, and mud.

One final significant mountain stood between me and Katahdin. I tackled Whitecap Mountain on a gloomy day going southbound on the advice of Poet. At 3,650-feet, Whitecap's peak is well above the tree line, has plenty of exposed bare rock, and from its north side on a clear day hikers can get their first view of Katahdin far to the north. But I started the climb in heavy mist that turned to rain, and I knew there would be no view of Katahdin from the summit. The rain stopped once I hiked over the top, but I was in thick clouds and could see only thirty or forty yards in any direction. The fifteen-mile hike was a long, tough slog. But in the afternoon, just as the heat began to drag down my pace, I met Popsicle coming toward me. We enjoyed a brief, cheerful reunion and I wished her well as she headed deeper into the One Hundred Mile Wilderness. Later I forded the west branch of the Pleasant River, wading across in my Crocs camp shoes, and a shuttle met me for the ride back to Shaw's.

The next day a shuttle deposited me at Logan Brook Road with fifty-five miles of the One Hundred Mile Wilderness behind me and five days of food in my backpack. Late in the morning I climbed a puny 1,980-foot bump called Little Boardman Mountain, and when I turned around to look back southwest, I saw an awe-inspiring sight—the Bigelow Range in the distance, Avery and West Bigelow peaks just discernible on the horizon. To look at such distant mountains and know I had hiked over them days earlier gave me a little shot of pride and courage, most of which would evaporate in the coming days, but on this day everything went right. I crossed a stream by rock-hopping, and the trail flattened out and soon brought me to Cooper Brook Falls Lean-to, which was set just above a big stream that featured rapids and a broad, deep pool of clear, cold water where several hikers had gone swimming and were now drying off in the sun on big flat rocks. Hikers had already claimed all the good tent spots, so I spent the night in the shelter, sleeping well after a fine day. The next morning, I was hiking before 6:00 a.m. under clear skies, feeling good and ambitiously considering a 15.7-mile day to Nah-makanta Stream Lean-to. Within an hour everything changed, and my hike threatened to crash to an ignominious end.

Loons' Lament

Pain in one form or another is a near constant companion for most long-distance hikers. Feet, knees, back, shoulders—these are the most frequent sources, but there are plenty of others, from cuts and bruises to insect stings and rashes to stomach upsets, chaffing, shin splints, and smashed toes . . . the list goes on and on. I had experienced mild pains since my third day out of Rattle River, but the odd thing was, out on the trail they moved around on my body from day to day and even from hour to hour. One day my neck would hurt in the morning from constantly keeping my head down and my eyes on where I was putting my feet. Then in the afternoon that would go away, and my left hip would feel pinched. And then I would adjust my pack straps and it would be fine for an hour, but my right hip would start hurting. Or my right shoulder. Then the next day it would be my upper back in the morning and my left foot that afternoon. It was as though the various parts of my body undergoing the stress of constant work took turns complaining about the abuse they were suffering and petulantly demanded that I stop.

I knew to expect this, and I figured out how to manage it. Midmorning was often time for an Ibuprofen. "Vitamin I" in the lexicon of thruhikers. Sometimes simply stopping for five or ten minutes and eating something while I sat on a log or rock would do the trick. Fiddling with the straps on my pack sometimes helped but sometimes was futile. In places the trail was so narrow and the spruce so dense that I had to push my way through, and the stiff branches would snag my pack and pull at it, loosening the straps or dragging my sleep pad to one side so the balance was off. On a particularly onerous day I might need another Ibuprofen late in the afternoon, or I would cut the day short if I came to a shelter or decent camp spot and spend a lazy hour or two just lying on my back. For twenty-one trail days these techniques, plus a day of rest at a hostel here and there, had mostly worked and the aches and pains were manageable. Just part of the deal I had signed up for.

Until day twenty-two. The trail that morning was just Maine being Maine—rocks and roots, rocks and roots, and then some mud. Nothing special. But after an hour of hiking, I was in trouble. Serious pain flared deep in my lower back, and I both knew and dreaded the new source: arthritis. This had happened to me once before, way back in Tennessee after crossing the Roan Highlands. I had endured an entire day on one of the most beautiful stretches of the Appalachian Trail that hikers can enjoy twisted and hobbled by lower back pain that had dialed up and up until by the time I reached the trailhead at US 19 I could barely walk.

This time, however, I was 32.6 miles from Abol Bridge by the time I eased myself into Potaywadjo Spring Lean-to, more than four miles short of Nahmakanta. I could not figure out what I had done to myself to cause this excruciating flare-up, but there it was, like a stiletto lodged near my lower spine, the point just waiting for a wrong move, a bend or twist or bad step, to jab into the bone. Walking out of here was the only option, and from the way I felt, that was going to take a long time. I decided to put up my tent instead of sleeping on the hard shelter platform, but the simple task of bending down to drive in the tent stakes brought stabs of pain in my back. I ate some lunch, carefully collected two liters of water from a nearby stream, slow-walked back to my tent, stripped off my sweaty clothes, and gingerly laid down on my inflated mattress for the rest of the afternoon, wondering how in the world I had managed to haul myself more than eleven miles in this condition. I lay as still as possible staring at the flies trapped between my transparent tent roof and the outer rain fly and tried not to think about Katahdin. This therapy, such as it was, would have to work; otherwise, how would I get myself out of the One Hundred Mile Wilderness? How far would I be able to hike tomorrow? Four miles to Nahmakanta Stream? Or the more than ten miles to Wadleigh Stream Lean-to? Or was that crazy?

This was one-day-at-a-time territory. In my head I went over the necessary distances to hike out of the Wilderness with the food supply I had: a little more than ten miles tomorrow, if possible, then maybe eight, and then either eleven miles to the final shelter on the Appalachian Trail at Hurd Brook or an additional four miles all the way to Abol Bridge. Then, if I had any hope of climbing Katahdin, another nine or ten miles across Baxter State Park. But the biggest test would be the day after tomorrow because the trail climbed Nesuntabunt Mountain, the last little bump before Katahdin. Any of these sections could end me if the arthritis went into the red zone and stayed there like it had over the Roan Highlands back in Tennessee.

During the night I heard loons calling, their eerie, mournful sounds very distant, then closer, then far away again, keeping me awake and wondering what was to come and whether I could walk in the morning. As if the loons were lamenting my condition.

The next morning, after a few hours of sleep, I felt better, but the simple tasks of breaking camp and taking down my tent emphasized my fragile state. I had to lean against a tree for a few moments to let the pain subside after pulling out the tent stakes. Everything I did—rolling up my sleeping bag and stowing away the tent and arranging my gear in my backpack—was slow and methodical and fraught with tension. I carefully hauled on my backpack, grabbed my trekking poles, and set out tentatively on the trail in the early light vowing to make zero mistakes with my footing this day, to survive the trail as much as walk it.

And then, after less than a mile walking ever so slowly under a perfect blue sky, testing every step like a man walking on ice, something magical and poignant happened. The trail brought me alongside Pemadumcook Lake, probably the place from which the loons had been calling during the night. A short side trail led to some rocks by the lakeshore, and a sign announced simply "View." By this point I had seen enough of Maine's ponds and lakes not to be terribly interested in seeing another of those lovely tableaus, especially in my damaged condition. But something about the sign and the morning light and the shimmering blue water attracted me. Maybe I would see a moose out there.

No, what I saw when I stepped out onto a rock and looked north was the ghost outline of Katahdin reflected on the still blue water and the great mountain itself looming on the horizon, its summit wreathed in fluffy white clouds, the gauzy profile instantly recognizable from the many pictures I had seen. But this was the real thing softly glowing in the early morning light. Katahdin was now real because I could see it with my own eyes. I stood on the rock mesmerized and grateful for what I was seeing but tormented by the idea that I had come all this way and now probably would be denied the opportunity to climb Katahdin because of the pain in my back. Would it be possible to recover enough in the next few days to try? Or would the pain only grow worse—was I being wildly and unreasonably optimistic? And if I did not get to go up this time, would I ever get another chance? And if I did not summit Katahdin, now or later, would I have to consider my entire Appalachian Trail section hike a failure? Of course, I would. The trail terminus, after all, was at the 5,268-foot summit and the famous sign, not down below at the campground at the base of the mountain.

I hiked the rest of the day to Wadleigh Stream Lean-to in a state of suspense and dread, every step over a root or around a rock a threat to my tender back. I remembered what Nimblewill Nomad had told me— "You'll make it. Don't worry." He had assured me with such confidence in his voice, as if there were no doubt. All I had to do was believe and get up every time I fell, like him. Miraculously, the trail was not difficult to hike. I forded a stream without a problem and filled up with water at a little brook that emptied into nearby Nahmakanta Lake. I tried with some success to concentrate on each footstep rather than worry about my back or fret about whether I would be able to climb Katahdin. I had my backpack perfectly adjusted and balanced—no problem there. The day was warm, and I was sweating a lot but also drinking plenty of water and feeling strong.

On a particularly gnarly stretch of roots my foot came down wrong on one and slipped sideways and down I went, but incredibly with no dam-

age to any part of me, not even a scratch or a twinge. And yet the simple
act of reaching for one of my trekking poles shot the blade into my lower
back and doubled me over. Minutes passed before I could risk getting
to my knees and then unbending myself enough to stand up. The un-
predictability of the pain and what provoked it was unnerving. At midday the trail that had paralleled Nahmakanta Lake popped me out on a
gravel road, and unbelievably a big RV was parked there, and a cheerful woman was dispensing hot dogs, cold drinks, and snacks to hikers.
Here in the middle of the One Hundred Mile Wilderness . . . how could
this be possible? It was because her daughter was thru-hiking here—I
had already met her once—and the mom wanted to help out. So the lady
had solved the maze of roads to find this trailhead and arranged her trail
magic on exactly the right day to rendezvous with her daughter. I gratefully ate one of her hog dogs and a few other snacks and, most enjoyable
of all, sat in a folding easy chair resting my back for ten minutes. It was
heaven . . . sheer heaven.

❦

The word "wilderness" has lost much of its meaning when applied to
anywhere east of the Mississippi River. Just because we proclaim an area
of forest or mountains a wilderness does not make it one. There was a
time, of course, when vast swaths of the Eastern Seaboard were wilderness, but that time is long past. Timber has been harvested over nearly all
of Maine. Plenty of square miles of the state are remote and rugged, as a
view from any of its mountain peaks will immediately confirm, but people have thoroughly explored and exploited those forests. Along the Appalachian Trail, which takes advantage of some of Maine's most remote
territory, very few stands of old growth trees remain. And encountering a
parked RV where the trail crossed a dirt road deep into the One Hundred
Mile Wilderness just put an exclamation point on the fact that I was not
wandering in the middle of nowhere. If the condition of my back pain
had crossed a red line, I could have been hauled out of there somehow
without having to walk myself all the way out to Abol Bridge, as I had
originally feared.

But after I left Wadleigh Stream Lean-to, the Appalachian Trail entered a region that truly had the feel of a wilderness, or at least a good approximation of one. The climb up Nesuntabunt Mountain wandered through a dazzling array of colossal mossy boulders, rock formations, and big trees. The trail went right over the forested summit and back down the north side. Then came a couple of ponds where I was certain I would see a moose at any moment. And then the sheer cliffsides of Pollywog Gorge, which I was grateful the trail sidestepped because from what I could see from its edge, going down in there would have been exponentially harder than the Mahoosuc Notch. And after lunch at Rainbow Stream Lean-to, the trail alongside Rainbow Lake for the better part of a mile was a mess that bore the informal name of "the root canal," a stretch that Poet had warned hikers about as they left Monson for the One Hundred Mile Wilderness. Here was where I began to hope with some slender supporting evidence that my back would be okay because every yard was a torture of tree roots and every step an opportunity to trip and fall flat on my face or twist my spine into a pretzel. And yet I managed the root canal okay. My shoes literally did not touch soil for an hour. I was actually grateful when the trail finally veered away from the lake for a short distance and just climbed awhile over rocks.

I finished the day at a camp spot called Rainbow Spring and pitched my tent underneath trees fifty yards or so up a hill from the lakeshore. Again, bending over to drive in the stakes without sending my lower back into wicked spasms was a difficult chore. As I settled in for the night, my assessment of the situation was that I had maybe fifty-fifty odds of climbing Katahdin if I could get there without doing any more damage to my back. I had one more day in the One Hundred Mile Wilderness, then another day from Abol Bridge to Katahdin Stream Campground. Two days and twenty-one miles. Then I would know.

⤝⤞

At the place where the Appalachian Trail enters Baxter State Park a trailhead kiosk displays various information sheets about the park rules, trails, and so forth. A sign-up sheet for thru-hikers to camp at The

Birches, which can accommodate only twelve hikers, is front and center. Tucked down in the bottom left corner is the daily weather report posted by the park rangers. When I arrived early on a sunny morning, I eagerly scanned the single-page weather sheet for the forecast for the next day. One hundred percent chance of thunderstorms at Katahdin Stream and The Birches campgrounds was penciled in. And then, for the summit of Katahdin itself, these ominous words: "Elevated risk of lightning." Which automatically ruled out climbing Katahdin the next day regardless of how my back felt. And I had only a single-night reservation at the Katahdin Stream Campground, my destination for this day. The following day I had scheduled a shuttle to the little town of Millinocket, where I would stay in a hostel, and then the day after that a shuttle to Bangor for the first leg of my long trip home to Georgia.

So, there it was—the end of the suspense of the last few days and the end of the hope that I could climb Katahdin this year. Next year? Maybe. But I would be a year older then and could not possibly hope to be in better trail fitness than I was now, after twenty-five days of hiking in Maine. A lot can happen in a year. A lot that might prevent me from ever returning to Maine.

I set out to hike the final nine miles from Abol Bridge to Katahdin Stream Campground digesting the news and adjusting to the reality of it. Enjoy this last day was my single thought as I walked alongside the Penobscot River. Enjoy the trail, the beautiful Maine woods, the river shining in the morning sun, the cool, sweet air. Enjoy the fact that my back was okay—just barely, but okay. Enjoy the fact that I had completed the One Hundred Mile Wilderness the day before, and done so in style, hiking well despite the handicap of my fragile back. Enjoy the improbability that I was even in Maine at all and the even greater improbability that I had hiked more than 1,900 miles of the Appalachian Trail during the past few years.

I ate lunch on a rock beside a lovely fork of the Nesowadnehunk Stream with white water surging past me and the roar of the rapids echoing through the forest. I hiked through pretty groves of tall spruce and hemlock and heard birds chirping in the branches. Hours went by, and I was alone, as if Baxter State Park had reserved the forest for me as its sole guest on this day. Away from the stream and its pounding rapids, the forest became completely silent except for the swoosh of my shoes over the trail duff.

In the afternoon the blue sky gave way to a high cloud deck, and I could feel the humidity rising. The predicted rain was coming. I stopped at Grassy Pond and walked down to the rocks on the shoreline, hoping maybe to see a moose or get a view of Katahdin. A large mountain loomed across the water, but it was not the great one. Katahdin was hidden. And there was no moose in sight. So it was not to be. I accepted this as a fact, although I knew there was a sliver of hope that something might change, that the forecast could be wrong, or I might wrangle an extra day at Katahdin Stream Campground to wait for better weather. Normally the campground was completely booked, but there was always a chance of a cancellation.

When I arrived in the midafternoon, the campground was buzzing with activity, the lean-tos appeared all taken, and the clouds were lower, the humidity almost oppressive. Rain was definitely on the way. I walked over to the ranger station to check in with the assumption that my hike through Maine was finished.

Is That You?

Great mountains have a long and nearly universal connection with human mythology and spiritualism. Olympus plays a prominent role in Greek mythology; Sinai is foundational for Judaism; and four religions proclaim Mount Kailash sacred and climbing it a sacrilege. The Navaho believe the four peaks bordering their ancestral lands in the American Southwest possess supernatural qualities. The list of sacred mountains and the cultures that venerate them would fill an entire volume and is so extensive that it might be a reasonable assumption that every high place on the planet has at one time or another been associated with the otherworldly spirits that drift through human memory.

The unique geology of Katahdin virtually guarantees that people will view it with respect, awe, and wonder, if not fear. The mountain range stands alone, rising out of a plain that is only five hundred to six hundred feet above sea level, and the 5,267-foot summit at Baxter Peak is just the beginning of a massive ridge that extends north to Hamlin and Howe Peaks. To the north of Katahdin is a bowl-shaped valley called the Klondike that is rimmed by South Brother, North Brother, Barren, Ford, and Owl Mountains. Weather systems dropping down out of Canada pick up moisture trapped in the Klondike and dump it on Katahdin, so that on an otherwise clear day the summit can be wreathed in clouds. Viewing the great mountain from afar, it is not difficult to understand why the native Wabanaki tribes would consider Katahdin a sacred place. Like Clingman's Dome in the Great Smoky Mountains, Katahdin, seen from a distance, seems an angry mountain, inhospitable, its face hidden and its breath exhaling clouds of steam. Why go up there? Why tempt the great mountain with trespass? Over many decades some of those who have done so have paid for the sacrilege with their lives.

The people of the Penobscot Nation revere the mountain. I heard about this from a hiker I met back in the One Hundred Mile Wilderness. He encountered a group of Penobscot who were walking toward Katahdin. They planned to arrive on Labor Day weekend and join other tribes who consider Katahdin sacred. But they would not go up the mountain—their ceremonies would take place down at the base, well below the tree line. Their advice for hikers who planned to go up Katahdin was to take with them a piece of cedar wood. Why? For protection from harm.

I did not think I would need a talisman when I checked in at the ranger station. The weather and the logistics of Baxter State Park had conspired against me, and I had already made my peace with the situation. Home beckoned, and the next day I would head in that direction. As I chatted with the ranger, I thought about all the things that had gone right on this hike. I had avoided serious injury or calamitous damage to my back; I had made the best use of the days I had here in Maine; and I had met wonderful people and experienced glorious days along with rough ones. All those miles and long days had toughened me a lot, had given me a taste of what the thru-hikers must feel. Not one of them that I had met and come to know would be deterred from climbing Katahdin. A small group of them had seen the weather report posted at the kiosk at the northern entrance to the park and had turned around to wait out the thunderstorms at Abol Bridge. The Birches campsite, which is where they would have to camp the night before climbing to the summit, was virtually empty. But tomorrow they would come streaming in and fill The Birches to capacity.

The ranger was a young man who had seen it all before, had climbed Katahdin many times, had even been caught in a terrifying thunderstorm up there and told stories of the ground shaking under his feet and the lightning bolts bouncing off the bare rock and flashing bright in the clouds with simultaneous blasts of thunder. This summer he had not yet gone on any rescue missions up there. Last summer was a different story—there were several. People tend to underestimate the mountain, he said. Getting up there is hard. Getting down safely is harder.

As we talked on the porch of the ranger station, I heard someone call to me. It was Popsicle, just returning from her summit of Katahdin. She was ecstatic, her face still flushed with excitement and pride. It had been hard, she said, so hard going up and back down, but so wonderful, so joyous to reach that famous sign and touch it, and now she would travel to Georgia to resume her flip-flop, floating on a wave of jubilant emotion and resolve. I wished her good luck and safe travels as she climbed into a shuttle van with her backpack.

I badly wanted to go up where Popsicle had gone, to the summit and that famous sign. I thought of Wanderer with his arm still in a cast. He and Merlot had already finished a few days earlier—no logistical snafu would have prevented them from climbing the great mountain and touching the terminus sign. Hammer and Ice Cube, Rodeo, Cogs and Coffee Bean, and all the other thru-hikers I had met—every one of them would find a way up there. Failure for them was not an option, not after coming so far and enduring so much. Why was I accepting my own failure so meekly? Fine weather was the forecast after the storms tomorrow. Could I possibly wait a day at Katahdin Stream Campground? Was there a way to arrange this?

The young ranger had silently watched my reunion with Popsicle. There were no cancellations, he said. The campground was full, booked up for the next week. But he bid me to wait a minute while he stepped into his office, then returned to the porch and squinted and stared at his boots a moment, then looked me in the eye. Maybe . . . no guarantees, but possibly, the ranger said, I could stay in a lean-to usually reserved for emergencies and other purposes if the park did not need it. He said this almost in a whisper, as though he didn't want anyone else to hear him. And even though cell service was unavailable here, maybe I could try to rearrange my shuttle to Millinocket and my hostel reservation, pushing them back by one day? Talking to the young ranger suddenly refired my hopes. Could it work?

Amazingly and improbably, in the space of two hours this all came together. I had a place in the park to stay and got word to the hostel to change my shuttle and reservation. Thru-hikers would have nodded their heads, not the least surprised by this minor miracle, and said the trail had provided. All I had to do now was wait.

⌁

The elderly man was gaunt and tall; his middle-aged son, a reporter for the *Los Angeles Times*, was even taller, lean and strong. We spent part of the next afternoon in conversation around a covered picnic table at Katahdin Stream Campground while the rain drummed on the tin roof and a few rumbles of thunder echoed down off the mountain. For forty years the old gentleman had been section hiking the Appalachian Trail, slowly working his way north, chipping away at the miles on vacations and weekends and stolen time whenever he could find it. His son had also found time to section hike the trail in the last few years and had caught up to his dad. And now they were one day out from climbing Katahdin in tandem to finish their epic hikes together by touching the iconic sign on the summit at the same moment.

We did not talk about tomorrow. We talked about the newspaper business and told stories about our experiences on the trail and discussed current affairs—mundane stuff to pass the time. We learned from other people hanging around that a couple of hikers had left the campground this morning, had hiked up the Hunt Trail, which is also the Appalachian Trail to the summit, had reached the tree line and turned around and come back down in pouring rain, chased by lightning. No one else had dared try. The elderly fellow was a year younger than me, and his trail name was Chester. His son's name was Blowout. The waiting was not so hard for Chester. Forty years is a long time to dream about a triumphant day. One more waiting out the rainstorm under a pavilion was no big deal. Only the light in his eyes betrayed his excitement. I said good evening to them as they headed to their camp spot at The Birches and we both wished each other good luck.

I was out of my sleeping bag at 4:00 a.m. and hiking the Hunt Trail fifteen minutes later guided by the pale beam of my headlamp. An average hike up and back down supposedly took between eight and ten hours. I had to be back down at the ranger station by 3:00 p.m. to catch my shuttle to Millinocket, and I wanted plenty of margin. The last thing I wanted on this day was to rush down Katahdin's treacherous slope, and missing the shuttle would strand me at the campground with no place to camp. I had already pressed my luck with the ranger by staying an extra day without a reservation. And I was out of food. An early start was thus mandatory.

The first mile and a half in the dark was standard Maine, the type of trail I now knew well, a steady climb with occasional rock features to surmount, none of them difficult. But at the tree line everything changed, and Katahdin quickly showed its true nature. The altitude gain from the campground to the summit is 4,168 feet, and the biggest chunk of that starts just beyond Katahdin Stream Falls in nearly vertical leaps up bare exposed rock. For the next 2.3 miles the trail rises a little short of three thousand feet, and every yard of gained height is hard-earned. At the steepest portion of this stretch, the trail ascends 860 feet in only half a mile of distance. This puts Katahdin in a class of four other Appalachian Trail mountains—Wildcat E, South Kinsman, South Twin, and Garfield. No other mountains on the Appalachian Trail come close to being both as technically and as physically challenging to climb as these five.

In the early morning sunlight, I ascended slowly, methodically, my route guided by the few white blazes painted on the rocks and all the previous experience on Maine's mountains that I could muster. Old Speck, Avery, the Mahoosuc Arm and all the others were just the opening acts. This one was the big show, the main attraction, the headliner. Just as in the Mahoosuc Notch, time warped into a slow drip of minutes. The concentration demanded of me to find the correct handhold, the best crease in the rock for my foot, the safest stretch of my leg to an iron rebar step, was total and continuous. No breaks, no stopping for pictures or to take in the enormous, heart-stopping view behind me or below me, no looking up to search vainly for a summit, because I knew it was not there yet. Just up, one rock ledge after another, one block after another, one scramble pulling up with both hands after another. For an hour and then another hour I climbed Katahdin with no thoughts rattling in my head, no voices, no words, and no sounds, no one else on the mountain, no memories or hopes or worries weighing me down, no buddha to kill. Just the feel of the rock through my shoe soles and on my hands and legs, my knees, and even my stomach. Not since the Whites had I done anything as remotely physically hard or mentally draining.

Something was driving me, but I could not get the sense of it. *Get up this mountain*, was all I could think about. *Get up this mountain*. Don't stop, don't hurry, don't despair, don't look at your watch, and don't wish. Just climb. Two yards here, three or four next, then another two. Find the white blaze up above you, there to the right, and angle toward it. How long I climbed in this mental and physical state of intimacy with Katahdin I do not know, only that it worked. At some point the rock faces began to slope in an arc instead of rising vertically. The climbing was still painfully hard; in fact, I was now very tired and in need of a break for water and food, but the realization that I was not going nearly straight up anymore drove me on. The first hiker of the day caught and passed me, but I paid hardly any attention to him. Finally, on a gap in the scattered rock where I could stand and turn around, I looked back the way I had come and gasped at the altitude. Far below on the narrow shoulder of the great mountain I glimpsed a speck of something red that was moving. A hiker climbing where I had been thirty minutes ago. Or an hour. Or maybe only ten minutes. I could not gauge either the time or the distance. And I felt an urge to push on, to keep going. *Get up this mountain*.

This was what made Katahdin so different. This time it was Newtonian physics, the classical path, straight from A to B, white blaze to white blaze, no fooling around, no guesswork or even much thinking. Above me in the clouds was a post bearing a sign. Getting there took an eternity, and it was not the summit, but it did mark the Gateway, where the shoulder of the mountain leveled off into a more gradual climb over a boulder-strewn alpine region called the Tableland. At Thoreau Spring the trail became a trail again, marked off by rocks stacked on either side and even strings to keep hikers off the delicate vegetation. Not that any of us wanted to go wandering, not now, when the summit was about a mile and a quarter beyond.

Another mile . . . another mile of dodging around rocks and the trail was still climbing, but now I had the sense of moving, of closing the distance, and I caught myself for the first time pushing too much, too fast, breathing too hard. Other hikers around me were doing the same thing now, catching and passing me on the Tableland and quickly dissolving into the clouds ahead. And somewhere on this last mile I heard a vaguely familiar voice from behind call out to me.

"Hey! Is that you?"

Bewildered, I turned around and saw coming toward me with powerful strides a man I recognized but could not believe was on Katahdin at the same moment I was.

Hammer! The hair on the back of my neck prickled at the sight of him. Hammer, the retired army ranger I had met in New York, the man who had carried out Wanderer's backpack when he broke his arm, the man who had worried about me and texted me to ask if I was okay. We grinned at each other like fools. We walked side by side for a few minutes, both of us talking excitedly, flabbergasted at this wonderful coincidence and with so much to catch up on, but I waved him forward, promising to join him at the summit, and he soon surged into the fog with those long strides and disappeared.

I saw the famous sign twice. First it was a distant dark line sticking up in the swirl of white cloud, just a glimpse and then it was gone. But the next time, from twenty yards, there was no mistaking the signboard marking the summit. Eight or nine hikers clustered around the wooden A-frame, Hammer among them, and my heart responded with a thumping in my chest. As I staggered the last few yards, they faced me and applauded. A young woman sitting on a rock with her face in her hands was sobbing, strangers hugged and high-fived, others were giddy with laughter and excitement. Emotions pent up for five, six, or more months overflowed and mingled with each other in a flood of pure joy. Hammer and I stood on either side of the sign and shook hands, still grinning at each other like fools. For a few moments the clouds thinned just enough for pale sunlight to brighten the summit and reveal some of the vast Klondike incredibly far below us. Then the white mist that so often veils Katahdin closed back over us, colors faded, and the hikers' voices became muted, as though the occasion had become a solemn ceremony.

Which in a sense, it was. A graduation, a matriculation, a benediction, and an ending. For the northbound thru-hikers their great adventure was over. They had hiked all 2,193 miles of the Appalachian Trail and there was nothing left of it. Time now to go home, or go somewhere, college, a new job, a new career, a new life. The abruptness of the ending was startling—even a surprise to some of them.

"I guess I'll have to figure out what to do next," I heard one young woman say to nobody.

"Will you go back to Colorado?" I asked Hammer.

"Maybe," he said. Like that part of his life was over and a new one was just beginning but he didn't know where it would take him. He was a new man, not the same retired army ranger anymore. He wasn't sure what he would do.

Two men approaching Katahdin as I began to hike down knew exactly what to do. Chester and Blowout marched side by side toward the famous sign at the summit. The old fellow was a bit unsteady among the rocks, as I had been, but his son was there to help him. They fixed their gazes on the summit, both grimly determined, just like I had been ten minutes earlier. Both were plowing forward in a rush, pulled by the anticipation. We fist-bumped as we passed each other, and they hurried on. They touched the sign together and hugged and cried and celebrated one of the most amazing father-and-son moments I could imagine, completing their great hikes together on the great mountain.

No one conquers a mountain like Katahdin. It would be sacrilege to think so, and none of the hikers I briefly shared the summit with would have dared such a claim. Climbing Katahdin is a privilege and a gift. Without resorting to spirituality or other metaphysical ideas, I can affirm that the great mountain is a sacred place, a place of veneration and awe. Whether it is a beginning or an ending or somewhere in between does not matter. The significance is the emotion that wells up on its summit. Katahdin did something to me no other place on the entire Appalachian Trail could do. It made me feel I was both very small and not so small, a man who was incredibly lucky to be alive, to have survived and endured and dared, to have failed and tried again, to have a home to go back to and a family waiting there. Katahdin was not the end for me, not a conclusion. I was grateful for that. It seemed right somehow that I was not done with the Appalachian Trail, nor it with me. Katahdin was my climax, but there remained a denouement, more trail, more mountains, more miles, more hikers to meet, more hours of forest solitude and silence. Maybe, I thought, when next I go out there on the trail, I will meet a buddha again striving toward the great mountain. The real kind. After climbing Katahdin, I would know what to say.

One Final Time

The final miles of the final day of my Appalachian Trail journey bundled bits and pieces of the entire five-year experience into a mishmash of nearly everything that makes the A.T. such a difficult challenge and so uniquely wonderful. I woke up in Maine long before dawn in a rain-soaked tent at Crocker Cirque Campsite. Two nights of rain had dampened all my gear except my sleeping bag, which while hiking I kept in a trash compactor bag stuffed in the bottom of my backpack to keep it as dry as possible. Twenty-one days of walking, first in the sweltering heat and humidity of Massachusetts, and then over southern Maine's toughest mountains, had brought me to within touching distance of the end, a mere 7.3 miles from the trailhead at Hwy 27 near Stratton. I was tired, nearly out of food, my right knee was acting up, my shoes and socks were wet, and I faced a hike up two big, steep mountains, one right after the other, and then a very long descent—altogether 4,483 feet of elevation change over those seven miles between me and completion of the entire Appalachian Trail. But the excitement and anticipation of my last day on the A.T. welling up in my head had me fumbling around in the dark, eager to pack my gear and start walking.

Slow down, I told myself as I rolled up the wet tent fly. Eat breakfast, even if you are sick of dry granola. Drink half a liter of water to hydrate before setting out. Make sure you don't leave anything behind. Ignore the mist and the mud. Stick to the routine that has gotten you this far. Only one more day on the trail, true, but make this day no different from the others.

Eleven straight days of hiking the rugged A.T. in southern Maine had extracted a lot of energy from me, as it must from any hiker. But I had crossed the twin open peaks of Baldpate Mountain in glorious weather. I had survived unscathed the sharp descent off Wyman Mountain and then scrambled and sweated most of a cool morning to climb Moody's rough, steep southern flank. Old Blue, an equally steep climb of 3,559 feet, had disappointed me at the tiny open summit because a fringe of head-high spruce blocked what should have been enormous views. On a foggy morning crossing Bemis Mountain, I had feasted on ripe blueberries picked from thick bushes right beside the trail. A three-mile alpine trek over exposed and weathered rock on Saddleback Mountain under blue skies and puffy white clouds driven by a thirty-mile-an-hour wind had been so magnificent I had lingered longer than I should have at the summit just gazing at the distant mountain ranges in every direction of the compass, marveling at the mountains to the south that I had already crossed and the mountains I had yet to traverse laid out in hazy rows up ahead. The ultrasteep and treacherous descent of The Horn had shocked me, as had the nearly as difficult descent off Sugarloaf, where the mountain abruptly sheared off into a col and the trail plunged down into ragged boulders and twisted into narrow defiles and vertical drops. I had crossed the South Branch of the Carrabassett River without getting wet thanks to a wobbly wooden plank stretched over rushing white water. I had endured long stretches of trail without good water sources, had pushed my way through dense, scratchy spruce lining both sides of the trail, and had admired the beauty of patches of deep-shaded evergreen forests between sparkling glacier lakes. I had smiled at the croak of a raven on Saddleback's alpine summit and had listened to loons on a lovely evening camped beside Little Swift River Pond. And, of course, mud . . . there had to be plenty of mud.

All of that was behind me. Just hike, I told myself as I set out in the dark from Crocker Cirque, my headlamp barely lighting the trail. Just climb, one foot in front of the other. The trail immediately gained altitude in a steady incline that rose into a dark forest. But soon weak yellowy light from a hidden sunrise over my shoulder replaced my headlamp's beam. I stopped to take off my rain poncho, wad it in a ball, and stuff it in a big pocket of my pants. Then pulled it out and put it back on thirty minutes later in more rain. Then the sun broke through, and I saw patches of blue sky ahead in the direction of the summit. The weather was playing games with me. I gave up on the poncho and just got wet when the clouds thickened and the drizzle resumed.

Partway up South Crocker, I angled across a massive boulder field where an enormous chunk of the mountain had long ago broken into millions of pieces that slid down off the summit. The footing among the boulders was tricky in the wet, but I stopped long enough to gasp at a vast mist-wreathed view of distant mountains laced with banded sunbeams and dark shadows. A few northbound thru-hikers passed me; they would hike into the Bigelow Range later this day, mountains I had climbed a year ago on my way to Katahdin. I wished them well and kept the fact that this was my final day to myself. Past the summit the trail dropped only a few hundred feet before quickly angling back up. My steps shortened and slowed to a monotonous trudge on the slope of North Crocker, the climb hard on my tired legs.

And then the long descent. Only five miles to go, all the climbing done now according to the trail profile. But, not for the first time, the map was wrong—the descent was instead choppy, dropping then climbing a little, then dropping more. Then a short rock scramble back up. Like the trail could not make up its mind where to go. A heavy shower caught me, and I wriggled back into the poncho. The trail instantly became a muddy stream that resoaked my shoes. Rivulets and seeps out of the mountainside became flowing braids of water inches deep. This was miserable. I was getting nowhere on a trail that I felt I should have finished by now. How much farther? Going down a wide patch that looked firm, my feet slipped in the slick mud, and I skidded helplessly toward a rock edge; I braked my momentum with my trekking poles just before a minidisaster would have sent me sprawling headfirst over an angled rock into mud and roots. The shower tapered off into drizzle and now I was sweating in my poncho as I ploughed on through the mud. How much more of this?

So, there he was, the buddha, the fat little man I knew so well, impassive and implacable, eyes closed, blocking my path like one of the rain-slick rounded boulders rising out of the mud. How appropriate that we should meet one final time, I thought. This time was different, though. I started laughing. At the buddha dissolving through no effort of my own, at myself, at the off-on rain and the mud and my tender right knee and the water dripping off my hat and trickling down my back. The laughter came from some deep place mingled with memories and miles, sunrises and sunsets, pains and thirst, exhaustion and exhilaration. I laughed until tears dripped down into my beard. Ridiculous . . . comical . . . and wonderful. Enough of this, I said to nobody as I wiped tears and sweat off my face. Pay attention. Just hike . . . just concentrate and walk. And don't carelessly slide again in the mud or you will wind up face down in it.

An hour later I met a pack of fifteen college kids headed up the mountain on some sort of freshman orientation activity, their bulging new backpacks strapped with extra gear that bounced and jangled as they marched toward me in their fresh, clean crimson T-shirts, khaki hiking shorts, and new boots. Some had unhappy, impatient expressions, some just seemed bewildered, and all of them were breathing too hard for conversation from the brisk pace of their leader. I stood aside in a mud puddle for them, the water seeping into my socks through the torn seams of my shoes. As they passed single file, most of them ignored me, but a few nodded or glanced my way with pity—a wet, bedraggled worn-down old man in mud-smeared pants and mud-caked shoes. But I had a smile on my face that no mud or rain or aching knee could wipe off, the manifestation of a powerful emotion they would not understand. I walked on, the trail leveled off, the sun came out, the last white blaze appeared ahead on a tree, and I emerged from the forest into the warmth of a bright Maine summer day at the trailhead parking area. I was done—2,193 miles hiked, all the way from Georgia to here, and the year before beyond this trailhead to Katahdin, and the years before then one foot in front of the other through state after state, printing indelible memories, if not peace and serenity, with every step. I could not stop grinning as I hauled off my backpack to wait for the shuttle. It was time to go home.

The Simplest Thing

The convention of Appalachian Trail hikers adopting and then using a new name for themselves during their hiking did not appeal to me at first. I thought it was a bit silly to call oneself Mumbles or Greybeard or Honey Bun, or any of the hundreds of other hiker trail names I had heard. In addition to sounding silly, I assumed that this was only something for thru-hikers, a kind of nomenclature reserved for the upper class of Appalachian Trail hikers. As a lowly section hiker, and a pretty poor one at that, I did not think I merited a new name.

Plenty of thru-hikers I met on my first hikes disagreed with me. If you are going to walk the walk, you need to talk the talk was their not-so-subtle way of putting it. And in time I began to come around to the idea. After all, writers adopt pen names, actors take stage names, monks and nuns take new names. Mark Twain, Marilyn Monroe . . . nothing silly about them. Thich Nhat Hanh adopted that Dharma name when he was ordained as a Buddhist monk in 1949.[1] And so the more I thought about it, the more I came to conclude that anyone seriously hiking the Appalachian Trail does in fact take on a type of new identity. For a period of time, maybe six months, maybe only a week or two, a hiker on the Appalachian Trail embodies a new persona as deeply as an actor on a stage becomes the character he or she is playing. The world of work and family, traffic jams and living room comforts, schedules and responsibilities and indulgences, all that falls away and is replaced by a routine more resembling that of a monk. Wake up, walk, eat, sleep, wake up, walk, eat, sleep . . . life strips down to those elementals and is measured more in miles than in hours of the day. The freedom of this new life, after a while, is both exhilarating and boring. You do pretty much whatever you damn well please in one sense, and in another you have tied yourself to a rigid, often uncomfortable, and always difficult conformity.

So a new name is appropriate. Strict convention holds that only a hiker can bestow a trail name on another hiker, but that is often contravened, and no one I ever met on the trail seemed to care. Some trail names bear a level of dignity and just seem to fit the person perfectly. Saint Pete was one. Hammer was another. As was Rodeo. Others hinted at some inner secret, like Cogs and Ice Cube. Some were descriptive—Quicktime was exactly that. Stump looked like one. Others were ironic—Stoneheart was anything but. Some were cute, like Popsicle. Others were funny, like the young woman who on her first night on the trail in Georgia had an accident with her camp stove just outside her tent, fortunately without injury or serious damage, and acquired an instant trail name—Explosion. And finally, others just seemed right. I gave Coffee Bean his trail name and it stuck to him like duct tape.

So I came around to the idea. It solidified the day I realized I might hike the Appalachian Trail with some degree of success, that maybe I could even go the full distance. It was a radical, ridiculous idea, but it would not go away, and I had to take it seriously. And to take hiking the trail seriously, I had to change. I had to grow a new streak of stubbornness, a harder edge when I found myself in trouble and discover a more open spirit for the fellow hikers I met. I had to adapt to the trail's demands and learn to live its moments one by one. Most of all, I had to kill those buddhas I met who looked like me, one after another, and bow to the genuine buddhas who graced the trail.

I had to become Raven, the old man who hiked all 2,193 miles of the Appalachian Trail. It was, in the end, the simplest thing.

NOTES

THE RAVEN

1. Robert Moor, *On Trails: An Exploration* (New York: Simon & Schuster, 2016), 14.
2. Moor, *On Trails*, 263.
3. Jeffrey J. Doran, *Ramble On: A History of Hiking* (New York: Doran, 2018), 20.
4. The length of the Appalachian Trail changes from year to year as sections are relocated.
5. Whether or not Shaffer walked every mile of the A.T. as it then existed has been disputed. Phillip D'Anieri, *The Appalachian Trail: A Biography* (Boston, Mass.: Houghton Mifflin Harcourt, 2021), 144. Given how rough and difficult the trail was in 1948, the actual number of miles he might have missed hardly matters.
6. Mrs. Emma Gatewood, *Sports Illustrated*, August 15, 1955.

BEARS

1. James Baldwin, "The White Man's Guilt," *Ebony*, August 1965.
2. Joe Fassler, "The Closest of All Possible Encounters," *The Atlantic*, November 14, 2018.

A DIFFERENT KIND OF BEAR

1. Martin Hägglund, *This Life: Secular Faith and Spiritual Freedom* (New York: Pantheon, 2019), 25.
2. Anthony Morgan, "The Time of Our Lives: A Conversation with Martin Hägglund," interview with Martin Hägglund, *Philosopher* 107, no. 4). Hägglund's use of the idea of "vertical" refers to the religious idea of eternity, but the principle applies equally well to an obsession with the personal freedom to do as we please.

3. The Georgia Appalachian Trail Club fields trained volunteers called "trail ambassadors" along the Appalachian Trail in Georgia to assist and advise hikers, report on trail conditions, and handle problems such as trash.

4. Brian B. King, "A Timeline of the A.T. and the Appalachian Trail Conservancy," *Journeys: The Official Magazine of the Appalachian Trail Conservancy* (Fall 2021): 4.

5. Mills Kelly, "The A.T. and Race," *Journeys: The Official Magazine of the Appalachian Trail Conservancy* (Winter 2021): 24–26.

6. Kelly, *A.T. and Race*, 24.

MANIACS

1. Paul Harper, *Me and the Boy: Journey of Discovery: Father and Son on the Appalachian Trail* (New York: Macmillan, 1986).

2. A Pulaski is a tool with an axe blade on one side of the head and a hoe on the other.

3. Murder on the Appalachian Trail is a rare thing. According to a statistical analysis by *Trek Magazine*, "The U.S. murder rate is more than 1,000 times higher than the equivalent rate on the A.T." That means a person is 968 times more likely to be murdered in the United States at large than while hiking on the Appalachian Trail. But no place in the United States is immune to violence. Records from the Appalachian Trail Conservancy show ten murders in eight incidents during the forty-five years between 1974 and 2019, when on May 11 army veteran Ronald S. Sanchez Jr. (trail name "Stronghold") was murdered between Little Brushy Mountain and Walker Mountain.

WE HAVE TO WAIT

1. This idea is different from and should not be confused with the Buddhist doctrine of two truths that holds that there are two ways of viewing the world: as things appear to be and as things are.

KISSING THE EARTH

1. Daniel Levin, *The Zen Book* (Carlsbad, Calif.: Hay House, 2005), 168.

2. The Roller Coaster is the name of a 13.5-mile stretch in Virginia that is a continuous string of short, steep climbs and descents.

3. Thich Nhat Hanh, *Peace Is Every Step: The Path of Mindfulness in Everyday Life* (New York: Bantam, 1992), 28.

4. Robert M. Pirsig, *Zen and the Art of Motorcycle Maintenance* (New York: Harper Collins, 1974), 205.

ROCKS

1. Robert Moor, *On Trails: An Exploration* (New York: Simon and Schuster, 2016), 263.

2. Bill Bryson, *A Walk in the Woods*, (New York: Broadway Books, 1998), 71–72.

3. Bryson, *Walk in the Woods*, 71–72.

4. Christopher Mole, *Attention Is Cognitive Unison: An Essay in Philosophical Psychology* (Oxford: Oxford University Press, 2011).

5. V. Collins Chew, *Underfoot: A Geologic Guide to the Appalachian Trail* (Harpers Ferry, W.V.: The Appalachian Trail Conference, 1988), 73.

6. Chew, *Underfoot*, 23.

7. David Miller, *The A.T. Guide*, (Wilmington, N.C.: AntiGravityGear, 2021), 131.

8. Chew, *Underfoot*, 85.

9. Chew, *Underfoot*, 85.

BEYOND BRAVE

1. Some bears have learned to chew or claw the cord that hikers use to hang their food bags from tree limbs, causing the bags to fall to the ground.

2. Many thru-hikers begin their northbound hike from Amicalola Falls State Park and hike the 8.8-mile Approach Trail to Springer Mountain, which is the official southern terminus.

3. Robert Moor, *On Trails: An Exploration* (London: Aurum Press, 2016), 35.

MIND OVER MUD

1. Jeffrey Marion, *Leave No Trace in the Outdoors* (Mechanicsburg, Penn.: Stackpole, 2014).

2. Moving rocks in a forest can disturb insects, reptiles, and microorganisms that live under them and is therefore a practice to avoid.

BITE OF THE WOLF

1. At this point in my section hike I had not even started the Virginia portion of the Appalachian Trail.

2. Dan Bruce, *The Thru-Hiker's Handbook* (Harpers Ferry, W.V.: The Appalachian Trail Conference, 1993), 128.

ALONE

1. The German word *Felsenmeer* means "sea of rocks," which accurately describes the high ridges and peaks of the White Mountains.

2. Bernd Heinrich, *Mind of the Raven* (New York: Harper Collins, 2009).

3. The Japanese Buddhist priest Dogen (1200–1253) founded the Zen Buddhist Soto School: "I came to realize clearly that mind is no other than mountains and rivers and the great wide earth, the sun and the moon and the stars."

SUPERSTARS

1. Author's interview with Doug Weilhrauch, August 16, 2019 at Lakes of the Clouds Hut, New Hampshire.

SUM OVER PATHS

1. The Dalí painting *The Persistence of Memory* depicts a melting clock.

2. For a concise description of Feynman's sum over paths theory, see Michio Kaku, *Parallel Worlds: A Journey through Creation, Higher Dimensions, and the Future of the Cosmos* (New York: Doubleday, 2004), 163.

3. Feynman won a Nobel Prize in 1965 for his sum over paths theory, which, through some complicated mathematics, revealed that our commonsense understanding of the universe coexists with an infinite number of possibilities—some of which go backward in time or to the edge of the universe—thus paths to Pluto, Alpha Centauri, or distant galaxies.

TRAIL BUDDHAS

1. This a secular interpretation of Buddhist teaching that is distinct from the religious goal of achieving nirvana, or enlightenment, which is the transcendent state of being sought by traditional schools of Buddhism.

2. Shunryū Suzuki, *Zen Mind, Beginner's Mind* (Waco, Tex.: John Weatherhill, 1970), 36.

DANGEROUSLY CLOSE

1. It did grow. In 2023, the Appalachian Trail Conservancy pegged the distance at 2,198.4 miles due to relocations and detours in New York and Maine, plus more precise measurements.

THE SIMPLEST THING

1. Seth Mydans, "Thich Nhat Hanh, Monk, Zen Master and Activist, dies at 95," *New York Times*, January 23, 2022.